THE
FORT WAYNE
STORY

In 1794, Anthony Wayne built the first American fort where the St. Joseph and St. Mary's rivers join to form the Maumee River.

THE
FORT WAYNE STORY
A PICTORIAL HISTORY

JOHN
ANKENBRUCK

Sponsored by Greater Fort Wayne Chamber of Commerce • Windsor Publications, Inc., Woodland Hills, California

Library of Congress Cataloging in Publication Data

Ankenbruck, John.
  The Fort Wayne story.

  Includes index.
    1. Fort Wayne—History.   2. Fort Wayne—
Description. I. Greater Fort Wayne Chamber of
Commerce (Ind.) II. Title.
F534.F7A67   977.2'74   80-53044
ISBN 0-89781-015-5

Published 1980
Printed in the United States of America

First Edition

CONTENTS

INTRODUCTION

The primary factor for the location and development of the city of Fort Wayne is the many favorable geographic advantages that the area enjoys. The source of the Maumee River, formed by the confluence of the St. Mary's and St. Joseph rivers, rises in the heart of the city. The early traveler could move by water from this point to the Atlantic Ocean. By means of a short portage to the west and south he could also travel by water to the Mississippi River and the Gulf of Mexico. The Indians who used the rivers as highways through the wilderness long realized the strategic importance of the location.

Here the Miami Indians located their village of Kiskakon (also known as Kekionga). This was the destination of many of the early travelers and coureurs de bois from Canada. The French and British struggled for many years to control the area. Near the end of the eighteenth century, after a series of bloody battles between the Indians and American forces sent here by President George Washington, the Indians were finally defeated by General Anthony Wayne and Fort Wayne was established as an important military outpost in the wilderness. This fort was the site of military action again during the War of 1812. After the defeat of the British the small village of Fort Wayne was securely established. After several decades of slow growth, the community was proclaimed a city in 1840.

The completion of the Wabash-Erie Canal, which was celebrated in 1835, furnished great impetus to the city's growth. Within the next two decades the first of a series of railroads was constructed through the city as the use of the canal rapidly declined. A number of men with vision, foresight, and entrepreneurial ability now became responsible for the initial commercial and industrial development of the city. All of this bustle and growth was fed by the successive waves of immigration from Europe. Many of the earliest settlers were Anglo-Saxon. The Irish came to build the canal and to work on other construction projects. Next we were favored by two periods of German immigration. They brought their crafts and skills from their homeland. Many became successful farmers, while others were skilled artisans and craftsmen. They became contractors, machinists, bakers, brewers, carpenters, and cabinet makers. The city enjoyed a reputation for a number of wood-oriented industries located here. By the end of the century the peoples from central and southern Europe began to arrive to work in the knitting mills, foundries, and shops devoted to metal work.

With the close of the nineteenth century the city's continued growth and progress was assured. Our population grew by 10,000 inhabitants between 1890 and 1900. The importance of agriculture now began to decline, and shortly after the end of World War I the establishment of a number of new large factories indicated that in the future emphasis was to be in the areas of industry and technology.

The period from 1900 to 1930 in the city's history might best be described by the German word, gemütlich. The community now was largely composed of people with a German background. The city supported two German-language newspapers. The German Lutherans and Catholics, who were a substantial fraction of the total population, were both supporting a large parochial school system. The city now was a transportation center for steam railroad lines as well as electric inter-urban transit. The many small stores and shops enjoyed a long period of prosperity, and streets were crowded until 10 o'clock on Saturday nights. The farmers' market on Saturday mornings was crowded with many conversations being carried on in German. The city supported a large number of secret fraternal societies. Many of the ethnic groups found a source of entertainment in their parochial school buildings where bowling alleys were frequently installed. There were five bands and orchestras in the city. The park system began to expand, and a number of theatres offered daily-except-Sunday vaudeville and legitimate stage productions. The population supported a surprisingly large number of saloons, but crime and drunkenness were never a serious problem. With the coming of Prohibition the saloon gave way to the speakeasy. The horsedrawn vehicle began to be supplanted by the automobile and motor truck. The chain-store system began to eliminate the small neighborhood store, and eventually a way of life enjoyed by all of the older citizens of this community disappeared from the scene.

The author of this history is thoroughly conversant with all phases of the development of the city. A journalist by profession, he writes in an easy flowing style that makes it a pleasure to read history. He has enjoyed a number of successes in this field. While one picture may not be worth 10,000 words, it certainly is worth many paragraphs. Mr. Ankenbruck's use of photographs in the preparation of this work adds immeasurably to the pleasure of reading it.

Fred J. Reynolds

The Wabash River, depicted in oils by George Winter, circa 1851. The Fort Wayne Museum of Art holds the original painting.

CHAPTER
I

HEART OF
THE
WILDERNESS

The recorded history of Fort Wayne begins with the Miami Indians and their meetings with French explorers. We first hear of the Miamis in the journals of the French. The way the French pronounced Miami sounded like mau-mee to the early English-speaking, thus we have Maumee River rather than the earlier Miami of the Lakes. When Jean Nicolet explored the rivers south of Lake Michigan in 1634, he may have visited the present site of Fort Wayne. It is clear, however, that he visited the Miami Indians along the western shores of Lake Michigan. The Miamis occupied the area extending from Green Bay, Wisconsin, to Chicago.

During the 17th century a struggle for the American continent developed between the English and the French, with the prime aim in the interior being the control of the fur trade. Over a thousand miles of wilderness, the Indians were the trappers and the soldiers. With them went the real control of both the land and the fur trade. The polarization of the Indian nations into two large, hostile groups ran parallel to the struggles between England and France in the New World. This polarization led to the founding of Miamitown, which would subsequently become the Fort Wayne community.

Even though Pere Jacques Marquette and Louis Joliet had found a trading route across Wisconsin to the Mississippi River in 1673, Rene Robert Cavelier, Sieur de la Salle, had already determined three years earlier that there was a quicker route from Lake Erie west. La Salle's plan called for use of the Maumee River, a short portage at the present Fort Wayne location to the Little Wabash, then eventually down to the Ohio and Mississippi rivers. The only obstacle to La Salle's plan were the Iroquois Indians, allied to the British traders, who had pushed the Ottawas out of the Maumee area and made life unsafe for French trading operations.

La Salle and Louis de Baude de Frontenac, governor-general of New France, decided on a number of moves to gain a strong hand in the area. La Salle began by building a fort in 1679, called Fort St. Joseph de Miamis, on a river flowing into Lake Michigan on the southeast shore. He set up a trading post at Chicago, and convinced a faction of the Miamis to move to the headwaters of the Maumee River. To secure the Maumee route down the Detroit River from Lake Huron, another post was built in the following generation. Fort Pontchartrain, at present-day Detroit, completed the first cycle in the cementing of relations with the Miami, Huron, and Ottawa Indians, and the extending of a trade route down the Mississippi. (Fort Pontchartrain was founded in 1701 by Antoine Laumet de Lamothe Cadillac and a band from Montreal.)

By that time, the Miamis had established themselves firmly at the source of the Maumee. They had driven out the homicidal Iroquois, at least temporarily. When they first made their way into the area between 1680 and 1682, they had found forests of oak, walnut, and wild cherry so dense that the

French alliance with the Indians (Miami, Huron & Ottawa) 1679-1701

Top
The portage between the Maumee and Wabash rivers attracted early explorers and trappers to the area which later became the city of Fort Wayne.

Right
La Salle claimed the Great Lakes area and Mississippi tributary lands for France. He had first met with the Indians of the Fort Wayne area in 1679.

sky was practically invisible much of the year.

Pierre Charlevois described the land between the lakes as "covered with trees of a prodigious height." Also, in his 1721 journal, he told of the ancestor of modern American games.

"The Miamis have two Games more, the first of which is called the Game of the Bat (Lacrosse). They play at it with a Ball and Sticks bent and ending in a Kind of Racket. They set up two posts, which serve for Bounds, and which are distant from each other according to the Number of Players. For Instance, if they are eighty there is half a League Distant between the Posts. The players are divided into two Bands, which have each their Post: Their Business is to Strike the Ball to the Post of the adverse Party without letting it fall to the Ground, and without touching it with the Hand, for in either of these Cases they lose the Game, unless he who makes the Fault repairs it by striking the Ball at one Blow to the Post, which is often impossible. These Savages are so dextrous at catching the Ball with their Bats, that sometimes one Game will last many Days together."

There were clearings at the confluence of three rivers where the St. Mary's River and the St. Joseph River formed the Maumee. The place was called Kiskakon, or Kekionga, usually thought to mean "blackberry patch." There were the sparse remains of corn plantings and thousands of beaver dams on the small contributory creeks and streams. Game was varied and included mountain lions, bears, turkeys, wild geese, buffalo, deer, and elk. But beaver was the main money crop.

A trading post was in operation by 1686, and it gradually came to be known as Miamitown — the oldest continually occupied community in subsequent Indiana and the general area to the south of the Great Lakes. Little is left to identify the French traders and individual Indians of that decade. Yet the French records in Quebec indicate Jean Baptiste Bissot, by then having been conferred the title of Sieur de Vincennes, came from his principal outpost of Fort St. Joseph near Lake Michigan to restore the post of the Miamis in 1697.

Captain Vincennes was to be the most influential figure in the possessions west of Quebec for a generation. He was the representative of the French crown to the Miamis and related Indian nations, and, apparently, an effective soldier and diplomat in a very turbulent period. The relations he cemented with the Indians were to last the French for half a century — right up to the time of the French and Indian War, when virtual control of most of the continent was decided.

Captain Vincennes continued to operate out of Fort St. Joseph of Lake Michigan, where his noted rescue of Detroit was undertaken in 1712. Under siege by British-backed Indian tribes, Detroit was taken over and partially burned. Vincennes led French soldiers, along with a host of Miami and other

Top
In the 17th century, beaver furs served as the money crop of the wilderness. After trapping the animals and removing their pelts, the Indians would sell the furs to French traders.

Right
Early settlers of the Fort Wayne area survived by hunting game such as geese, turkeys, buffalo, deer, and elk.

Indians, to save the garrison of Captain Renaud Dubuisson, who had succeeded to the position of post commander at Detroit in 1710. Captain Dubuisson was later sent to Miamitown to protect French interests there.

The records of 1715 indicate Captain Vincennes was instructed to move his headquarters to Fort Miami on the Maumee. This evidences the fact that the Maumee-Wabash trade route between the St. Lawrence and the Mississippi rivers had surpassed in importance the older routes along the upper lakes.

Vincennes spent the last four years of his life in the community that was to become Fort Wayne, and he was the area's first prominent citizen of record. It can be safely presumed Captain Vincennes was buried at the Miami villages, putting the grave near the middle of the present city, but the approximate location is unknown.

Burial grounds from the early days of the Fort Wayne settlement continue to raise intriguing questions for historians. The Indians were known to have had several resting places in the area; a military plot was located in the American fort near present-day East Main Street; the early churches often had midtown plots, and the remains from some of these were later moved to regular cemeteries as they came into existence.

But while the records on many of the early burial sites are sketchy, an extensive Indian burying place is known to have existed on the bank of the St. Mary's River, approximately where Rockhill Avenue now approaches West Main Street. It is reasonable to place the Vincennes grave at that location, as well, even though only Indian artifacts have been uncovered in later diggings.

Just two years after Vincennes's death, the French chose a site for a fort only 100 yards to the north. The great upsurge in the building of military posts, which the French undertook to secure their growing political and trading interests, was well underway by 1721. In that year Captain Renaud Dubuisson was instructed to proceed up the Maumee and down the Wabash to establish permanent military presences. One of those posts, located along the St. Mary's River, was called Fort St. Philippe. It was completed and garrisoned by 1722. This stockade, later called Fort Miami, stood at what is now the west terminus of Superior Street in midtown Fort Wayne.

The other fort, called Fort Ouiatenon, was erected by Captain Dubuisson just south of the present city of Lafayette along the Wabash in 1721-1722. Fort Ouiatenon derived its name from the Ouia (or Wea or Wabash) Indians, who had a village and trading center there. The Ouias were kindred tribes with the Miami and Illinois Indian nations and remained allies through the crucial era.

France, during this period of colonial expansion, was the strongest nation in the world. Its explorers in the New World were the most adventurous and intrepid. They seized the principal waterways of the interior. Their dealings

This bas-relief panel in the Allen County Courthouse depicts Angeline Chapeteau, a member of an early French trader family, meeting with Indians. The Chapeteau family lived near the old fort. Courtesy, Fort Wayne and Allen County Public Library.

with the Indians were even-handed and produced lasting bonds. Various French adventurers married Indian maidens, the offspring of whom number among Fort Wayne's population to this very day.

Only in the Quebec-St. Lawrence area did the French allow settlers in large numbers. Everywhere else they carefully restricted land grants, mostly to reserve for themselves the profits from the fur trade. The strict limitation on the size of their immigrant population eventually put the French at a numerical disadvantage to settlers of other nationalities, especially the British along the Eastern seaboard.

Yet there was one advantage to the French policy of discouraging immigration and land grants: The Indians were pleased to have trading partners who did not pose an inordinate threat to their land. A half-century later, Miami chiefs at Fort Wayne would tell American treaty negotiators that the Indians considered the period from the 1680s to the 1750s to be a

"Golden Age." Their trade relations with the French brought them tools, weapons, and many commodities previously unknown to them. Their experiences with the French removed these Indians still further from the stone-age habits of the tribes of the Southwest.

This "Golden Age" was not without military incident, however. When King George's War broke out in Europe in 1744, some of the hostility moved to the New World. The trouble centered in the Great Lakes area, where the war is remembered as the "King Nicolas War," named after the Huron chief who led the attack. Under the influence of the British, King Nicolas enlisted some of the tribes in what he hoped would be a surprise attack against various French posts.

On Pentecost Sunday, 1747, the Indians rushed Fort Miami at the headwaters of the Maumee. The small eight-man garrison of French soldiers was overpowered, and the stockade burned. This uprising at Miamitown was unusual, given the generally good relationship between the Miamis and the French. Old records note, however, that the two main Miami chiefs, Coldfoot and Hedgehog, were at Detroit at the time. The fort's commander, Ensign Douville, and part of his command were also away on a visit to Montreal.

A far more serious calamity befell both Indians and French in the years of 1752 and 1753, when a smallpox plague swept across the Indian country. With little natural resistance to the imported disease, Indians died in such great numbers that entire villages became deserted. From one-half to two-thirds of the native population between the Appalachian Mountains and the Mississippi was estimated to have been lost. It is quite possible that disease broke the power of the Indians more than all the military campaigns of the epoch.

The building of the second French fort at the present site of Fort Wayne followed a visit in 1749 of a force of over 200 soldiers headed by Captain Pierre Joseph Bienville de Celeron. Accompanying Bienville was Jean de Bonnecamps, a Jesuit mathematician, explorer, and missionary, who was professor of mathematics and astronomy at Quebec. In De Bonnecamps's letters he described the "decayed" condition of the original fort and the "eight miserable" hovels of the traders. "The French there number 22, and all of them, including the commandant, had the fever. Monsieur Raimond (Captain Charles Raimond), did not approve the situation of the fort and maintained it should be relocated on the bank of the St. Joseph, a scant league from the present site." Bonnecamps reported Captain Raimond wanted him to survey the new fort site, but Celeron and Bonnecamps were anxious to depart. "All I could do was trace for him the plan of his new fort," Bonnecamps wrote, giving the latitude as 41 degrees, 29 minutes. By the following year, 1750, the new Fort Miami was erected — on the St. Joseph River's east bank, a half-mile north of three rivers.

During his first term as President, George Washington launched a war against the Miami Indians at the location of present-day Fort Wayne.

When Bienville and his soldiers stopped at Fort Miami, they were on the return trip of a sweep down the Ohio River, the aim of which was to destroy posts of the English and drive them east of the Alleghenies. The offensive was highly successful, as colonial records show, and led directly to the French building of Fort Duquesne (later Pittsburgh) and the French and Indian War. Upon completion of Fort Miami, a new commander arrived. He was Louis Coulon de Villiers, destined to be the winning commander of the initial engagements of the war. Coulon came up the Maumee in July, 1750, and strengthened the garrison to fifty men. Three years later, in 1753, he left Fort Miami, returned to Quebec, and began preparations for the campaign in Pennsylvania. He was later knighted for his efforts by the Marquis de Montcalm.

Coulon in 1754 led an army of French regulars and Indians, including Ottawas, Miamis, and Hurons, against a colonial force under Colonel George Washington which was threatening the newly-built Fort Dequesne. With 650 soldiers and warriors under his command, Coulon caught the Virginians on July 4, 1754, at a place called Great Meadows. Washington, who had been retreating for two days, made a stand at a hastily constructed stockade called Fort Necessity. Coulon's forces made immediate attack, during which, according to Washington's report, "was the most tremendous rain that could be conceived." A third of Washington's 150 effectives were killed or wounded. The next day Washington capitulated, and after signing away the rights of the English for a year in the Ohio Valley, was allowed to take his defeated troops back east.

Only weeks before, Washington, on May 29, 1754, had written to Lieutenant Governor Robert Dinwiddie of Virginia: "I have neither seen nor heard any particular account of Twightwees (Miamis) since I came on these waters. We have already begun a palisades fort and hope to have it up

In 1747 Indians burned Fort Miami, the stockade built by the French in 1721 along the St. Mary's River. Artist James McBride illustrates the uprising.

tomorrow." Then a few days later, on June 3, he wrote "the French early in spring sent a speech to the Wyandots (Hurons), Twightwees (Miamis) and their allies, and desired them to take up the hatchet and start to the Ohio and cut off the inhabitants with the English." Then, and for the next 40 years, Washington recognized the Twightwees or Miamis as a prime Indian element in resisting American expansion.

It was the following year, 1755, that a large army, outfitted in England to operate in colonial America, landed. General Edward Braddock led the 2,000-man force into the wilderness, complete with cannons to reduce Fort Duquesne. Sailors from the ships handled the heavy lines used to drag the big guns over mountains and down the precipices. Colonials under Washington joined in the march. They hardly worried about Indians interfering with such an army; and wrongly figured the fading Iroquois (friendly Senecas, Mohawks and Onondagas, Cayugas, and Oneidas) would cancel out the Indians to the west. But an army of another kind was moving east from an area stretching from the Straits of Mackinac on the upper lakes to the Maumee. Led by a young Ottawa chief named Pontiac and a half-breed frontier fighter named Charles Langlade, more than 1,000 Indians moved in front of Fort Duquesne, together with a small brigade of French regulars from the fort. They caught Braddock's army in a steep ravine a few miles short of its destination. Braddock never got a chance to even see the fort he had come so far to reduce. The surprise attack disoriented the English forces. More than a third died. The balance of the army fled. Among those dying of wounds was General Braddock.

But the war continued, and Washington survived to participate. It also became uglier, if that was possible. I found an entry in Washington's papers of peculiar interest regarding early Fort Miami (Fort Wayne) personalities. Following a skirmish, Washington wrote to the Virginia governor on April 7, 1756: "Monsieur Douville, commander of the party, was killed and scalped. Mr. Plaris sends the scalp by Jenkins, and I hope, although not an Indian's, they will meet with adequate reward." The scalped Douville mentioned by Washington was apparently the same Ensign Douville who was commandant at Fort Miami when it was burned by the Indians in 1747 along the St. Mary's River.

The grisly business of taking scalps became common during this period, and was by no means a practice only by Indians. Virginia left the fixing of rewards for scalps to the discretion of the governor. Later a reward of 10 pounds sterling was established by law — but only for Indian scalps. In Maryland, at one time, the bounty for Indian prisoners or scalps was as high as 50 pounds. All New England states offered bounties. The colonial governor of Pennsylvania in 1764 offered bounties of $134 for every scalp from Indian males over 10 years of age, and $50 for scalps taken from females over 10. In this hateful climate, it was with resignation that Washington wrote Dinwiddie in late 1756: "Military threats will not deter the (Indian) butchers . . . I fear it is scarcely practicable to get Indians to go now to the Twightwees (meaning to counsel for peace with the hostiles at Miamitown).

As successful as they were in the early phases of the war, the French met a series of disasters in 1759 and 1760. Quebec fell to the British in the celebrated battle on the Plains of Abraham in 1759 and Montreal was taken in 1760. That same year Major Robert Rogers took possession of Detroit and Fort Miami, coming up the Maumee River in a December sleet storm. He left Ensign Robert Holmes in charge of the fort on the St. Joseph River, just north of Miamitown. In one of the startling reversals in colonial times, France ceded all its continental North American possessions east of the Mississippi to the British, then gave its possessions west of the Mississippi to Spain.

British relations with the Indians of the Great Lakes area, however, quickly deteriorated. In just three years after taking charge, an Indian uprising of wide proportions swept the English forces from nearly every stronghold west of Niagara. This was the celebrated Pontiac uprising. Among the forts destroyed were Sandusky, Fort St. Joseph, Fort Miami, Fort Ouiatenon, Fort Venango, Fort Le Boeuf, Fort Presque Isle and at the straits of Mackinac. Only Detroit and Fort Pitt survived after long sieges.

The attack at Fort Miami developed on the night of May 25, 1763, when three soldiers outside the stockade walls were killed by Miamis from nearby Kekionga village.

Ensign Robert Holmes, the post commander, immediately closed the gates of the fort and put the garrison on alert. The following day two English traders, approaching Miamitown and unaware of the sudden hostilities, were grabbed from their boats and imprisoned at Miamitown. One of the traders, Robert Lawrence, subsequently related the events of May 27 — the day the fort fell to the Indians.

"A young Indian girl who lived with the commandant came to tell him that a squaw lay dangerously ill in a wigwam near the fort and urged him to come to her relief. Having confidence in the girl, Holmes forgot his caution and followed her out of the fort. Pitched on the edge of a meadow (the present Lakeside section of Fort Wayne) stood a great number of wigwams. When Holmes came in sight of them, the treacherous conductress pointed out one in which the sick woman lay. He walked on . . . two guns flashed from behind the hut and stretched him lifeless on the grass." Lawrence said he was shown Holmes's scalp later the same day.

There are some who doubt this rather romantic tale; yet fifty years later, during the period of American garrisons at the location, it was curiously confirmed. An old Indian woman admitted to the wife of a sutler (wagon master) that she was the Indian girl who had lured Ensign Holmes to his death.

She told Laura Suttenfield a Miami chief (presumably Le Gris or Vesculair) had cast a spell of fear over her to get her to draw Holmes out of the fort. She also told Mrs. Suttenfield that she wasn't aware at the time that she was with child — Holmes's child. Mrs. Suttenfield said that, sitting with the aging crone, was a middle-aged male Indian with blond hair.

In the subsequent decade, British relations with the Indians improved, but at a cost in relations with the Atlantic colonies. Some history texts emphasize various stamp and taxation acts, but the more immediate cause of the outbreak of the Revolution may have been the Quebec Act of 1774. It limited the colonies to the Ohio River, cutting off large areas claimed by Pennsylvania, Virginia, and other colonies; gave a privileged position to the Catholic Church; and declared lands west of the Ohio to be part of Canada administered directly by the crown. The act at once placated the French Canadians and satisfied the Indians, who were resisting colonial expansion onto their territory. But it was declared an "intolerable" measure in the colonies. This act, together with the "quartering act" which would permit British soldiers to occupy buildings in the colonies, led directly to the calling of the First Continental Congress.

But by that time, the Indians were already on the warpath; and a major staging ground for raiding parties was Miamitown. This situation developed in part with the driving out of the Delawares and Shawnees from the Virginia and Pennsylvania territories. By 1775, there were seven villages at Miamitown: the two Miami villages on either side of the St. Joseph River (one at the present Lakeside district and the other across the river to the west at the present site of the Filtration Plant); two Delaware villages a couple of miles up the St. Mary's River; and three Shawnee villages short distances down the Maumee. All were violently hostile to colonial intruders and were launching raids across the Ohio River into Kentucky (then part of Virginia) even before warfare opened on the East Coast.

Still another type of man was drawn to Miamitown in the months after the opening of the American Revolution — the partisan fighter from the Colonies who joined the British cause. Today they might be called guerrillas, but that term had not yet been coined. The best known were Alexander McKee, Matthew Elliott, and Simon Girty.

All three were deserters from Fort Pitt. McKee and Elliott worked closely with the English commander at Detroit. But even the British were wary of Simon Girty, whose name became a dirty word on the frontier for several generations. There are those who claim Simon was blamed for many crimes, however, that were probably committed by others — including his two brothers, George and James. George Girty had a cabin along the Maumee a couple miles downriver from Miamitown. James Girty married a Shawnee woman and traded for years in the vicinity. Simon's whereabouts were usually

See "Fifty Stories from Ohio History"
by Clement Martzoff (1917)
p. 103-110
also Simon Girty p. 100-107

a mystery, but he often joined Indian raiding parties on western settlements of the newly declared states. What is known, however, is that he founded a place called Girty Town, which later was renamed St. Mary's, Ohio, and took for his wife a girl named Catherine Malotte, whom he kidnapped off a flatboat on the Ohio River. An insight into Simon Girty's habits can be gained from a letter received later in the war by General Washington from the Fort Pitt commander. Dated July 11, 1782, he tells of the fate of Colonel William Crawford, a childhood friend of Washington from Virginia, and others among Crawford's force of more than 300 rangers who had hoped to attack the Maumee villages. "Dr. Knight, a surgeon I sent with Colonel Crawford, returned and he brings a melancholy fate of poor Crawford." The note described a surprise attack on the Americans near the south shore of Lake Erie by Shawnees who scattered the intruders. Crawford and his young son were among those captured. "Crawford and nine others," the letter continues, "were taken back to Sandusky. The unfortunate Colonel, in particular, was burnt and tortured in every manner they could invent. The doctor adds that a certain Simon Girty, who was formerly in our service and deserted with McKee, was present at the torturing. The Colonel begged of Girty to shoot him, but he paid no regard."

In 1778 George Rogers Clark began an adventure which was to have a considerable effect on the fact that Fort Wayne and the territory became part of the United States. Traveling from Virginia to the Mississippi, Clark and a force of 400 irregulars swung east to the Wabash and surprised the old French town of Vincennes. Nominally under British control, the post capitulated without much difficulty. This stroke didn't appear to be a matter of great concern that summer of 1778, except that it provoked Colonel Henry Hamilton, the British commander at Detroit. Hamilton was known widely among frontier Americans as "the hair buyer" because of his practice of paying Indians a bounty for American scalps. His chief agent in hair trading at Miamitown, incidentally, was Charles Beaubien at Miamitown, whose wife was the sister of a rising young warchief named Little Turtle. Upon hearing the news of the Virginians at the post on the lower Wabash, Hamilton decided to erase the impunity.

In early chronicles, Little Turtle was said to be the son of a Miami chief and a Mohican mother. His village was at Devil's Lake, twenty miles northwest of Fort Wayne. His Indian name was Mi-Che-Ki-Nah-Quah and he spoke French in addition to the Algonquin dialects, (he learned English in his later years). At that time the chiefs of the two Miami villages at three rivers were Pacan, a relative of Little Turtle, and Le Gris. Le Gris was first among equals and his influence extended to the Great Lakes and lower Wabash. Little Turtle became known as the "chief warrior" of Le Gris. Both Le Gris and Little Turtle were very militant in stemming the invasion of whites into the

Chief Little Turtle

Northwest Territory. Their activities ranged from Canada to below the Ohio River. Building from this base during the Revolutionary period, and with the help of British arms, Little Turtle became warchief for the confederated Indian nations in the 1790s.

The British force from Detroit, including a small number of regulars and a large number of Indians, traveled across Lake Erie and up the Maumee to Miamitown. In the fifteen large boats, and numerous pirogues and canoes, were 180 troops and many times that number of Indian volunteers, mostly Ottawa and Chippewa. They arrived at the present site of Fort Wayne on October 24, 1778. "At the Miamis Town," Colonel Hamilton wrote in his journal, "we met several tribes of Indians previously summoned to meet there and held several conferences, made presents, and dispatched messengers to the Shawnees, as well as the nations on our route, inviting them to join us." He told of meeting Le Gris, "the great chief of the Miamis." A number of Miamis and Shawnees joined Hamilton's campaign as it moved across the portage to the upper streams of the Wabash. Within weeks, Hamilton took Vincennes; but Clark and most of his force were not there, having returned to Kaskaskia on the Mississippi.

With the onset of winter, the Indians returned to their villages and hunting grounds. Unlike their counterparts in the towns and villages of the white man, where activity was curtailed in cold weather, the Indians were especially active. Particularly in the Great Lakes area, the warriors turned to hunting game that could more easily be tracked in the snow. Besides, fur-bearing animals had full pelts only in the winter season. But this disappearance of the Indians from Vincennes proved to be a disastrous circumstance for Colonel Hamilton and his British force. Across the icy wastes of the Illinois country, and wading half-frozen streams, came George Rogers Clark and 170 riflemen. They attacked Vincennes on February 7, 1779, completely surprising the British. The following day the garrison capitulated and Hamilton was taken prisoner. He was to spend the balance of the Revolution in a Williamsburg, Virginia dungeon.

A little more than a year later another expedition was mounted at Kaskaskia on the Mississippi. This one, led by a French officer named August Mottin de La Balme, had as its aim the sacking of Miamitown. From there, it was presumed, the force would move north and make contact with French Canadians. Colonel La Balme had been commissioned in Paris and had come to this country with the Marquis de Lafayette, though his adventure in the back country was free-booting for personal gain. La Balme followed the Clark route to Vincennes, then proceeded up the Wabash River to Ouiatenon, then on to Miamitown. On November 3, 1780, La Balme and 102 men crossed the portage from Aboite Creek and sacked the surprised village. There is no record of loss of life in the raid, but the large stores of furs at Miamitown, owned by both French traders and Indians, were taken. After setting fire to some of the wooden storehouses, the intruders retired about eight miles to the west to their encampment along the Aboite.

What followed has ever since been known as the "La Balme Massacre." A large party of Indians led by Chief Little Turtle, then twenty-eight years old, surrounded the Aboite camp in the middle of the night. The Miamis raked the sleeping forces of La Balme with rifle shot, then jumped them with knives, axes, and stone-embedded clubs. The battle was chaotic, but brief. Forty Americans were killed by rifle shot or beaten to death. Most of the others were taken prisoner, though some escaped into the swampy wilds. After the taking of scalps, the Indians made their way back to the Kekionga village at three rivers. As for the scalps, the Miami warchief would be paid later for them by Colonel Arent Schuyler de Peyster, a New York Tory who had succeeded Hamilton as the British commander at Detroit.

Back at the torture grounds, where Fort Wayne's Lakeside residential district is located today, the surviving prisoners had an opportunity to "show their bravery," as the Indians termed it. To the Indians, burning at the stake was not necessarily considered cruel. Quite to the contrary, there are reliable records indicating Indian warriors, when captured by enemy tribes, would request trial by fire. Stoicism in the face of pain and privation was an essential ritual in the establishing of an Indian brave's manhood. It remains a mystery of mind over bodily senses, but Indians could and did suffer burning and other tortures for hours and sometimes days without uttering a sound, or even evidencing a change in facial expression.

Presumably the captives in La Balme's group were not equipped to handle such treatment. The main work of the burning was performed by women, and sometimes children, as the warriors sat around and watched. Among those who failed to survive the La Balme massacre was Colonel La Balme himself. But his aide, a Frenchman named Rhys, was taken to Detroit for questioning. He eventually made his way to Niagara, where he described the end of La Balme and his fellow adventurers.

There is a bizarre postscript to the practice of the Miamis. There was recorded the existence of a man-eating clan within the tribe, some of whom lived at Eel River some twenty miles west of Miamitown; others were located at Calumet Lake, an area presently on Chicago's South Side. There are those who prefer to discount this unpleasant practice, but it is clearly a part of Fort Wayne's early history. A French trader named Jean Battiste Bruno left a detailed eyewitness account of a cannibalistic ritual at Miamitown. The practice was later confirmed by several reliable sources: General Lewis Cass, governor of the Michigan Territory; Jean Richardville, a later Miami chief; and Father Stephen Badin, a missionary to the Indians who subsequently was instrumental in the founding of the University of Notre Dame.

ittle Turtle stands opposite Anthony Wayne at the signing of the Treaty of Greene Ville in 1795.

CHAPTER
II

MIAMI INDIANS
VS.
UNITED STATES

Finally, in 1789, Congress appropriated funds for a small army to invade the Indian country. Its goals were the defeat of the Indians along the Wabash and Maumee, and the establishment of a fort at Miamitown. Treaties forced on several minor chiefs had failed to secure land as had been promised veterans of the Revolution. It was politically expedient to remove the dangers of Indian raiders from the path of the settlers.

The expedition to clear the "savages" from the newly won lands northwest of the Ohio River was commanded by General Josiah Harmar, a veteran of the American Revolution. Harmar's troops began to stream north from Fort Washington at Cincinnati during the last week of September, 1790. The force included 320 regular federal troops and 1,133 militia, mostly from Pennsylvania and Kentucky.

The march of the troops began soon after the return of an emissary named Antoine Gamelin from an extended trip to the various Indian chiefs. President Washington had hoped for a last-minute agreement with the tribes. In his journal Gamelin said, "I went to the great chief of the Miamis, called Le Gris. His chief warrior (Little Turtle) was present." The emissary said Le Gris wanted all the proposals in writing and would consult with the British commandant at Detroit and the lake nations. "He promised me that in thirty nights he would send an answer. He asked me in private discourse what chiefs had made a treaty with the Americans at Muskingum [Fort Harmar on the Ohio River]." Le Gris would seek out and eliminate chiefs coming to terms with American intruders. His answer to U.S. peace proposals (giving over of Indian lands) was an attack on Ohio River settlements. The war was on.

The army of Josiah Harmar marched for sixteen straight days. On the afternoon of October 15, an attachment of mounted Kentucky riflemen "stole in upon the Miami villages, only to find it deserted by men, women and children," according to the journal of Captain John Armstrong of the regulars. At the direction of the Warchief Little Turtle, the Indians themselves had burned Miamitown, a century-old post, to the ground. Nothing was left for the 1,453-man army to plunder in the immediate vicinity. During the following three days the troops became restless, and began straying about the vicinity in search of trophies. This resulted in the first official U.S. communication at the future site of Fort Wayne. Over the signature of General Harmar: "Camp of the Miami Village, October 18,1790. The General is much mortified at the unsoldierlike behavior of many of the men in the army, who make it a practice to straggle from camp in search of plunder .... The army is to march tomorrow morning early for their new encampment at Chillicothe, about two miles from hence (an old Indian post down the Maumee)."

On October 19 Colonel John Hardin led a unit of 300 regulars and militia along a trail leading to the northwest. They had learned of a trading post and village some twenty miles away at Eel River. They also learned, too late, that

General Josiah Harmar (1753-1813). The Miami Indians, led by Little Turtle, defeated General Harmar and an army of 1,450 soldiers in 1790 along the Maumee River. Courtesy, Fort Wayne and Allen County Public Library.

Miami warchief Little Turtle (1751-1812) led the confederation of Indian nations against the invading armies of the United States. Courtesy, Fort Wayne and Allen County Public Library.

they were victims of a cat-and-mouse game. In a swampy area partway to their destination, the troops were hit and scattered by Indian war parties under Little Turtle. Thirty-one soldiers were killed and the rest ran. This setback prompted the second official proclamation: "Camp at Chillicothe, one of the Shawnee towns on the Omee (Maumee) River, October 20, 1790. The party under the command of Captain Strong is ordered to burn and destroy every house and wigwam in this village, together with all the corn. A party of 100 men, properly officered, under the command of Colonel Hardin, is to burn and destroy effectually, this afternoon the Pickaway town (further down the Maumee) with all the corn." General Harmar announced the army would start its march back toward Cincinnati.

The evening of the following day, when the army was camped about seven miles south of Miamitown, a scout named David Williams brought Harmar some news. He said the Indians were returning to Kekionga in considerable number. The officers decided on a quick surprise attack. Harmar ordered Colonels John Fontaine and Hardin and Major John Wyllys to lead a force of 400 in a nighttime march back to Miamitown. The balance of the army would follow for the mopping up.

Drawing close to the Miami villages in the cool light just before sunrise, the Americans sought to surround the Indians. Colonels Hardin and Fontaine led the horsemen across the St. Mary's River to the west of the villages and, finding no resistance, went north to the St. Joseph River. The infantry company under Major Wyllys headed directly toward a Maumee crossing. But instead of squeezing the Indians, the horsemen to the north of the villages found themselves victims of a sudden rush of warriors near the banks of the St. Joseph River. Colonel Fontaine was shot from his mount and reportedly was scalped while still alive. The horsemen, breaking out, raced south toward the Maumee. In that direction, they could hear rapid gunfire.

Little Turtle and his warriors, armed with British rifles, caught Wyllys's infantrymen midstream with a withering ambush. Only a few of the soldiers managed to scramble up the slick clay bank and escape south. The fleeing horsemen joined the remnant of the regulars. The spot of the ambush, on the Maumee just east of Fort Wayne's present downtown, has ever since been known as Harmar's Ford, even though General Harmar wasn't there on the crucial day. Harmar, with the major portion of his army, was still several miles to the south when the fleeing raiding party was met. All turned and began the march back to Cincinnati.

President Washington addressed the joint houses of Congress (twice) regarding the desperate circumstances in the Northwest. It was decided, after the failure of still another peace mission, that the young government had little choice but to raise a larger army to punish the Indians. Word was relayed to the Indian chiefs at Miamitown (after a report from a British diplomat at

Philadelphia) that on March 3, 1791, the Congress passed legislation providing for a new frontier expedition. It called for a 3,000-man army commanded by General Arthur St. Clair.

To weaken the Indians before the main onslaught against Miamitown, two quick thrusts were made against the villages along the Wabash. On May 23, 1791, General Charles Scott led 850 horsemen across the Ohio River from Kentucky. They struck a course through what is now the hills of southern Indiana during a series of rainstorms — possibly the reason the Indians were taken by surprise. Scott's raiders completely destroyed the old post of Ouiatenon, built nearly a century earlier by the French just south of the present city of Lafayette. The Indian villages of the Weas, the Kickapoo, and the Eel River Miamis were put to the torch. Killed were thirty-two Indians and taken prisoner as hostages were fifty-eight Indians, including a number of women and children. On August 1 of the same year, Colonel James Wilkinson led 500 mounted riflemen from Fort Washington at Cincinnati and made a second attack on the Indian tribes along the Wabash; and like Scott, escaped back to the Ohio River without serious losses.

If the hope was to divide and strike fear in hostile Indian camps, the running attacks had something of the opposite effect. The Miamis, the Shawnees, and the Delawares gathered along the Maumee. From the Michigan and Ontario regions to the north came Ottawa, Chippewa, and Huron warriors. Streaming in from the shores of Lake Michigan came the Potawatomis, a tribe usually not especially friendly with the Miamis. The remnants of the Kickapoo nation came from the stricken Wabash area. The Kickapoos would remain so hostile to the Americans that they would eventually fight to their virtual extinction.

Into the face of the growing Miami Confederacy marched the army of Arthur St. Clair. Starting from Cincinnati on September 17, it was a step-by-step movement of fort building to protect the army's rear. Twenty-five miles north of Cincinnati, Fort Hamilton was erected. After another twenty miles movement north, Fort St. Clair was established. Another day's marching distance along the same line, Fort Jefferson was built. From there St. Clair began the serious thrust toward the Miami villages. In addition to slightly more than 2,000 regulars and militia (including the garrisons left at the strongpoints) St. Clair had cannons for use at "a strong and permanent military post ... at the Miami village intended for awing and curbing the Indians," as Washington had put it in his instructions relayed to St. Clair through Secretary of War Henry Knox.

The Indians were watching. The first mention of a Shawnee chief named Tecumseh appears during this campaign. He would lead an Indian uprising in a later generation. It was the function of Tecumseh and a number of others in his party to raid the supply trains of the U.S. forces and report movements

Governor of the Northwest Territory, General Arthur St. Clair. In 1791 Miami and Shawnee Indians led by Little Turtle defeated St. Clair and his army in western Ohio. It was the worst defeat an American army had ever suffered at the hands of North American Indians.

A haggard-looking General Wayne in 1796, the year he died.

back to Little Turtle and the other Indian strategists. By November 3, 1791, the invading army had reached a stream in present western Ohio where camp was set up. St. Clair said in his journal that it was the upper reaches of the St. Mary's River, which flowed northwest to Miamitown. But it wasn't. St. Clair actually was along a tributary to the Wabash, somewhat more distant from his destination than he thought. But that aspect was academic.

At daybreak, November 4, 1791, the Indians struck in what was to be the greatest rout in the history of U.S. arms in North America. Because of some desertions and companies sent after deserters, there is some question as to the exact number in camp at the date, but the number was between 1,400 and 1,600. They were caught in complete surprise. The Indians first hit the militia encamped on the north side of the stream. The militia broke and ran across the creek to the regular encampment. Another war party struck from the side, over-running the large gun emplacements. It was at that site that General Richard Butler was cut down. Butler, second in command to St. Clair, had been a commander with Anthony Wayne's Pennsylvania troops during the Revolution. Butler on this day had the honor of being the first and only known American general to be scalped by Indians. He was among 632 U.S. soldiers to lose their lives on November 4, and nearly a thousand to die during the campaign up from the Ohio and the flight back south. St. Clair survived.

After the Indians had taken control of the battleground, Chief Little Turtle ordered clay be stuffed in the mouths of the fallen. It was meant as a warning to the land-hungry intruders upon the lands of the Indians. The Indians then departed for Miamitown and the victory celebrations. Left at the site was a treasure of $30,000 in gold coins buried by Colonel William Darke, who covered St. Clair's retreat. Long sought in later diggings, the treasure remains one of the mysteries of the disaster. If it really never was found, it still lies today under the small village of Fort Recovery, Ohio.

When the legions of General Anthony Wayne reached, late in 1793, the site of St. Clair's defeat, they found hundreds of skulls and other macabre remembrances. Wayne ordered a fort built during the winter months of 1793-1794 on the battleground. Wayne named it Fort Recovery, and meant this name to be a warning to the Indians of the determination of the Republic.

Just the year before, Wayne — then a faded Revolutionary War hero facing bankruptcy — had accepted command of the American land forces. At the age of 47, going thick around the middle, he still carried in the back of his thigh the musket ball from the Revolution days. His nomination for top command of the Army was confirmed by Congress, but "rather went against the bristles," in the words of James Madison. Wayne's inordinate self-esteem, roistering ways in Philadelphia nightlife, estrangement from his wife Polly, and affair with the beauteous Mary Vining all affected attitudes concerning Wayne. Yet George Washington suggested, "the trust which is committed to him will correct his foibles."

The declining fortunes and disasters of the American military in the face of Indians in the Old Northwest Territory required a proven officer to rekindle an effective army. The serious choices for the top command were reduced to two: Wayne and Baron Von Steuben, the "Prussian drill master." Von Steuben lost out in part for the same reason as the legendary Von Steuben clause in the Constitution: the part which requires U.S. Presidents to be native-born. So popular was Von Steuben at the conclusion of the Revolution that Benjamin Franklin suggested the clause against a foreign-born as the most diplomatic bar to a potential Von Steuben move for the Presidency.

Immediately upon the appointment of "Mad Anthony," the British minister, George Hammond, warned his home government the reputation of Wayne meant the likely attack on British forts in the Northwest — such as, along the Maumee, Detroit and the Straits of Mackinac. He appraised Wayne as "the most active, vigilant and enterprising officer in the American army."

The Battle of Fort Recovery, sometimes called the "second battle" because of the earlier American defeat at the location, was perhaps the most significant of the era, though peculiarly unheralded today. "At 7 o'clock in the morning of the 30th of June [1794] one of our escorts consisting of 90 riflemen and 50 dragoons commanded by Major McMahan was attacked by a very numerous body of Indians under the walls of Fort Recovery, followed by a general assault upon that garrison in every direction." The 140 dragoons and riflemen with the pack-train made it into the fort and joined the garrison of some 300 soldiers and artillery under Captain Alexander Gibson.

The Indians continued the attack through that day and into the night. "The savages were employed during the night, which was dark and foggy, in carrying off their dead by torch light, which occasionally drew fire from the garrison," Wayne reported. "The enemy renewed the attack on the morning of July 1st but were ultimately compelled to retreat." The number of Indians was variously estimated between 2,000 and 3,000 — something of a high point in any Indian army sizes. In addition to the Miami, Shawnee, and Delaware, there were the Ottawa, Chippewa, Huron, and Potawatomi from the upper lakes and a number of Kickapoo and, reportedly, white observers from Canada. The defeat was a disaster to Indian hopes for a number of reasons. Some of the upper lakes Indians withdrew in disappointment. The British used the occasion as an excuse to withhold arms supplies to the Indians. The London government wanted no provocations that might lead the United States onto the side of France in the European war. The repulse at Fort Recovery and the hedging of the British on guns and ammunition caused the Miami warchief Little Turtle to consider for the first time the coming to terms with the Americans. Little Turtle did not go to war with bows and arrows.

Instead of marching on Miamitown to the northwest, or heading northeast toward the new British Fort Miami near present-day Toledo, Anthony Wayne went directly north to the Maumee where it is joined by the Auglaise River. He arrived August 8 and founded Fort Defiance, a strong bastion which controlled the vital river. For the final onslaught, Wayne's legion numbered approximately 3,500 men in arms — 2,000 regular federal troops and 1,500 militia, mostly mounted. Other soldiers, of course, consisted of the garrisons at posts to the rear. At a council of war further down the Maumee toward Lake Erie, the Indians had a falling-out. Little Turtle and some of the Miamis opted for avoiding a battle. This resulted in the naming of the Shawnee chief, Blue Jacket, and the Ottawa, Turkey Foot, as Indian war chiefs. The warriors, numbering about 1,700, took up a position on the north bank of the Maumee, some ten miles up river from Lake Erie, at a spot called Fallen Timbers. (A tornado had felled large trees there, thus the name.)

Wayne waited three days before moving on the Indian positions on August 20, 1794. "At 8 o'clock on the morning of the 20th the army again advanced in columns — the legion on the right, its right flank covered by the Miamis (Maumee), one brigade of mounted volunteers on the left under Brigadier General Todd and the other in the rear under Brigadier General Barbee," Wayne reported. "After advancing about five miles, Major Price's corps received so severe a fire from the enemy, who were secreted in the woods and high grass, as to compel them to retreat."

At that point, Wayne formed the infantry in two lines for a broad advance, and sent the 1,500 mounted riflemen into the wilderness to his left in a flanking effort. The frontal assault with rifles and bayonets was successful and "the savages and their allies abandoned themselves to flight and dispersed," according to Wayne. After chasing the Indians some two miles, the American army marched on the British post, Fort Miami. The 450-man garrison was commanded by Major William Campbell. The British had given the Indians no visible aid on the day of the Battle of Fallen Timbers. Wayne rode his mount up to the gates of the fort, calling for its surrender, and saying it was built illegally in U.S. territory. Campbell refused. There was no exchange of fire. Wayne began his march back up the Maumee, after destroying various buildings in the vicinity. In the battle of August 20, the Americans lost thirty-three; some 100 were wounded. The Indian losses are unknown, but they were presumed to be several times those of the U.S. Army. Chief Turkey Foot of the Ottawas was killed, but the Shawnee chief Blue Jacket was among the survivors.

When news of the victory reached the capital at Philadelphia and other cities, there were great celebrations. Vice President John Adams, speaking for the Senate, called it "so momentous in the affairs of nations." The House sent a message to Washington: "We rejoice at the intelligence of the advance of the army under the command of General Wayne."

The hero of West Point, Stony Point, Yorktown, and now Fallen Timbers, still had several jobs to complete. These included the reduction of Indian power and the building of a fort at the Miami villages.

The march of the legion up the Maumee amounted to a scorched-earth policy. Over the 100-mile route along the river, every Indian village and trader's post was leveled. Fields of corn were put to the torch. The British to the north became increasingly worried about their weakened position. John Graves Simcoe, governor of Upper Canada (Ontario), wrote to Lord Dorchester (Guy Carleton of Revolutionary fame) who was governor-general of Canada. Simcoe told Dorchester, "If Wayne be permitted to establish himself at Detroit, it may occasion the loss of both Canadas." Dorchester asked in return if Simcoe could muster sufficient forces to resist Wayne's attack.

But by that time, Wayne was going in the opposite direction. The legion reached Miamitown at sundown, September 17, 1794. The army came along the north bank of the Maumee, and upon reaching the desolate clearing, Wayne "reconnoitered" the vicinity.

He inspected the remains of the old French fort on the east bank of the St. Joseph River, then crossed over the St. Mary's River and chose a spot there for the building of a new stockade. The site was on raised ground overlooking the Maumee, just to the south of the confluence of the St. Mary's and St. Joseph rivers into the Maumee. Today the location is at the approximate intersection of Berry and Clay streets. Two other American forts were later built, in 1800 and 1815, about a block north.

An interesting sidelight of Wayne's occupation of this area concerns a man named Robert McClellan, who came to Fort Wayne with the General and had a special job. A number of movies have been made about the "last of the Western badmen." But could McClellan have been the first?

A curious entry is made in the diary of Captain John Cooke while the fort was being built. "A man deserted from Captain Thompson's company, now commanded by Captain Bines. This desertion seems somewhat extraordinary after McClellan's report to the commander. He had, in accordance with orders, killed one of the deserters he was sent after and had seen two more who were killed and scalped."

This was but a hint of Wayne's use of a hired gunman to discourage desertions from his legion, desertions having been all too common in earlier frontier campaigns. McClellan was still a young man in 1794; but his name would be mentioned again and again in west-of-the-Mississippi annals. Washington Irving tells of McClellan in his volume, "Astoria," about the development of the fur trade as far as the Pacific Coast. Irving was a friend of John Jacob Astor, and perhaps for that reason was vague about what McClellan was doing in Astor's employ in the Far West. He portrayed the

Top
The second United States fort was built in 1800 in the dimensions indicated in this 1808 drawing. It was this fortification which withstood the Indian siege in 1812. Courtesy, Allen County-Fort Wayne Historical Museum.

Right
The original town plat of Fort Wayne shows the location of the United States forts in relation to the rivers. Courtesy, Fort Wayne and Allen County Public Library.

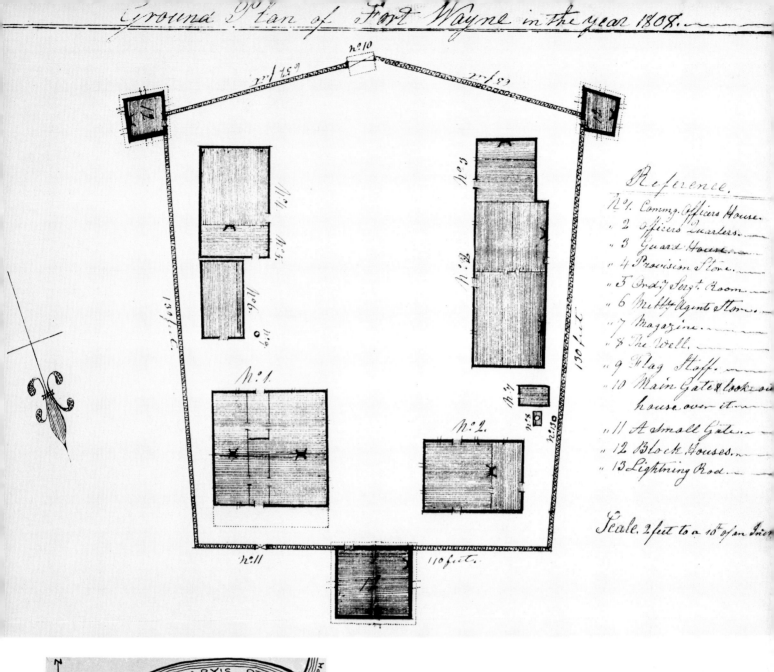

Ground Plan of Fort Wayne in the year 1808.

Reference.

No. 1. Commg. Officers House.
" 2 Officers Quarters.
" 3 Guard House.
" 4 Provision Store.
" 5 Ordny Sergt. Room.
" 6 Military Agents Store.
" 7 Magazine.
" 8 The Well.
" 9 Flag Staff.
" 10 Main Gate & lookout house over it.
" 11 A Small Gate.
" 12 Block Houses.
" 13 Lightning Rod.

Scale. 2 feet to a 10th of an Inch

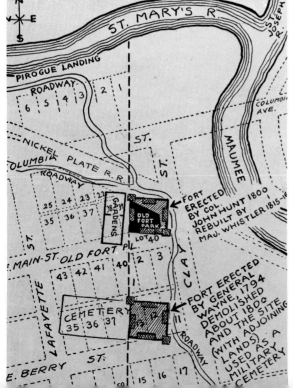

gunman as a sort of eccentric woodsman.

After his stint with Wayne, McClellan hired on with the Astor enterprise, which was trying to gain a monopoly on the Western fur trade. Astor's American Fur Company had moved into the area after Wayne drove out the British interests. In Colonel Frank Tripplett's "Conquering the Wilderness," there are numerous references to McClellan. He was short in stature, a tough man with instincts of an animal, and a loner. Traders and other early wilderness travelers were inevitably wary of McClellan, and apparently for good reason. One of Astor's aims was to supplant a Spanish trader named Manuel Lisa who operated out of St. Louis, and who had extensive connections with trappers and Indians up the Missouri River and in the Rockies. McClellan acquired a quick antagonism toward Lisa, who was seldom heard from again. That was in 1811, and there were similar episodes following in McClellan's wake. Yet, unlike the romances of the West, the first of the Western hired guns didn't die in boots at the hand of a faster draw. McClellan expired in bed years later in a small-town shack along the Mississippi, just downriver from St. Louis.

Explorers Meet

The names Meriwether Lewis and William Clark are remembered best for the expedition to the Pacific in the years 1803 to 1806. But long before that they were in the frontier wars and at Fort Wayne when the stockade was built. That was in 1794 and Meriwether Lewis was 20 years old at the time. In the drive up from the Ohio River to the Maumee with General Wayne's legion, Lewis became acquainted with Lieutenant William Clark, whom he would later choose as his partner for the Western explorations. Lewis was a family friend of Thomas Jefferson, and while the Louisiana Purchase was being contemplated, President Jefferson turned to Captain Lewis, by then Jefferson's secretary, for leadership of the expedition up the Missouri River.

William Clark, the younger brother of George Rogers Clark, was part of the Kentucky faction in the frontier army. He was something of a partisan in the pro-Wilkinson and anti-Wayne group in the 3,500-man legion. General James Wilkinson, second in command, was trying to enlist Congressional allies in bringing various charges against Wayne, the aim being Wilkinson's advancement to the top command.

Clark, twenty-four years old when he observed the building of Fort Wayne, reflected his attitude in letters written during October, 1794. "The ground is cleared for the garrison just below the confluence of the St. Joseph and St. Mary's. The situation is tolerably elevated and has a ready command of the two rivers. I think it much to be lamented that the commander-in-chief is determined to make this fort a regular fortification, as a common picketed one would be equally as difficult against the savages," he carped.

It is significant that these sentiments about the fort reflect those of General Wilkinson who, for reasons of his own, opposed permanent fortifications in the western wilderness. The use of the word "savages" indicates the attitude of Clark's renowned older brother. Though a national hero and Indiana's hallowed and honored patron saint, George Rogers Clark was seen by the Indians for what he really was: a hard-drinking frontier butcher whose high days were those of sweeping onto Indian villages with fire and knife. More women and children than warriors were the usual victims of Clark-led raids. Infant Indians were reportedly tossed into fires. About the only thing which could be said in the elder Clark's defense was that the "savages" in both Clark's bands and those of Little Turtle and the Shawnee Snake were doing the same thing. If anything, the Indians were the kinder regarding the children, which they often only kidnapped. The phrase, "The only good Indian is a dead Indian," had its roots in these campaigns, and typifies the attitude of Clark.

Zebulon Montgomery Pike is best remembered as the discoverer of Pike's Peak in Colorado. Years earlier, while a teenager, he was at Fort Wayne. Young Pike worked with a company of suppliers who were carrying the materials needed by the several garrisons in the Old Northwest frontier. This was even before his father, Major Zebulon Pike, was named commandant of the Fort Wayne post. Major Pike arrived in June, 1803. Like most other early commanders at Fort Wayne, he had served in the Revolutionary War.

The younger Pike, while working in the fort supply system, came under the influence of General James Wilkinson. When Wilkinson succeeded to the top command after the death of Wayne, Pike moved up in the pecking order. Wilkinson was already busy weaving a scheme to set up for himself a wilderness empire, an aim that was broadened when he was named military governor of the vast Louisiana Territory. Pike moved with Wilkinson to New Orleans.

It is often supposed Aaron Burr initiated a conspiracy in the American West for an inland state separate from the United States. It is even referred to as the "Burr Conspiracy." But actually Wilkinson brought Burr into the scheme rather later in the game. By that time Pike, who acted as Wilkinson's advance man in the unchartered territories, had explored as far as the Spanish settlements in New Mexico. These forays of Pike were secret surveys for Wilkinson. On one of these trips in 1806 he traveled up the Arkansas River, which brought him into view of the 14,110-foot peak that bears his name.

When Wilkinson later saw his land scheme was failing, he declared martial law in the entire area west of the Mississippi and had Burr arrested, blaming him for treasonous activities. Subsequently lawyers for Burr dug into Wilkinson's record, which resulted in accusations against Wilkinson and Pike. Both were exonerated, yet the court records clearly gave evidence that General Wilkinson, while at Fort Wayne during the building of the fort in

1794, was in the pay of Baron de Carondelet, Spanish governor-general of Louisiana.

Naming a Fort

On October 22, 1794, Colonel John Hamtramck marched his troops to the garrison at 7 A.M. After a discharge of fifteen guns, he named the fort, by a garrison order, Fort Wayne. He then marched his command into it. After the reading of the speech and the running up of the Stars and Stripes, there was a volley of cheers from the assembled troops. It was four years to the day since the morning when the Indians under Little Turtle had cut down the soldiers of General Josiah Harmar as they attempted to cross the Maumee.

Wayne had left Hamtramck as commander of Fort Wayne. Hamtramck, a native of Canada, had earlier headed the garrison at Vincennes, and after two years at Fort Wayne, would become commandant at Detroit when that stronghold was handed over by the British. On October 27, 1794, General Wayne and the main army began the march back to Fort Greene Ville (present Greenville, Ohio). With the building of the fort, the place immediately became of less significance in international politics. For a century prior to the coming of Wayne, Miamitown had been a bone of contention in power plays which not only involved the Indians, but also the French, the British, in remote degree the Spanish, and finally the new Republic. Once secured, the Fort Wayne area lapsed into a rather routine and unremarked role in the general domestic development; and with the exception of several critical moments during the War of 1812, never again figured directly as a field of contest among nations.

But that wasn't obvious in the cold winter of 1794-5. The Indians were still a force to be reckoned with. The intentions of the British were still mistrusted. Several chiefs of the Ottawas, Chippewas, Sacs, and Potawatomis came to Fort Wayne and were sent along to Fort Greene Ville in January, 1795, to talk peace terms with Wayne. Hamtramck remarked at the time, however, that the Miami, Delaware, and Shawnee remained hostile. Chiefs of these nations suggested that any parley be held at Fort Wayne rather than Greene Ville the following summer. Wayne, in a letter to the War Department, said he opposed meeting with the Indians at Fort Wayne because of supply problems and also because of apprehension at the isolation of the remote outpost "should these overtures for peace be only artifice."

The treaty of Greene Ville was remarkable because it set the pattern for most of the agreements forced on the Indians in the following decades extending across the plains and mountains to the West Coast. It was signed on August 13, 1795. Like most others to follow, it provided for the taking of desirable lands and money allowances to the Indians. It was the beginning of the reservation system, with its enforced welfare. Indians who took up the

Above
Old Fort Wayne as it appeared in 1797. From *Photo-Gravures of Fort Wayne*, 1889.

Right
A rather idealized portrait of young General Anthony Wayne. From *Photo-Gravures of Fort Wayne*, 1889.

subsidized life changed radically from the resourceful independence which characterized the tribes in their hereditary environment. Even at that, large numbers of the Indians avoided the reservations, found means to sustain themselves, and joined the mainstream of the new civilization. Today, most Americans with Indian blood would fall in the latter category.

The Treaty of Greene Ville followed lines set by Congress in 1790 in the Indian Act. It said that only Congress could make treaties with the Indians — not the various states, as previously. The main reason Congress acted in 1790 was because the Miami Confederation was putting worrying military pressure on the new Republic. It was thought that direct negotiations between the federal government and the Indians might lead to agreements and avoid war. The Act failed in that respect, but became a model for all treaties written since then. It still remains the basis for litigation and the paying over of treasury funds on Indian claims. At the treaty of Greene Ville, the Indians ceded to the United States about 25,000 square miles of land, plus sixteen other tracts or strong points. The Indians were given $25,000 and the promise of annual allowances. The strong points signed over included the sites of the present cities of Detroit, Toledo, Fort Wayne, Lafayette, Chicago, and Peoria.

After the signing of the treaty, Anthony Wayne returned to Philadelphia. He came west again the following spring, ostensibly to accept the posts of Fort Miami and Detroit from the English. The real reason was probably to gain evidence regarding the possibly treasonous operations of General James Wilkinson. The turning over of the forts was effected by Colonel John Hamtramck, who took possession of Fort Miami on July 11, 1796, and Detroit

Surveying confiscated Indian lands became a major occupation leading to government land sales and settlement by pioneers.

38 Miami Indians vs. United States

on July 13 of the same year.

Hamtramck had departed from Fort Wayne on May 17 at the head of an armed force assembled for the purpose. Wayne, by way of Fort Greene Ville, met Hamtramck at Detroit for the formal acceptance of the post from Colonel Richard England, the British commandant. In one of his last letters, Wayne referred to William Wells as rendering "very essential services to the United States from early in 1793 until this hour." Wells, who had been kidnapped at the age of twelve from a farm near Louisville, was later adopted by Little Turtle. He was married to Little Turtle's daughter, Sweet Breeze. As a young man, however, he joined Wayne's army as a spy and served the United States thereafter. Wayne asked that a military pension be granted to Wells. Rights to land just north of the St. Mary's River across from Fort Wayne were later granted Wells. He subsequently became Indian Agent at Fort Wayne. A creek next to the Wells property has ever since been called Spy Run Creek. This name is usually attributed to Wells and his wartime occupation.

There is another story on the origins of the name of Spy Run Creek. In the winter months of early 1794, two Choctaw spies in Wayne's employ were captured by Shawnees along the Maumee River. The pair were hung between two old oaks near the stream — and left to wither in the breeze for months thereafter.

Wayne left Detroit in the middle of November, 1796, and sailed across Lake Erie in the sloop *Detroit*. He became ill during the voyage and was put ashore at Presque Isle. He died there on the morning of December 15, at the age of fifty-one.

After Perry's victory on Lake Erie, General Harrison took his army directly across the lake and invaded Canada where he finally defeated Tecumseh and British forces at the Thames. Courtesy, Louis A. Warren Lincoln Library and Museum, Fort Wayne.

CHAPTER III

THE LAST GREAT TEST

In the year 1800 a special officer arrived at Fort Wayne with a particular mission — the building of a new fort. He was Captain John Whistler, and his story is one of the more fascinating of the Revolution and the aftermath. John Whistler came to America with the army of General John Burgoyne, which invaded the United States from Canada in 1777. He was with the British forces defeated by Americans under Benedict Arnold at Saratoga. After the war Whistler returned to the United States and joined the U.S. Army. He became an adjutant under General Arthur St. Clair when that expedition met disaster at the hands of Indians under Little Turtle in 1791. Whistler was severely wounded, but survived that battle. He turned up again in the legions of Anthony Wayne, as a lieutenant, and was at Fort Wayne during the building of the first American fort at the three rivers.

When Captain Whistler returned to Fort Wayne in 1800, the commander of the garrison was Colonel Thomas Hunt. For that reason the second fort is sometimes called Hunt's Fort, though its construction was apparently designed and directed by Whistler. During that same year John Whistler and his wife, Ann, had a baby boy, whom they named George Washington Whistler.

After the completion of the fort, at the location of present Main and Clay streets in Downtown Fort Wayne, Whistler went on to Detroit in 1802.

Major Whistler's final assignment at Fort Wayne followed service at Detroit, Fort Dearborn and, several posts in Ohio. He, his wife, two daughters, and son came up the St. Mary's River to take up residence in the stockade in 1814. As commander, Whistler began the construction of a third U.S. fort at the site in 1815. The plans he drew for this fort still exist and were used 160 years later for the rebuilding of the Old Fort on the north bank of the St. Mary's just across the river from Whistler's original site. A railroad elevation made the original site unusable for the recent restoration.

George Washington Whistler, the boy who was born in the fort in 1800, soon went off to West Point for a military education. He became a recognized master of railroad building in that infant industry in the 1830s and 1840s. His international repute caused Czar Nicholas of Russia to contract for his services to build a rail line from St. Petersburg to Moscow, a link which exists to this day. With him went his small son, James Abbott McNeill Whistler, who was educated at St. Petersburg until his father died there in 1849. Young Whistler subsequently moved about Europe and became one of the most celebrated artists in the second half of the 19th century. So it happens that "Whistler's mother" wasn't born at Fort Wayne, but his father was. And his grandfather built Fort Wayne — three times. His grandfather, the Major, had possessed another unusual distinction: in the heart of a virtual wilderness, he enjoyed the services of not one but two German chefs.

The years prior to the outbreak of the War of 1812 were ones of contrast between the foul and the beautiful. Colonel Hunt was occasionally accused of leniency in the operation of the fort, a situation that his successor, Captain Thomas Pasteur, was bent on correcting. The log book is loaded with entries in which the commanding officer ordered prisoners to receive as many as seventy-five lashes from a cat-o'-nine-tails. Often the punishment was meted out for visiting French Town, the place where wayward soldiers went for diversion.

French Town was located across the river from the fort at the present site of Lakeside. The mixture of Indian huts, traders' shacks, and whiskey mills grew up on land burned out in 1794 by Wayne's legions. So foul was its influence on the garrison that it was declared off-limits, except for two hours in midday, and then only with "particular leave."

Yet the records of John Johnston, an agent at Fort Wayne, indicate the area was a paradise for those inclined to the outdoor life. In the spring of 1808, he listed furs going East: deer skins numbering 1,140; raccoon, 26,938; beaver, cats, and foxes in large number; 94 bear skins; as well as the pelts of wolves, buffalo, elk, mink, and lynx. Coming back from the East across the lakes was scarlet cloth, indigo, silk, spices, German steel, wine from France, scarves from China, gunpowder, trinkets, screws, and Bibles.

But before that time something else was brewing in the wilderness and along the streams of the Indian villages. Of the major nations of the Indians, only the Shawnees had refused to sign in the Treaty of Greene Ville. It probably was only natural that out of their number would rise another who would lead the many tribes against the hated intruders.

The Shawnee medicine man, known as The Prophet, was said to have been the twin brother of Tecumseh, though there is some dispute on the twinship. He was of unstable habits and a conjurer. In the first decade of the 1800s he gained considerable following by railing against the whiskey traffic. The justification for this course can readily be seen in records at Fort Wayne during the period, when hosts of whiskey traders would flock to take advantage of Indians receiving their annual annuities. "It was a raucous scene," in the words of one traveler.

The Prophet, a reformed drunkard, had all the zealotry of that breed. Gradually the focus of his hate changed from spirits to white men. Joined by his brother, Tecumseh, The Prophet set up camp along the Wabash near the outlet of the Tippecanoe River. Francis Lafontaine, a French trader with an Indian wife, reported the following in 1809: "The Prophet had 1,000 souls under his control, perhaps 350 to 400 men, principally Kickapoos and Winnebagoes, but some Potawatomis and Shawnees and a few Chippewas and Ottawas." The following year Tecumseh called for the war dances and began a series of trips in the upper lakes region and as far south as the lower Mississippi. By early 1811 hundreds of warriors were finding their way to

Prophetstown.

Word spread like wildfire across the frontier areas. Fear, because of the terrible death tolls of the previous generation, brought widespread calls for government action against the Prophet. British guns began appearing in the hands of the Indians — a sure sign of bad times ahead. The natural choice for settling the difficulties was William Henry Harrison. Harrison, a one-time aide to Anthony Wayne and governor of the Indiana Territory since 1800 (that territory originally comprised the states of Indiana, Illinois, Michigan, Wisconsin, and part of Minnesota), had been the government's chief military figure and treaty maker in the area. He immediately met with Tecumseh and a large party of Indians, but the talks became testy and provocative, with the barest veneer of expressed good intentions able to be preserved.

Harrison decided to take the initiative. On October 5, 1811, he assembled troops numbering about 1,000 at a camp some sixty miles north of Vincennes, the territorial capital. The army moved up the Wabash on a rather indirect route on the northwest side of the river. By November 5 the Americans encamped some nine miles from Prophetstown, foolishly believing they were undetected by the Indians.

The next day, as Harrison's troops moved closer to the Indian concentrations, they were met by scouts of Indian war parties. Both sides restrained actions, however. Harrison and The Prophet exchanged verbal pleasantries about their mutual peaceful intentions. Almost immediately, both leaders returned to their own camps and prepared for attacks.

In the cold drizzle of that night, The Prophet called on the spirits of darkness to blind the enemy. He told the warriors the hour had come for the great sweep of the white man from the Indian lands. Standing high on the side of a hill, known to this day as The Prophet's Rock, he waved on more than 600 warriors toward the pickets of Harrison's soldiers. Alert sentries discovered the creeping Indian advance at 4 A.M. First there were shots; then the Indians made a headlong attack on the emplacement of the soldiers. The Battle of Tippecanoe lasted until daybreak, when the Indians scattered into the woods. The Americans suffered 38 dead and about 150 wounded. The Indian losses were slightly higher. Harrison reported he had won a decisive victory and had broken the power of the Indians. Tecumseh, however, had not been present on the day of the battle.

The victory, together with evidence of British guns in the hands of the Indians, were all Henry Clay, John C. Calhoun, and the other War Hawks in Congress needed to stir support for a war against Great Britain. It is still erroneously reported in some school texts that the cause of the War of 1812 was the impressment of American seamen and Atlantic trade squabbles. Actually, the record shows the senators and representatives of the maritime states voted against war, and those states were so divided they withheld

Top
The third United States fort, often called Whistler's Fort after its designer and builder, is shown in these plans drawn by Whistler.

Right
William Henry Harrison, governor of the Indiana Territory, rescued Fort Wayne in 1812. Courtesy, Louis A. Warren Lincoln Library and Museum, Fort Wayne.

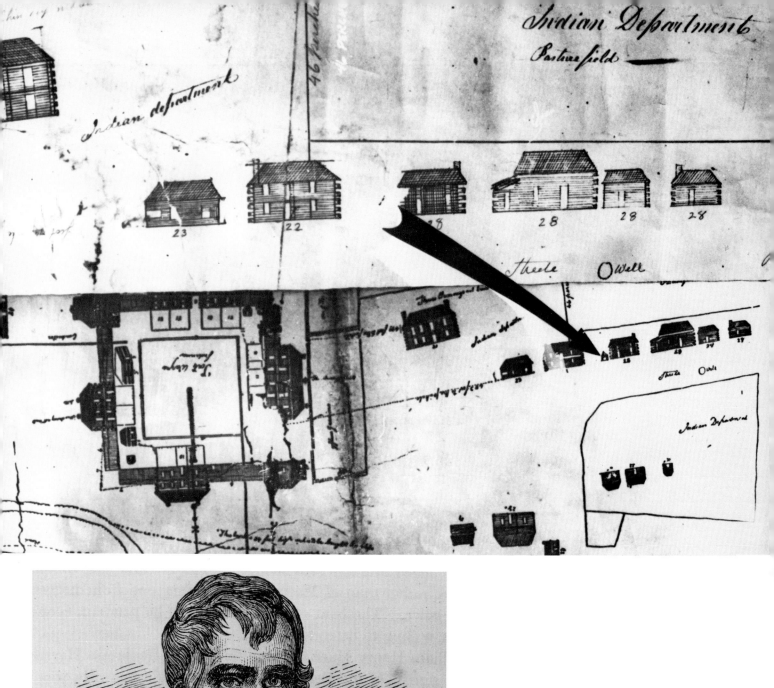

conscripts from war service. It was the Western and Southern blocs in Congress that voted for war. The aims were clear and in keeping with the temper of the times: land hunger, hate for the Indians, and hopes of annexing Canada were the ruling factors.

When Tecumseh returned to Prophetstown, he found the site burned out and the Indians gone. He made his way up the Wabash and across to Fort Wayne. There, according to the federal agent, Benjamin Stickney, he had the characteristic audacity to ask for guns and powder. His request was refused. The following spring he declared he was on his way to the British in Canada and would return to restore the power of the Indians. Congress declared war on June 18, 1812.

Though the Americans had declared the war, the British and the Indians were far quicker to move. General William Hull wasn't even at Detroit when hostilities opened. He quickly assembled some additional troops in Ohio and hurried back to the Michigan strongpoint. Hull took an army of 1,800 men across the Detroit River with the aim of taking Fort Malden. But learning British reinforcements were on the way, he returned across river to Detroit. The British, under General Isaac Brock with a large number of Indians under Tecumseh, pursued Hull across the river. Bringing up both land batteries and gunboats, the attack on Detroit commenced. Hull surrendered on August 16.

By that time a fearful episode was being played out at Fort Dearborn (Chicago). William Wells, at Fort Wayne, had been asked to take a party to Fort Dearborn, to help with the evacuation and bring the small number of military personnel and their families back to the safety of Fort Wayne. The commander at Fort Dearborn, Captain Nathan Heald, was married to Wells's niece. When Wells arrived along the shores of Lake Michigan, the fort was already being evacuated under pressure of more than 1,000 Winnebago and Potawatomi Indians. An attack began in the sand dunes where downtown Chicago is now located. It is remembered as the Fort Dearborn massacre. Few of the seventy soldiers or twenty-seven women and children survived. Wells was made a particular example. His head was put on a pole and his heart cut out on August 15.

The siege of Fort Wayne began on August 21, 1812. At first communications and supplies were cut off. For weeks the government to the south and east had no way of knowing whether its most advanced remaining military post was still in operation. In fact Captain James Rhea and a garrison of 100 men were to hold off Indian raiders of up to 1,000 for nearly a month. Following long weeks of almost unbelievable indecision on the part of the Madison administration on military appointments, General William Henry Harrison finally received confirmation of his command in the West on September 3.

On September 5, he posted this notice at his headquarters at Piqua, Ohio:

Though the relentless Shawnee, Tecumseh, turned a thousand miles of frontier land into a bloodbath in the War of 1812, he failed in his attempt to take Fort Wayne. Courtesy, *News-Sentinel*.

"Mounted Volunteers: I have now a more pressing call for your services. The British and Indians have invaded our country, and are now besieging (perhaps have taken) Fort Wayne. Every friend to his country, who is able to do so, will join me as soon as possible, well mounted, with a good rifle, and twenty or thirty days' provision. Ammunition will be furnished at Cincinnati and Dayton."

Harrison's army grew as he moved north. He had 2,200 men en route out of Piqua and 3,400 by the time he drew within seventeen miles of Fort Wayne on September 11, 1812. At that point he had a friendly Shawnee named Logan scout the area and bring back a report that some 1,500 warriors were besieging the stockade. That night there was sporadic gunfire, as Indians tested Harrison's hastily fortified camp. The Indians made a last attempt on Fort Wayne, described as a hail of bullets, and numerous fires started along the palisades. At daybreak Harrison made his move over the final miles. The Americans covered the seventeen miles and reached Fort Wayne two hours before sunset. But the Indians had slipped away in the swampy thickets of the area.

After the rescue of Fort Wayne, there were marches and counter-marches by both American forces, under General James Winchester, and British under Colonel Henry Procter. Nothing had been decided, but the Indians controlled most of the Maumee and Lake Erie area. Finally in the cold of January 1813, the Americans moved toward Detroit as far as the Raisin River, near the outflow into Lake Erie. A force of 900 soldiers occupied a place called French Town. A larger number of British and Indians surrounded the Americans. The attempt to escape was frustrated by heavy snow. Among the Americans killed was Colonel John Allen, after whom Allen County is named. General Winchester was taken prisoner. He was taken across the frozen Detroit River to Fort Malden. Some 200 wounded were left behind at French Town. The following morning the Indians moved in and killed everyone, then burned French Town.

By 1816, the year Indiana became a state, Fort Wayne had entered a rather peculiar and barbaric period. The garrison was declining in discipline and numbers. The fort became the central dispensing point of Indian annuities to tribes for hundreds of miles around. There was a heavy illicit whiskey traffic and many fights for advantage in the declining fur trade. Murders were commonplace and the area was replete with renegades and refugees from more civilized climes.

"The insatiable thirst for intoxicating liquors that appears to be born with all the yellow-skinned inhabitants of America, and the thirst for gain of the citizens of the United States appears to be capable of eluding all the vigilance of the government," remarked Major Ben F. Stickney, agent of the council house for Indian affairs. Thomas Scattergood Teas, a visitor from

Philadelphia, said, "It has been the custom of the traders to bring whiskey by the kegs, and hide in the woods a half-mile from the fort, a short time previous to the paying of the Indians" who after trading away money, guns and bracelets "squat on the ground and pass the canteen rapidly around, and sing, whoop and hallo." Fort Wayne was closed as a military post on April 19, 1819, the day the last commandant, Major Josiah Vose, marched the garrison out of the stockade. They went down the Maumee to Detroit.

The main government representative remaining was Dr. William Turner, an Indian agent who had married Ann Wells, the daughter of Captain William Wells and the granddaughter of Chief Little Turtle. (Little Turtle, incidently, had died on July 14, 1812, and was buried on Wells's property across the river from the fort.) Dr. Turner attempted to halt the liquor traffic and get the Indians to take up agriculture and assimilate into the new culture.

His successor in 1820, John Hays, reported greater successes in these efforts. Hays, the first Jewish resident of the community, was succeeded as agent by General John Tipton in 1823. But except for a few families related to the Miami chiefs who were granted land tracts, little of permanence was accomplished.

Isaac McCoy arrived in 1820 with his family and took up residence in the abandoned fort. McCoy, a Baptist missionary, established the first school. The linguistic mix of the children says much of the fort's heritage. Of the twenty-five pupils from the frontier village, ten were English-speaking children of American government and pioneer families; six were French-speaking children of the old traders; eight were Indian children who possibly spoke some French in addition to the Indian dialects (Algonquin); and one was a Negro child who presumably spoke English. A record of the names of the children is no longer available. Classes were in the Council House, which stood just west of the fort about where Main and Lafayette streets intersect today. In the second year, McCoy received federal aid and expanded his class to forty-two pupils. The nearest school or settlement, McCoy reported, was "nearly 100 miles distant."

Left
An engraving of the Indiana State Seal.

Opposite
Top
Colonel John Allen, for whom the county was named, was killed at the Raisin River Massacre in January of 1813. Courtesy, Fort Wayne and Allen County Public Library.

Right
Indiana gained statehood in 1816. The first capitol building was at Corydon, but was later moved to Indianapolis where it was more centrally located.

STATE HOUSE OF INDIANA.
1876

Traffic along the Wabash-Erie Canal. The canal, which extended 400 miles, was started at Fort Wayne.

CHAPTER
IV

A
TOWN
EMERGES

During the same years McCoy was teaching school, in the 1820s, others observed the Fort Wayne environment. Captain James Riley wrote: "There were at least one thousand whites here from Ohio, Michigan, New York and Indiana trading with the Indians. Horseracing, gambling, drinking, debauchery, extravagance and waste were the order of the day and night."

In 1823, Major Stephen Long, a topographical engineer, wrote: "At Fort Wayne we made a stay of three days, and to a person visiting the Indian country for the first time, this place offers many characteristic and singular features. The confusion of tongues owing to the diversity of Indian tribes which generally collect near the fort make the traveler imagine himself in a real babel. The business of a town of this kind differs so materially from that carried on in our cities that it is almost impossible to fancy ourselves within the same territorial limits; but the disgust which we entertain at the degraded condition in which men appear is perhaps the strangest sensation."

Yet in this "awful scene," as a visiting churchman termed it, there was the beginning of a permanent town. The adventurers and the hangers-on shifted out to the West. A twenty-two-year-old named Samuel Hanna came to Fort Wayne from St. Mary's, Ohio, in 1819. He figured in a remarkable range of interests for the next half-century: merchant, town planner, judge, legislator, canal builder, railroad builder, and banker. Another notable was Colonel Alexander Ewing, who had been with General Harrison's relief expedition to lift the siege of Fort Wayne in 1812. He returned with his four sons and three daughters in 1822. His wife, Charlotte Griffith, was the sister of Captain William Griffith, victim of the Fort Dearborn massacre.

The Ewing sons included Charles W., who became the president-judge of the Circuit Court; William G., the first man to be admitted to the bar in Allen County; George W., whose trading empire eventually spread to an area extending from Detroit to St. Louis, supplanting John Jacob Astor's American Fur Company; and Alexander H., prosperous Cincinnati merchant. The daughters included Charlotte, married to William Hood; Lavina (for whom Lavina Street in Fort Wayne is named), married to George B. Walker; and Louisa, married to Charles E. Sturgis (Sturgis, Michigan, is named for him).

A number of French-Canadians became permanent fixtures in the infant community. Francis Comparet and Alexis Coquillard were resident agents for the American Fur Company. James Peltier and Louis Bourie traded with the Indians and later were storekeepers.

Jean Baptiste Richardville, son of Canadian Drouet Richardville and Tacumwa, [the astute sister of Little Turtle] doubled as chief of the Miamis and operator of the portage concession. Richardville became the richest Indian in the United States by virtue of the tolls over the seven-mile strip of land between the St. Mary's River and the Little Wabash River. Fort Wayne's other name — Summit City — stems from this portage. The St. Mary's flows

NOT TRUE

Top Left
Sam Hanna, the mover behind the Wabash-Erie Canal. This photograph, circa 1848, is the earliest known photograph associated with Fort Wayne.

Top Right
William G. Ewing, along with his brothers, broke the fur-trading monopoly of John Jacob Astor.

Right
Jean Baptiste Richardville, Little Turtle's nephew, grew rich from the portage trade near Fort Wayne. He also served as a Miami chief.

northeast, to the Maumee-Lake Erie-St. Lawrence route to the Atlantic. The Little Wabash flows southwest, eventually to the Ohio, Mississippi, and the Gulf of Mexico. In an era when water was the chief commercial right-of-way, the key portage was richly significant.

The federal government finally agreed in 1822 to sell the old plat, or the lands where the fort stood and its immediate surroundings. The city's downtown area is located on this land. John T. Barr and John McCorkle purchased the original fort plat for $2,838 — or about $5 an acre for the 600 acres. Paul Taber, a former sea captain, bought 240 acres west of the town plat for $1.25 an acre. The sale was held on October 22, 1823. Robert Young surveyed and laid out the town. Taber's daughter, Lucy, married Colonel Thomas Swinney, who built a house on the west plat, a house that later became the home of the Historical Society. In the old fort plat, the most desirable lots were along Columbia Street. Most of these went for $100 each to Alexander Ewing, Sam Hanna, and Allen Hamilton. Hamilton was named the first sheriff and later started the first bank. Hanna had been named the first postmaster in 1822.

Allen County was formed by a state act on December 17, 1823. The Allen Circuit Court was activated on April 1, 1824. Samuel Hanna and Benjamin Cushman were elected judges; William Rockhill, James Wyman and Francis Comparet were named commissioners, and Anthony L. Davis, clerk. Charles Ewing was appointed by the court as prosecuting attorney. In 1824 Barr and McCorkle, original purchasers of the old plat, donated a square of land for the courthouse at Main, Court, Berry, and Calhoun streets.

In 1837 David Wallace was elected governor of Indiana. In addition to fathering Lew Wallace (who would later serve as a Union general in the Civil War, govern Southwestern territories, and author *Ben-Hur*), David Wallace was distinguished by presiding over Indiana's great canal-financing disaster. So great became the debt service on the notes, that it threatened to surpass the entire tax income of the state. The state went bankrupt; one result of this was to bring about legislation forbidding bonded indebtedness by state government in Indiana, a restriction that exists to this day.

The Wabash-Erie Canal, which became the longest manmade waterway in the history of the world, was started at Fort Wayne. It extended 400 miles from Toledo on Lake Erie to Evansville on the Ohio River. The moving spirit behind the canal was Samuel Hanna.

Congress passed legislation in 1828 for the sale of public lands for such waterways. But even before that, at Fort Wayne in 1826, a treaty with the Miami Indians provided land for waterways; and, at the direction of President John Quincy Adams, a survey was begun. Colonel James Shriver was detached from the War Department to manage the survey, and he chose Fort Wayne as the starting place. By action of the Indiana Legislature, Sam Hanna, David

Top
A 19th-century view of the Maumee River showing traffic between Fort Wayne and Lake Erie.

Right
The Wabash-Erie Canal crossed over the St. Mary's River near West Main Street.

Burr, and Robert John were appointed canal commissioners. The following year, in 1829, the Ohio Legislature enacted provision for its part of the route.

So little of the canal structure remains that it is difficult to visualize in the 1980s that which was initiated 150 years before. The concept was monumental. For the most part the route was through a wilderness of thick forests, swamps, and sparse population. Indians were still the most numerous inhabitants in some of the villages along the way. Yet the construction spurred immigration, particularly from Germany and Ireland. Soon newspapers in London were reporting the great enterprise in the American wilderness, and editorially asking what was wrong with the English regime and slow public works at home. Due to the canal the westward movement of the U.S. population was phenomenal. In Indiana the growth shifted from the south to the north. The state population went from 350,000 in 1830 to 684,000 in 1840 and to 988,000 in 1850. Many more settlers went through Indiana to Illinois and the outlying territories.

The first shovel of dirt turned for the Wabash-Erie Canal was in the spade of Sam Hanna at Fort Wayne on February 22, 1832. Jesse L. Williams, who had canal experience to the East, was employed as chief engineer. There were celebrations, and the era of land speculations was launched.

More than a thousand men were working on the canal by 1834. They outnumbered the regular population, and changed forever the atmosphere and commerce of the area. The Irish hands soon comprised two rather hostile groups — those from County Cork and those from Ulster. It was the same combination that plagues Irish affairs today, and in the 1830s "the Irish war" raged in the Indiana back country. At one point, the state militia was called out to restore the peace.

The first section of the canal was completed in 1835 between Fort Wayne and Huntington. A celebration on July 4 marked the occasion. A canal boat for the initial trip was jammed, and included thirty-three girls in costume. The festive group moved at the usual pace of a canal boat — three miles an hour. These boats were pulled by mules that walked along the side on the towpath. At that rate it took approximately eight hours for the twenty-four-mile trip to Huntington.

The canal digging proceeded mile by mile through swamp lands and wooded areas, where the trees often had trunks ten or more feet in circumference. Mosquitoes plagued the sweating workers in the hot summer months. Double rations of whiskey were issued to ward off malaria. It was said a man died for every 100 feet of canal. Wages were advanced to $12 a month to attract more laborers. Land speculation grew to a mania. Fortunes were made by the shrewd and lucky at Evansville and Lafayette.

But in 1837 a panic caused land sales to dry up and banks begin to fail. Jesse Williams said it would cost $23 million more to complete the canal.

Jesse L. Williams, chief engineer for the building of the Wabash-Erie Canal.

Opposite
Top
An 1871 map of downtown Fort Wayne shows the rivers, rail routes, and canal.

Bottom
The original plat of Fort Wayne, drawn in 1823.

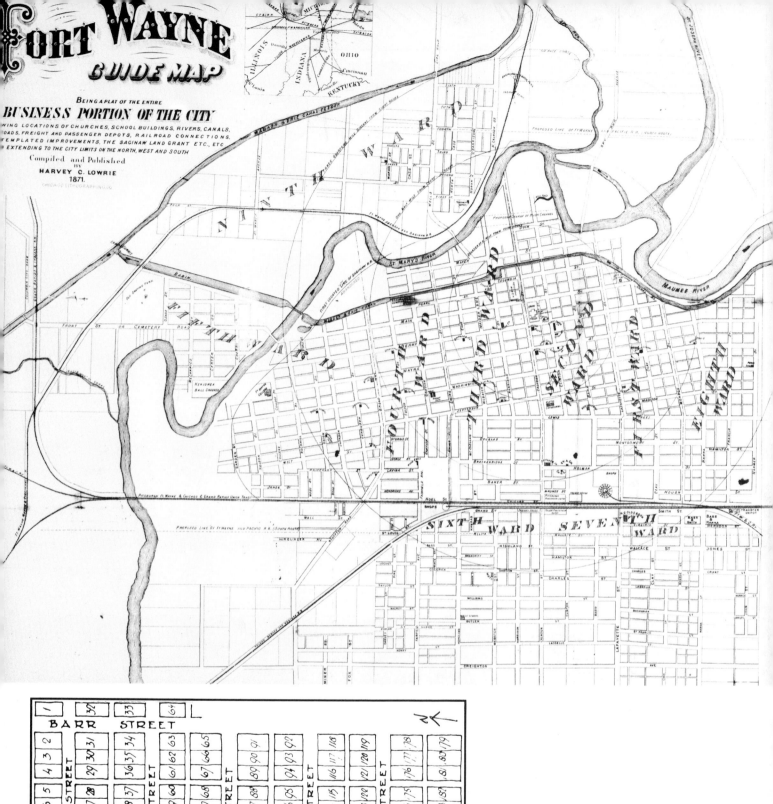

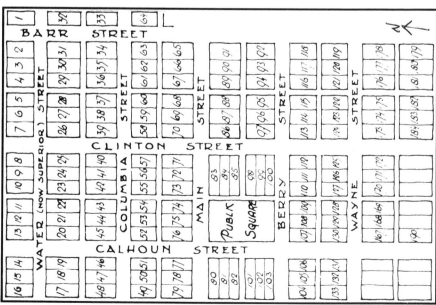

Governor Wallace said the entire state income wouldn't pay the interest on the notes. About this time rumors spread, and it was later shown to be true, that $2 million of the canal funds had been embezzled and the New York firm of Morris Canal and Banking Company had been able to buy notes greatly discounted. But the canal was continued on scrip money, called "red dog" after the color of the paper. The canal was finally finished in 1843. Presidential candidates and other noteworthies attended the July 4 dedication event at Fort Wayne. There were bands and torchlight parades. Taverns, already the town's biggest industry, did a swinging business.

People were packed on the boats by the hundreds, sometimes forty or more to a room. Lucy Beste, a traveler from England, remarked on the mosquitoes "that swarmed on the windows and inside our berths." She noted the "miles of woodland which had never seen an ax ... magnificent timber ... great sticks of black oak." There was one bathroom for the entire packet, with water in a bowl and a comb for the gentlemen. The main canal cargo, however, was the freight — coal, limestone, pork, flour, hides, wool, and wood products. Plank roads were built from the canal trading centers to outlying communities. These roads with oak cross timbers carried regular stages and droves of cattle. Tolls were charged at various gates, as they were built and maintained by private enterprise. Sam Hanna, Allen Hamilton, James Barnett, and the Ewing brothers financed the first one out of Fort Wayne: the Lima Road which went north as far as Sturgis, Michigan.

But before and after the building of the canal, a large portion of the travelers came overland from the East. Families in ox carts and horse-drawn wagons, or just lone men on foot. One of the latter was a man named John Chapman, known then and afterwards in pioneer lore as Johnny Appleseed.

When John "Johnny Appleseed" Chapman came to town, he didn't come as a stranger. He had been in and out of the area since the days of the War of 1812. In fact, during that war, he was one of the few whites who could wander safely in the Indian country. Indian children would run after him, as did other children. He would always find some kind of gift or ribbon, or at least kind words. Sometimes he would stop and tear out a page from his Bible, explaining the meaning of holy writ to anyone who would listen. The Indians regarded him as a medicine man.

Chapman was born on September 26, 1776, in Springfield, Massachusetts. He first appeared in the Ohio country in 1801 and already had the habit of carrying horse-loads of appleseeds and plantings from Pennsylvania. His earliest known nursery was nine miles below Steubenville, Ohio. He never carried a weapon and was especially fond of horses. In the fall he would round up old or lame horses and shelter them through the winter. He existed on milk, grain, and, of course, apples.

George Brackenridge, an early resident, recalled seeing Johnny Appleseed

Top
Artist Jim McBride shows a typical canal boat and mule tied up at the Fort Wayne landing in this ink drawing.

Right
The deteriorating interior of a canal warehouse built at Fort Wayne in 1856. Courtesy, Fort Wayne and Allen County Public Library.

on Fort Wayne streets in the early 1830s: "He was simply clad, in truth like a beggar. He went on foot — seeking the small fractions of land that occurred in the surveys of public lands. He would not sleep in a bed, but on the floor or the ground. For undershirts, he wore coffee sacks." In his old age he roamed the areas of the St. Joseph and Maumee rivers northeast of Fort Wayne. Thus it happened on a cold March night of 1845 that he learned of cattle invading one of his orchards some 20 miles up the St. Joseph River. He set out on foot, but was overcome by fatigue and exposure. Finding lodging at the home of William Worth, he sat on the cabin floor and had a bowl of bread and milk. The family joined him in a reading of the Sermon on the Mount. He emphasized the beatitude: "Blessed are the poor in spirit for theirs is the kingdom of heaven." He died the next day.

The *Fort Wayne Sentinel* published his obituary on March 25, 1845, saying he had died on March 18. The report noted he had been a regular visitor to the city for more than twenty years, and had been seen on the Fort Wayne streets a day or two previous to his death. The body was taken on the feeder canal, which ran from a dam six miles north of town on the St. Joseph River to supply water for the canal, to the burial ground of the David Archer family. The site rests today in Johnny Appleseed Park on the city's north side and is known as the Johnny Appleseed Gravesite.

In the years of Johnny Appleseed and other wanderers in the new lands, most people lived close to the earth. They provided their own food. Corn stalks served as a mattress for sleeping. Many people would go for a year at a time without any real money, with barter often providing the only extras.

It wasn't until 1827 that the first grist mill was built. James Barnett and Sam Hanna located it on the east bank of the St. Mary's River, just south of the present Broadway Bridge. It was destroyed by fire in 1888. A second grist mill was erected by Henry Rudisill and Henry Johns on the opposite side of town in 1830. The Rudisill mill was on the west side of the St. Joseph River, south of the present State Boulevard Bridge. The ruins were still standing in 1910; and when the river water was lowered by Maumee dam roller lifting in 1979, remains of the wooden Rudisill mill dam were uncovered, causing a stir of curiosity in the community.

Pioneers had to live through the winter and much of the following spring and summer on the previous growing season's produce. The solution to saving apples, vegetables, and other produce was the root cellar. Even today an occasional root cellar can be found in old farm houses near Fort Wayne, and in early town houses. Root cellars were also built onto hillsides some distance from a settler's hut. Along the slopes of the St. Mary's River on Fort Wayne's south edge are several relics of root cellars dug during the days when Indians still roamed that vicinity.

The procedure for making a root cellar was to dig a hole or wide trench

Johnny Appleseed, as carved by Dean Butler in 1976. Courtesy, Fort Wayne and Allen County Public Library.

Opposite
Top Left
The St. Joseph River, below the Rudisill Mill dam, 1889. Courtesy, Fort Wayne and Allen County Public Library.

Top Right
Johnny Appleseed reading a bible tract to a farm family just north of Fort Wayne.

Center
The grave of Johnny Appleseed lies in the David Archer family graveyard near the St. Joseph River. Courtesy, Fort Wayne and Allen County Public Library.

Right
The residence of John Archer. Archer was the eldest son of David Archer, the close friend of Johnny Appleseed. Courtesy, Allen County-Fort Wayne Historical Society.

into the side of a hill, piling the displaced earth where it could easily be reached to throw back on top of the cave roof. If the ground was very firm, no side walls were necessary. A peaked roof of logs was built over the cavity with supports in the center to keep the roof from collapsing from the weight of the ground on top. The earth — about two feet thick — kept it cool in the summer and reasonably warm in the winter. This type was completely frost-free. These underground mud chambers also served as the community's first ice houses. That may explain why some of them were built along slopes to the St. Mary's River, where ice could be cut in February, with the reasonable expectation some of the ice would last to the Fourth of July.

Until just the past couple of decades, motorists were likely to see curious small barns with drive-through centers in farm areas. These were the storied corn cribs, where little boys hid joke books and first learned the facts of life. The original corn cribs were built of logs and consisted of storage places on either side of the pass-through and with a roof over the whole arrangement. The farmer could simply drag his wagon under the roof, unload on either side, then continue on out. That was a lot easier than making the ox or horse back out, as would have been necessary with a closed-end barn. The spaces between the logs of the crib let the air circulate and dry the corn. Corn was the staff of life, both for early settlers and their cattle. The cribs developed before barns did, and such sheds were often the only building on a pioneer's lot, other than his hut or cabin.

On the grounds of the Swinney Homestead at West Jefferson Street, about a mile from downtown, can be seen a log cabin. It is a fine example of a pioneer house and was moved to its present location from an original rural site some miles to the southwest. Several other early log houses survive in the immediate area.

These timber houses, rustic as they are, were probably fancy when compared with most of the huts of the first pioneer families and traders. The earliest abodes were little more than four sides, with a thatch or shake roof over a dirt floor. There were no windows, and the only light came through the door when it was open or from the fire.

Early log huts were dark and dank places, causing a high rate of "consumption" (tuberculosis) and childbirth deaths. Most early fireplaces in huts of northeastern Indiana were made of timbers, with mud packed on the inside to keep the fire from burning the logs. When the mud cracked off, it had to be quickly reapplied or the house would burn down — a common tragedy for the negligent.

The pioneer's cabin was made from the timber readily at hand. Most often, the wood chosen was black walnut, oak, or maple, and occasionally elm. The preferred timbers were of white oak — the same wood Anthony Wayne chose for his fort. Heavy and almost impregnable, white oak when properly dried,

Opposite
Top
By the 1870s Indiana farmers had more sophisticated equipment to cut wheat in the fields.

Bottom
Henry Rudisill employed German women to help with the corn husking in Fort Wayne during the 1830s.

Below
Plowing with oxen in the 1830s.

was particularly resistant to earthy rot. We often imagine early cabins had stone fireplaces and chimney. Sometimes they did. But more often the harried pioneer didn't have time for such fine points in the face of a gathering winter.

Life had few amusements for the early settlers; maybe that is why hangings were widely attended events both prior to and after the Civil War period. There were a number of them in Fort Wayne. However, only one double hanging is mentioned in the records. And the job was botched. In that era people streamed into town from miles around for these public affairs. So it was on a sunny morning in April, 1855. "The Mad Anthony Guards under the command of Colonel George Humphrey and a large police force were stationed around the place to keep back the crowd," the *Fort Wayne Sentinel* reported. The high scaffold was standing bare at the center of the square — known then and now as the Jailhouse Flats along Calhoun Street. Out of the jail and into the center of attention were brought Benjamin Madden and George Keefer, convicted of murdering old George Dunbar at a lumber yard.

Two ropes were tightened over the crossbeam, and one each attached around the necks of the condemned pair. When the word was given, the platform was released, leaving Keefer suspended in the air. "Horrible to relate," the news account reported, "the rope by which Madden was suspended snapped in two and dropped him to the ground with a deep red gash at his throat. The miserable wretch walked around among the horror-stricken and almost paralyzed witnesses, saying: 'Don't murder me, boys.'" Joel Forbush took Madden and led him again to the scaffold. Keefer was still hanging, preventing them from lifting the platform. So Forbush climbed to the top of the crossbeam, and, holding the rope with his strong arms, literally hanged Madden himself.

Saloons and churches competed for souls early in Fort Wayne, and for a long time the saloons seemed to have the stronger hold.

The Reverend John Ross, a Presbyterian, began a mission in 1822. The Reverend James Holman, a Methodist minister, began services in his home along the St. Mary's River in 1824. The Reverend James Chute formed the first permanent Presbyterian fellowship in 1831, which led to the building of the first Presbyterian Church on East Berry Street in 1837. The Reverend Jesse Hoover, a Lutheran, with backing of Adam Wefel, Henry Trier, Henry Rudisill, and Conrad Nill, began construction of St. Paul's Lutheran Church in 1839 on Barr Street, the site of the present church. The Second Presbyterian Church was started in 1844 because of a fight over the pulpit of the first one. Henry Ward Beecher, abolitionist and brother of *Uncle Tom's Cabin* author Harriet Beecher Stowe, split off some of the First's congregation and became preacher of the Second.

Father Stephen Badin came to Fort Wayne in 1830 and helped pick out a site for a Roman Catholic church in 1831. This land along Calhoun Street is the present Cathedral Square. A log building was erected in 1837 and was called St. Augustine's Church. Father Julian Benoit, a native of France, succeeded in 1840 the first resident pastor, Reverend Louis Mueller. Father Benoit drew the plans and began construction of the cathedral in 1859. It is the same cathedral which stands today — the city's oldest remaining church. John Henry Luers was named first bishop of Fort Wayne in 1857. The first Episcopal congregation was formed in 1839, and shared a church with the Methodists built in 1840 at the northeast corner of Berry and Harrison streets. The present Trinity Episcopal Church at Berry and Fulton streets was erected in 1865.

The first Jewish congregation, known as The Society for Visiting the Sick and Burying the Dead, was formed in 1848. Officers of this first Jewish congregation in Indiana included Frederick Nirdlinger, Sigmund Redelsheimer, Isaac Wolf, Isaac Lauferty, and Rabbi Joseph Solomon. They met in the Nirdlinger house in the 200 block of West Main Street, which was also a way station on the "underground railroad" which spirited runaway slaves north prior to the Civil War. The name was changed to Achduth Vesholom Congregation in 1861.

It may have been more than coincidence that Beecher was in Fort Wayne very soon before it became a station on the underground railroad. Fort Wayne, being between Cincinnati on the Ohio River and Detroit across the river from Canada, was about midway along the shortest route from slave states to freedom. It was illegal to help slaves escape, thus travel was by night and records rare. What is known, however, is that the Nirdlinger house among others in Fort Wayne provided hiding for the fugitives. A number of Jewish families in LaGrange to the north along the Lima plank road, and families in towns to the south, participated in the link. There are no figures on how many slaves were brought through in those years. They were hidden in wagons or in the holds of boats. It also should not be presumed only altruistic motives were involved, though that was certainly one aspect of the work. Funds were raised by organized interests, particularly in New England, to finance the flights. Rewards were offered for capturing a fugitive and fines up to $1,000 were levied against citizens aiding in the escapes.

All this happened in a northern town that was unusually pro-Southern in sympathy, and remained so right through the Civil War. The city's first newspaper, the *Sentinel,* was strongly Democratic. It was founded in 1833 by Thomas Tigar and S.V.B. Noel. A Whig paper was established in 1841 by George Wood and passed into the hands of John Dawson, a super-patriot on one hand and conservative on slavery on the other. A German-language weekly, *Der Deutsche Deobachter Von Indiana,* was started in 1843 and remained strongly Democratic in tone. This situation might partially explain why Abraham Lincoln, when running for President in 1860, failed to carry

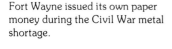

Fort Wayne issued its own paper money during the Civil War metal shortage.

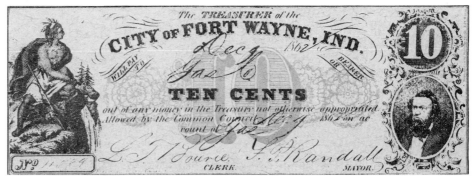

Allen County. The town and county cast 3,224 ballots for Stephen A. Douglas and 2,552 for Lincoln. President Lincoln, when running for reelection in 1864, did even worse in Allen County. General George McClellan, the Democrat, received 4,932 to Lincoln's 2,244. That surely was unusual for a sizable Northern community. An organization called the Order of the Sons of Liberty opposed the war and advocated states in the Northwest secede from the Union. As late as June of 1864, it assembled at Fort Wayne to affirm states' rights and opposition "to this unholy and unconstitutional war."

Abe Lincoln stopped in Fort Wayne only once — in the middle of the night to change trains. By contrast Stephen Douglas came to town on October 2, 1860, to address a huge throng from the balcony of the Rockhill House, a large hostelry on Broadway which later became the St. Joseph Hospital. A parade in his honor went down Main Street to the iron Wells Street Bridge, and a large saw log, representing Lincoln, was tossed into the river. At nightfall a torchlight parade swung around the County Courthouse, where the Democrats hanged a straw figure of Lincoln and cheered when it went up in flames.

Regardless of these Confederate sympathies, Allen County sent more than 4,000 men to the fields of battle during the war. Many received their training at Camp Allen, near West Main Street, just west of the St. Mary's River.

Sion Bass, founder of Jones, Bass & Company and brother of John Bass, died at the Battle of Shiloh on April 7, 1862. Colonel Bass was one of 489 Allen County men killed during the war.

In the wake of the death of Sion Bass developed one of the more human stories to come out of the Civil War. To thousands of wounded and dying Union soldiers there was a woman known simply as, "Mother George." She is mentioned in various journals and historical recollections dealing with the terrible final campaigns.

Her maiden name was Elizabeth Hamilton Vermont; she had been widowed by a W.L. George. It is believed that her daughter, Eliza, was married to Sion Bass. After the body of Bass was returned to Fort Wayne in 1862, Mother George joined the Union army as a nurse. She was with the forces in the Wilderness Campaign and in front of Lookout Mountain at Chattanooga. She reported in her letters, "An ambulance train brought in 1,200 wounded men . . . amputated legs and arms . . . some wounded in the head . . . from Hooker's Division." A graying woman of 54 years, she was one of the few nurses to move with Sherman's army across the bloody miles from Kennesaw Mountain to Atlanta. From there Mother George crossed Georgia and was still working with the suffering and dying in 1865 in North Carolina. There under her care came the 11,000 prisoners from the terrible stockade at Salisbury — footless, dying of typhoid, frostbitten. Mother George herself contracted typhoid and died there on May 9, 1865.

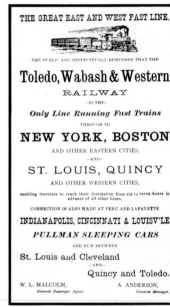

Abraham Lincoln came into Fort Wayne by way of the Wabash Railroad while en route to New York to deliver his Cooper Union address.

Opposite
A large crowd was on hand when Ben Madden and George Keefer were hanged in 1855.

The city of Fort Wayne, viewed from Fort Wayne Female College. The college, built in 1847, faced West Wayne Street. Courtesy, Fort Wayne and Allen County Public Library.

CHAPTER
V

A TIME OF
GROWTH
&
INVENTION

The population of Fort Wayne reached the 10,000 figure just as the Civil War began; but the population of Allen County as a whole was about three times that number since the majority of people were still farmers or farm laborers. "Hired hand" and "handy man" were terms applied to thousands of rural laborers, often of the temporary variety. According to the census report, Allen County's population in 1850 was 16,919. In the subsequent decade the population nearly doubled to a figure of 29,328. By 1870 the county had 43,494 people.

We know that from the 17th century there were various small trading posts, crossing points, and temporary cabins scattered along the rivers near Fort Wayne. It wasn't until the land surveys were completed in the early 1830s, however, that large numbers of farms were established. Prior to that the land holders were called squatters, though most of their claims were honored. This contrasted to nearby Kentucky, where corrupt government and legal sharpsters drove out Daniel Boone and many other original pioneers. In Allen County it was only natural that the Maumee area would receive the early interest of settlers. Joseph Gronauer and Jared Whitney established farms in 1832 and 1833. This land was along the right-of-way then being marked out for the Wabash-Erie Canal. The area still contained deep forest, roving wolf packs, and a few remaining Indians. (Whitney, together with William Harper, Aretas Powers, and Christian Wolf built the first log cabin

Right
Fort Wayne was a point of departure for passengers on the Fort Wayne, Cincinnati & Louisville Railroad bound for Indianapolis and the West.

Below
An 1856 panoramic view of Fort Wayne looking south from the St. Mary's River. Courtesy, Fort Wayne and Allen County Public Library.

school in Jefferson Township in 1838.)

The rural inhabitants survived by more than the products of farming. The 19th century was a period of cottage industries. The first was the product of the sharpshooter. Henry Castleman, who built the first tavern along the old Ridge Road, claimed to have shot 1,678 deer and 23 bears. He and others hauled loads by sled into Fort Wayne for marketing. One of the methods of hunting was floating pirogues silently along the Maumee, picking off game that gathered at the forest edge by the river.

In the meantime Fort Wayne had become a rail center and, during the Civil War, the site of heavy industry related to rail development. Construction began in 1852 for a line between Fort Wayne and Crestline, Ohio. To finance the railroad, the Ohio and Indiana Railroad Company was formed in 1850. It merged with others to form the Pittsburgh, Fort Wayne, & Chicago Railroad by the time operations began with the first run on November 15, 1854. The first engine, however, didn't come in on rails: in 1852, when work was started, an engine was brought in on a barge on the canal and hoisted onto tracks that had been built on Lafayette Street from the canal to the regular east-west rail line nearly a mile to the south.

William H. Jones and Sion Bass began a foundry and machine shop related to rail equipment, which they sold to the Pittsburgh, Fort Wayne and Chicago Railroad in 1857. This was the beginning of the "Pennsy" shops, which were

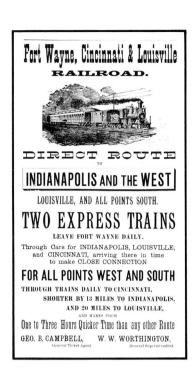

to remain an important local industry until the 1930s. The following year Sion's brother, John Bass, leased another plant that eventually became the Bass Foundry and Machine Works. Huge, red brick buildings just south of the Pennsylvania rail tracks occupied a large labor force for nearly a century. Combining these with Bass plants subsequently built at St. Louis, John Bass became the world's largest supplier of railroad wheels and axles — not only for the Eastern railroads, but also for those going west of the Mississippi to the Pacific.

With the development of the canal and the great foundries of Bass and others at Fort Wayne, another cottage industry dotted the countryside. Kilns for the making of charcoal sprang up everywhere. When historian Henry Howe came through Allen County, Indiana, and neighboring Paulding County, Ohio, in 1886, he recorded the dying vestiges of an industry based on plentiful hardwoods. He saw "lines of structures shaped like beehives, about 15 feet at the base and about as high. These were on the line of the railroad and Wabash Canal. The beehive structures were white as snow (constructed, I believe, of brick and plastered with lime)." He was told they were kilns for the burning of charcoal. The ores smelted in nearby furnaces were from Lake Superior. One beehive oven would yield forty-five to fifty bushels of charcoal in four days of burning. The ore from the upper lakes region was brought by ship to Toledo, then by canal, and later railroad. By 1886, however, the operation was no longer running. All the furnaces in the United States originally used wood-based charcoal; but by the 1880s it was replaced by coal and coke. Yet, a century later, an occasional relic of these beehive-like kilns can be spotted in the corner of some remote field.

Barrel-stave making, as had the kilns, depended on hardwood and thus depleted the vast forests of virgin timber, which were characteristic of the Fort Wayne area. Howe spoke of "the grand primitive forest, waiting its turn to sink beneath the labor of man." He said the few trees left were "like sentinels on duty, have the look of trees grown in the Black Swamp, where they run up like naked poles." The Black Swamp, extending from Fort Wayne for 100 miles into Ohio and mentioned in the military diaries of the earlier period, was gradually drained in the second half of the 19th century. The timber was the largest stand of fine furniture woods in the world, but only recognized as such when it was nearly gone. Black walnut, white oak, bird's-eye oak and wild cherry were all cut down and remain today only in the furniture that they were used to build. Hardwood trees of those sizes are all gone.

The Amish community in Allen County still supports itself by working the land. Of all the Anabaptist groups surviving in the United States in 1980, the Old Order Amish in Allen County have retained some of the most austere codes and customs. Unlike the Pennsylvania Dutch with their colorful decorations, or the more liberalized Mennonite congregations, the Allen

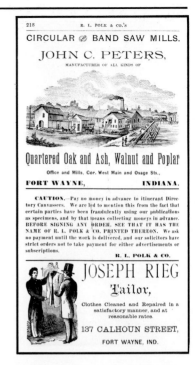

The mill of John Peters was pictured in an 1868 advertisement. Peters was the grandfather of actress Carole Lombard.

Opposite
Top
The Bass foundry, expanded during the Civil War era, became the world's largest manufacturer of railroad wheels.

Center
This engine, the John Bull, pulled the first passenger train into Fort Wayne on November 15, 1854. Courtesy, Fort Wayne and Allen County Public Library.

Bottom
A scale drawing of a Pittsburg, Fort Wayne & Chicago Railway Co. steam engine built at the Pennsy shops in Fort Wayne. The train carried both passengers and freight. Courtesy, Fort Wayne and Allen County Public Library.

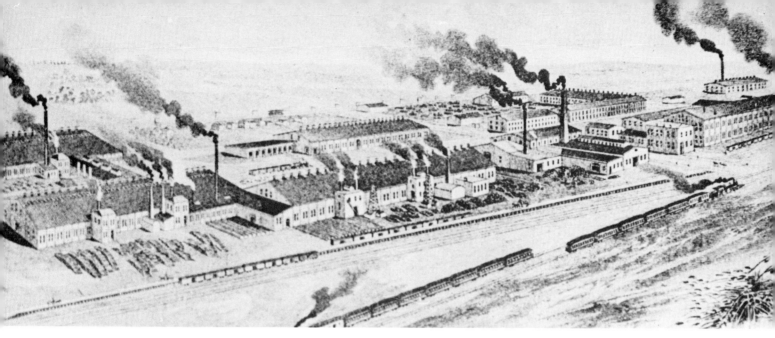

PITTSBURG, FORT WAYNE & CHICAGO RAILWAY CO.
WESTERN DIVISION.
STANDARD PASSENGER and FREIGHT LOCOMOTIVE
BUILT AT THE COMPANY'S WORKS.
JAMES M. BOON   MASTER MECHANIC
FORT WAYNE,   INDIANA.

County Amish have held the line on frills of any kind. They use neither electricity nor automotive equipment. Even in the coldest weather conditions, their carriages are open rather than closed, as adopted by some related groups. Yet from a small band a century ago, they have flourished into a community of nearly two thousand, mostly in the eastern rural section of Allen County.

The congregation "is the only one in the Indiana-Michigan Conference which was made up almost exclusively of European immigrants," according to Mennonite historian Christian Wenger. After sailing across the ocean from France, the original Amish settlers moved from the coast to Starke County, Ohio. After a stay at that place, Peter Graber and two brothers came to Allen County in 1852. In April, 1853, a party of fifty-two European Amish made the trip in eleven teams from Starke County, Ohio, to the Indiana area just northeast of Fort Wayne, which remains their home to this day. The family names included Gerig, Graber, Hostetler, Klopfenstein, Ledermann, Liechty, Miller, Neuhouser, Richard, Schlatter, Stalter, Stoll, Stuckey, and Witmer.

Bishop Sam (Spot) Graber recently talked about the progress of the Amish. At seventy-three years old, Sam-Spot, as he was always called, had been bishop for thirty years, and had had three previous wives. Like most of the Amish, he was a farmer. His grandfather, Daniel Graber, had also been a bishop and his great-grandfather, Peter, had been the founding bishop in Allen County. He said he believed the original immigrants walked in with oxen and carts across Pennsylvania and Ohio. They had some horses and covered wagons while coming from Starke County, Ohio, and "bought land near Grabill," a small town later developed about ten miles northeast of Fort Wayne. Over the years the families used Percheron and Belgian draft horses for the heavy farming. Draft horses, the best-known variety of which is the Budweiser Clydesdale, are some of the original horse strains that work the Amish fields to this day. "We never had mules," Bishop Graber said. They also had other horses, such as the two driving horses of Sam's father — "Spotted horses, Arabians, that gave me my middle name."

A falling-out among the Amish community almost immediately following its establishment in Allen County caused many church members to leave and join with the Mennonites nearby.

The dominant group remaining was led by Bishop Peter Graber and was Old Order Amish. His great-grandson, Bishop Samuel L. Graber said: "When I was a boy only two church districts existed. Now there are seven of them." Each church district has thirty to thirty-five families, which are usually large with the norm being seven to ten children. Church services are held in the home. "When houses won't hold the number, we divide the district," Bishop Graber said.

While the Amish movement became extinct in Europe, it persisted and grew in Allen County and other American rural areas. For more than a century

Top
Horses are used to perform the heavy farm work on the Amish countryside, about ten miles northeast of Fort Wayne.

Right
A little Amish girl studies a big horse in eastern Allen County. Photo by John Sorenson.

their horses and buggies have been a familiar sight along the roads and parked at the curbs of Fort Wayne markets. The Amish pay taxes when they have to, but refuse government services. A traveler has little trouble picking out the Amish properties. The house is inevitably white and there is a distinctive neatness about the farm yard. No poles or telephone lines intrude. Horses can be seen in the fields, sometimes in considerable number.

Amish marry only among the Amish, or are expelled. Amish children do not attend public schools, but go to their own elementary variety until they are sixteen. During the 1950s and 1960s, the Amish of Allen County fought a running battle with the State Department of Public Instruction, which attempted to close the Amish schools. The Amish eventually won in court. The Amish continue their Old Order costumes and customs, which include speaking old German dialect and having High German Bible readings. In matters of morals and rules, the bishop is absolute. The Amish accept no government benefits, not even social security. They do not serve in the military, nor do they use the courts to sue for damages. So firm are they in their beliefs, the Old Amish would not even contact police authorities if one of their number was murdered by an intruder. Just such an incident was reported in nearby Berne, Indiana, during 1979.

At the same time the Amish started to arrive, the first meeting of the Fort Wayne Board of School Trustees was being held. April 30, 1853, marked the beginning of the system of public schools, or free schools as they were then called. Prior to that time schooling had been limited to that offered by several church groups and a few private-venture school operations.

After a few arguments on the local and state level regarding school tax money and levies, two public schools were begun on October 3, 1853. One school was established in a house made available by Alexander McJunkin, the township trustee, on Lafayette Street between Wayne and Berry streets. The other school was in the Hulburd house on West Wayne Street at Ewing Street. According to an enumeration in 1853, there were 1,233 children of school age in the city. In that first term, however, there were 240 boys and 160 girls attending the free school. The first public school building constructed was Clay School in 1857.

One of the strongest proponents of public schools and legislation to support them was Hugh McCulloch, Fort Wayne banker and lawyer. In 1863 Hugh McCulloch became the first controller of the currency, an office created by the federal government to regulate Civil War financing and inflation. Two years later, in 1865, President Lincoln appointed McCulloch to be his Secretary of the Treasury — a cabinet post McCulloch retained during the administrations of Andrew Johnson and Chester Arthur. McCulloch's home in Fort Wayne, built between the Wabash-Erie Canal and the St. Mary's River, was an imposing Greek Revival structure. It still stands today on west Superior

Top
Amish children study in a contemporary version of the one-room school house at Milan Center east of Fort Wayne. The Amish successfully fought the State Department of Public Instruction to maintain their own schools in Allen County. Photo by John Sorenson.

Center and Bottom
Wheat stacked under the summer sun and horses grazing calmly in a winter snowstorm provide a rural seasonal contrast at Amish farms. Photo by John Sorenson.

Street, a street that didn't exist at the time of the house's construction, and that was first named Water Street before becoming Superior Street.

McCulloch played a role in the founding of one of the city's early colleges — Fort Wayne Female College in 1846. This institution was at the west end of Wayne Street and later became known as Methodist College. Samuel Bigger, a former Indiana governor, William Rockhill, who donated the land, and Dr. Alexander Huestis, the first college president, were also key figures. The academy was combined with the Fort Wayne Collegiate Institute, which the same group established for young men, between 1852 and 1854. The combined college was later moved to Upland, Indiana, where it operates today as Taylor University. St. Augustine's Academy, a Catholic girls institution, was founded in 1846 along Calhoun Street at what later became Cathedral Square. A counterpart for boys, known as The Brothers School, was founded in 1856 just to the south in Library Hall. The Lutherans, who had opened a school for children in 1837 headed by the Reverend Jesse Hoover, founded the only early college here that has lasted to the present day. Concordia College was established on a 25-acre campus along Maumee Avenue in 1861. Concordia expanded at that location until 1957 when it was relocated at the present site on the city's north edge along the St. Joseph River. The old campus property was taken over by Indiana Institute of Technology, a college organized in 1930 in the 200 block of East Washington Boulevard.

The Fort Wayne College of Medicine came into existence on March 10, 1876. Located at the southwest corner of Broadway and Washington Boulevard, a scant two blocks from St. Joseph Hospital, the medical school was an important factor in the advancing of medical skills in a three-state area. Doctors B.S. Woodworth, I.M. Rosenthal, W.H. Myers, C.B. Steman, H.A. Clark, and Miles Porter were key movers and staff heads. When the school was in its early years doctors were intellectuals with far-ranging interests, compared with the more narrowly directed but, perhaps, more skilled specialists of today. Both Rosenthal and Porter were pillars in the cultural life of the community; the latter was the brother-in-law of novelist Gene Stratton Porter — author of many popular books, including *Freckles* and *A Girl of the Timberlost* — who also lived in Fort Wayne for a few years.

Body snatching was a fellow traveler of medical education during much of the 19th century. No sooner had the college been set up at Fort Wayne than a plague of grave robberies besieged cemeteries over a wide area. The situation became such a scandal that the Allen County Grand Jury was called in to investigate the matter. The report of the jury noted the practice "produced and is producing great excitement, anxiety and indignation, expecially among those who have families or have recently lost friends." The college was particularly criticized for "depositing, concealing and dissecting human bodies, a portion of which are stolen from cemeteries and graveyards in this

Top
By 1884 Female College had become Fort Wayne Methodist College. In 1889, when this photograph was taken, this building was new. Courtesy Fort Wayne and Allen County Public Library.

Right
A Fort Wayne College commencement program from April 23, 1856.

Far Right
In 1861 Concordia College was established along Maumee Avenue. Though the campus was later expanded and relocated, at the time of its establishment it covered 25 acres. Courtesy, Fort Wayne and Allen County Public Library.

FORT WAYNE COLLEGE
COMMENCEMENT EXERCISES
BY
THE SENIOR CLASS,
FOR APRIL 23rd, 1856.

Order of Exercises

1. PRAYER......................................
2. LATIN SALUTATORY..........................
             Miss JOANNA M. KIMBERLY.
3. ESSAY.—EARTHLY FAME.—Shadowy Dreams.....
             Miss CELINA E. JOHNSON.
4. ESSAY.—HAPPINESS, A Life Dream..........
             Miss LAURA S. McMAKEN.
5. ESSAY.—Force of mind and character must rule the world.
             Miss JOANNA M. KIMBERLY.
6. ESSAY.—The days of originality—are past...
             Miss FRANCES E. SWINNEY.
7. ESSAY.—Would you conquer—press on......
             Miss JANE M. TAM.
8. VALEDICTORY..............................
             Miss CELINA E. JOHNSON.
9. DEGREES conferred by the President........
10. BENEDICTION..............................

VOCAL AND PIANO MUSIC,
WILL BE INTERSPERSED WITH
THE EXERCISES.
Fort Wayne, April 23, 1856.

[Daily Times Job Office Print, Fort Wayne, Ind.]

vicinity, in violation of the law, common decency and the proprieties of life." Even the bodies of the rich were not sacred. In 1877 ghouls dug up the body of a young girl at Lindenwood Cemetery. She was the daughter of the prominent Ewing family and a $1,000 reward was offered for information leading to the capture of the culprits.

Two years later a more bizarre case drew the curiosity of the town. Odor led to the discovery of the body of a man in a battered trunk on the baggage platform of the Lake Shore Railroad. This depot, which later became the property of the New York Central Railroad, is still located on Cass Street near the Wells Street Bridge, and remains the only original rail station in the city. The body, in the 1879 incident, was returned to Waterloo from where it had been taken; but was reportedly stolen a second time.

The rash of grave robberies continued despite precautions taken to prevent them. Guards were posted at cemeteries; watch towers were erected; and clever contraptions such as spring guns were employed to trip up the robbers. All that didn't stop ghouls from snatching the body of the father of the President of the United States. This occurred at Cincinnati where the father of Benjamin Harrison (and son of an earlier president, William Henry Harrison) disappeared from his grave. William Henry Harrison, of course, figured in Fort Wayne's early history. It is usually reported his son's body went to a medical school in the Cincinnati area. Peter Certia, an authority on all things antique in Fort Wayne, told me before he died, however, that the Harrison body disappeared on the dissecting tables of the Michigan School of Medicine at Ann Arbor. His report was more in keeping with the later sophisticated practices of the body trade. To avoid detection and prosecution, the medical schools didn't use local bodies. They traded them with those of other medical schools some distance away. The Fort Wayne College of Medicine lasted until 1905, when it was merged with the Indiana College of Medicine.

St. Joseph Hospital was started in 1868 with the purchase of the Rockhill House Hotel at Broadway and Main. The Reverend Julian Benoit and Henry Monning headed the association. It underwent numerous rebuildings and expansions at the same location, the most recent being completed in 1980. The family of Jesse Williams donated funds in 1893 to build Hope Hospital at Washington and Barr streets, after the hospital had operated in a house at Main and Webster since 1868. The institution became known as Methodist Hospital when relocated at Lewis and Harrison streets in 1917; and finally Parkview Hospital, which was dedicated November 8, 1953, and located at East State Boulevard, and Randalia Drive. The Evangelical Lutheran Hospital Association founded Lutheran Hospital in 1904 on Fairfield Avenue at Wildwood Avenue in the former residence of Lindley M. Ninde. Building programs in later years expanded the hospital from Fairfield to South Wayne

Fort Wayne Medical College was located on the upper two floors of the Remmel Brothers' building located at Broadway and Washington. Courtesy, Fort Wayne and Allen County Public Library.

Avenue. In 1888 the Indiana School for Feeble-Minded Youth was moved from Knightstown to Fort Wayne. Large gothic structures were built on East State Boulevard, the main building which remains standing to this day. Known as the State School during most of its existence, it was renamed Fort Wayne State Hospital and Training Center, in keeping with changing tastes and programs for retarded persons of all ages. An extensive building program was started in 1956 to relocate the institution at a 270-acre tract at Parker Place on St. Joe Road, northeast of the city. The institution had about 2,500 patients at that time.

The curious involvement of a local doctor in one of the startling events of 1881 was not revealed until nearly a century later when Laverne Ankenbruck and Kay Fishering bought several trunks sold in an estate auction in New Haven, Indiana. The trunks contained letters and other papers having to do with the career of a Dr. William B. Brittingham, a New York-born physician who practiced in Fort Wayne, New Haven, and Lafayette in the late 19th century after medical service in the Civil War.

The event was the lingering death of President James A. Garfield after an assassination attempt on July 2, 1881. (Garfield was shot while waiting in a Washington railway station by Charles J. Guiteau, a disappointed office seeker.) Dr. Brittingham, then a practicing physician in New Haven, was apparently a consultant in the treatment of the wounded president. A letter to his wife, Mary, dated July 7 says in part:

"Well we have had a lively time of it here. I knew from the start General Garfield would not. I knew it 12:30 Saturday [July 2]. I immediately sent word to Dr. Bliss, who I know, not to hunt for the bullet, as it was down in the abdomen. I have been in constant communication with Dr. Bliss [the attending physician]. Now this is private. Only to Dr. Rutherford ... [Dr. E.E. Rutherford was a medical associate of Dr. Brittingham's.] There is at the side of the President a Homeopathist. Garfield is one; and don't forget the reason he has not had distress and is so much better, he has been taking [illegible] and [illegible]. I know this and so does Dr. Bliss. The rest are ignorant of it. Well he will get well; and if things work well, it will be good for me. Yours, W.B.B."

Apparently the numerous doctors (at one time twenty) neglected to take many sanitary precautions, which alarmed Dr. Brittingham. "They continued to poke dirty fingers and instruments into the President's wound," was the comment at the time. Some of the attending physicians spoke of quantities of "healthy pus" issuing. After Garfield was taken from Washington to the New Jersey Shore on September 6, Dr. Brittingham seems to have had a more direct hand in the care of the patient, though to no avail. The next letter dated September 18 said, "I expect this man will die. No telling. It seems impossible to do anything right. I will write again." President Garfield died at 10:30 the

Dr. William B. Brittingham of Fort Wayne, circa 1870. Dr. Brittingham was one of the doctors at the deathbed of assassinated President Garfield in 1881.

Opposite
Top Left
A letter sent by Dr. Brittingham from New York to his wife, Mary, at New Haven, Indiana, on July 7, 1881, just prior to his joining the staff tending the stricken President.

Top Right
The residence of Judge Lindley Ninde on South Fairfield Avenue became the first home of the Lutheran Hospital in 1904.

Bottom
A locomotive in service in 1890 on the Lake Shore & Michigan Southern Railroad. Courtesy, Fort Wayne and Allen County Public Library.

New York July 7

Dear Mary, I have not received any letter from Jon for 2 weeks. I am quit well again. well we have had a lively time of it here. I knew from the start Gen Garfield would not. I knew it 1230 Saturday. I immediately lent word to Dr. Bliss who I know not to Hunt for the Bullet as it was down in the abdomen. I have been in Constant Communication with Dr. Bliss, now this is private. Only to J. Rutherford and Leonard. there is at the side of the President. a Homeopathist Garfield is one: and don't forget the reader he has not had intense and is so much better. he has been taking tonics & Laudunula I know this and so does Dr. Bliss. the rest are ignorant of it. well he will get well. and if things work well it will be good for me

Yours
W.F.B.

following night.

We probably will never know what the doctor said in the other letter or letters, or why Dr. Brittingham happened to be a consultant in the case. It appears that the doctor's comments, however, tell us more than we knew before about the fallen president's illness — in particular, that he was a victim of unsanitary conditions and that the narcotics he was given (this seems to be what Brittingham was referring to in the first letter) may have worsened his condition; they certainly masked it. As for Dr. Brittingham himself, other papers indicate that he lived at 429 East Washington Street while he resided in Fort Wayne. Two known children include John W. and Minnie Brittingham (later married to John R. Hartzell, an early New Haven merchant).

Horses, Baseball, and Beer

Industry in Fort Wayne moved from lumber, hides, and woolen mills of its early years to the heavy rail-related works of the mid-19th century, then diversified into beer, pumps, and electric lights and motors during the later decades of the 1800s. C.L. Centlivre started his brewery between the St. Joseph River and the Feeder Canal, north of the city on Spy Run Avenue in 1862. It was originally called the French Brewery, but was renamed the Centlivre Brewery by the time of expansions in the 1870s and 1894. Nearby Centlivre Park was Fort Wayne's circus grounds in the 19th century and until the post-World War II period. The Berghoff Brewery, located on Grant Avenue, was begun by Herman Berghoff and his brothers — Gustav, Henry, and Hubert. Herman later established the Berghoff restaurant in Chicago, which remains a landmark on Wabash Avenue to this day. The Berghoff family also operated another brewery, makers of Hoff-Brau, after the repeal of prohibition in 1933. The original Berghoff properties were sold in 1954 to the Falstaff Brewing Corporation of St. Louis.

The Fort Wayne Organ Company owed its existence to the Great Chicago fire. Isaac Parkard, burned out at Chicago, came to Fort Wayne and built a large brick plant, employing 300 workers, at Fairfield and Packard Avenue. The name was later changed to the Packard Piano Company, since pianos were its best-known product.

The city of Fort Wayne also has become a center for production of gasoline pumps and is especially known today for Tokheim pumps and Wayne pumps. But the original pump maker was Sylvanus Freelove Bowser. His rise and eventual demise had the rags-to-riches quality of a Horatio Alger story. A country boy who grew up in Allen County, Bowser had only three months of schooling. In his youth he sold ice and wrapping paper, but was often idle and was subject to nervous spells. At home one morning he became annoyed with the task of lifting water with a bucket from a seventy-foot well. That day in 1885 Bowser got the idea for a pump that was to revolutionize the oil and gasoline pump industry and make a fortune for himself. The principle involved

Top Left
The Old Fort Wayne Marble Works was established by P.S. Underhill and Elliot Smith in 1857.

Top Right
The L.C. Zollinger & Brother Company advertise their "celebrated Fort Wayne Wagon."

Center Left
An 1868 advertisement shows the brewery of Charles Centlivre along the feeder canal just north of town.

Center Right
After suffering a loss in Chicago's great fire, in 1871 Isaac Packard moved his organ business to Fort Wayne.

Bottom
This 1889 advertisement shows the tank factories of Sylvanus Freelove Bowser which were located on East Creighton Avenue. In 1894 these plants burned down but a large pump-making firm replaced them.

was as simple as forcing liquid down one pipe to force it up another.

He and his brother, Alexander, began a plant on East Creighton Avenue, making oil tanks and pumps for the measuring out of kerosene in grocery stores. It was an immediate success; and, with the coming of automobiles, Bowser expanded into a worldwide marketing operation for fuel pumps, first for garages then service stations. By World War I sales had passed the $6 million mark, then doubled and tripled that figure in the 1920s. In addition to massive plant expansions, Bowser began paternalistic employee payroll and financing operations, and established his own bank on Creighton Avenue. The minor empire came tumbling down in the bank panic and depression of the early 1930s, along with protracted disagreements with unions over rights of workers. Bowser, in his old age, lost control of the S.F. Bowser Company.

But even before Bowser began making pumps, the old Wabash-Erie Canal through Fort Wayne vanished. Victim of faster, year-round rail transport, the canal was sold in 1880 to the New York, Chicago and St. Louis Railroad, known as the Nickel Plate System. The canal was filled in and tracks were laid over the right-of-way. The system got its name from William H. Vanderbilt, who bought the line in 1882. "The price we paid for it, it ought to be nickel-plated," Vanderbilt reportedly remarked.

James A. Jenney, an inventor of an electric-arc lamp and a small dynamo, came to Fort Wayne in 1881 looking for a place to make his products. He formed a company with Ronald McDonald, H.G. Olds, Perry Randall, and Oscar Simons. The company eventually grew into the city's largest employer with a payroll of more than 10,000 workers in the 1940s. Jenney Electric was first located in old brick buildings along Superior Street. Among its early successes, Jenney lighted the World's Fair grounds in 1884-1885 at New Orleans. In 1885 the firm bought the building and land of the Gause Agricultural Works on Broadway, the present main location of General Electric plants. Mergers resulted in several changes in name and management for the company, but finally in 1916 it was taken over by General Electric Company, under which name it operates today.

An earlier merger of Fort Wayne Electric with the Edison interests had some nostalgic connotations. Seventeen-year-old Tom Edison was transferred to Fort Wayne in the summer of 1864, where he worked as a telegraph operator for the railroad. Edison reportedly stayed in a room above one of the Columbia Street business houses for several months before moving on to Indianapolis and Louisville.

Major-league baseball began with a game played at Fort Wayne on May 4, 1871. The National Association of Professional Baseball Players (now the National League) was organized earlier that year in New York on St. Patrick's Day. Nine teams were chartered the first season: the Philadelphia Athletics, the Boston Red Stockings, the Troy Haymakers, the Washington Olympics, the Rockford Forest City, the Fort Wayne Kekiongas, the Chicago White Stockings, the New York Mutuals, and the Cleveland (Indians) Forest City.

Though it is often believed that the first pro league game was played in old League Park between Clinton and Calhoun streets, the actual location was near West Main Street next to the canal. As might be expected, a host of baseball firsts were established. The Official Encyclopedia of Baseball reports: "It is ironic that the Kekionga club, the only one not to weather the season, won the opening game by 2 to 0. Not only was this noteworthy as the first pro league game of record, but it was also the lowest-scoring game in the first four seasons of the league."

Fort Wayne won the toss and sent Cleveland to bat. Bobby Mathews, bought from a barnstorming club of Baltimore, Maryland, threw the first pitch — a ball. James (Deacon) White was the first batter, and he led off with the first major league hit — a double. Gene Kimball followed with a fly to second, but when White took a long lead, Tom Carey pulled an unassisted double play. Jim Lennon, the catcher, scored the first run for the Fort Wayne team. He doubled and came in on Joe McDermott's single. Mathews tossed six strikeouts.

Chicago had the best league record that season, but lost to the Philadelphia Athletics in a playoff series. By that time, however, Fort Wayne's team was history. The Kekionga franchise wilted in August, and was bought for $10 by a Brooklyn organization. That team prospered and became known as the Brooklyn Dodgers, and subsequently the Los Angeles Dodgers.

Fort Wayne and other cities of the world were never the same after the disappearance of draft horses, which were used to haul heavy loads of all kinds. The term, "teamsters," now used for truck drivers, also was applied to the men who oversaw the labors of the draft animals, although the term, "drayman," was more frequently used in the 19th century. It was a common occupation. While the industrial revolution would eventually do away with the need for draft horses, at first it created more demand for them. Huge, sweaty beasts dragging ever-heavier loads churned down muddy and dusty streets. The weighty products of the age — coal, pig iron, bricks, lumber — had to be hauled into and through the more populous cities. Where there were canals and railroads, the need for draft horses was even greater. Hardly a block in the core of old Fort Wayne was without a stable for the horses. In addition to the draymen and the stablemen, the occupations of blacksmith and veterinarian flourished.

Through most of the 1800s the city streets were made of dirt. Until rather late in the century, only Calhoun Street was paved with red bricks that can still be observed occasionally. With the churnings of the huge horses, plus the leavings of thousands of oversize digestive tracts, it takes no imagination to envision the condition of the muddy right-of-way.

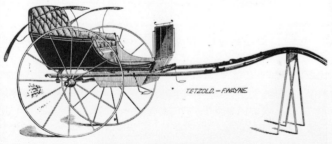

Above
In 1889 West Berry Street was equipped with utility poles, yet it remained unpaved. On the right is the Georgian mansion of early trader George Ewing, which was built in 1838. Courtesy, Fort Wayne and Allen County Public Library.

Opposite
The horse and buggy meant big business in the old downtown area. Advertisements from the 1870s show manufacturers of carriages, horse collars, graders, and numerous stables.

Right
A quiet afternoon in the summer of 1889 on East Jefferson Street; St. Mary's Church is in the distance. Courtesy, Fort Wayne and Allen County Public Library.

Another measure of the town atmosphere and its street condition can be seen in an ordinance passed in 1885. The law was aimed at ending the practice of letting cows run at large in the streets. But when Fred Woenker, the poundmaster, attempted to enforce it, he was attacked by cow owners, particularly housewives. It was a time when most families kept cows about the place for milk requirements.

Into this mess, on January 6, 1872, came one more horse-drawn vehicle down the streets of Fort Wayne. At 3:45 that afternoon the first city streetcar labored down Calhoun Street as far as the Aveline House. It, too, was drawn by a team of draft horses. At the reins were Charles Breckenridge, city engineer, and John H. Bass, president of the Citizens' Street Railroad Company. The firm had been started the previous September with a capitalization of $50,000 at the direction of Bass, Sam Hanna, S.B. Bond and G.E. Bursley. They gained approval of the city council for the laying of tracks on Calhoun Street from Main Street to Creighton Avenue, then as far west as Fairfield Avenue. A track was also run from Calhoun east on Wallace, where the huge Bass iron works were located.

Two small horsecars with open decks fore and aft were the operating equipment. Within weeks the number of cars was expanded to four, and tracks were added east and west along Main Street. It would be incorrect to suppose the attraction of the horse-drawn streetcars was speed. Rapid transit remained

Opposite
Right
Operated by the privately-funded Citizens Street Railroad Company, the first horse-drawn streetcars began laboring along the avenues of Fort Wayne in 1872. This form of transportation was used until 1892. Courtesy, Fort Wayne and Allen County Public Library.

Opposite
Bottom
Calhoun Street as it appeared in the 1880s. At left is the Transfer Building. Courtesy, Fort Wayne and Allen County Public Library.

Below
In 1880 the 100 block of Columbia Street dead-ended into the Randall Hotel. Courtesy, Fort Wayne and Allen County Public Library.

for a later era. A prime motive for taking a streetcar was the saving of shoe leather and skirt bottom from the ravages of the streets. Mud, slime, and worse formed the ordinary walking surface during much of the year. Sidewalks made from boards or stone slabs were to be found only in choice locations. A gentleman or a lady now could ride with dignity.

Troubles with the new service started almost immediately. An epidemic of horse fever took its toll and mules were employed for awhile. The practice of scattering salt to melt snow drew community ire. "No sooner did the snow begin to fall this morning than the streetcar employees began to scatter salt on Calhoun Street. This is the way sleighing is spoiled on the main thoroughfare and businessmen cut off from their trade. How long will the authorities permit this outrage?" the *Fort Wayne Sentinel* asked in an editorial during this period. County commissioners refused to allow the "newfangled" streetcars on the bridges over the rivers. In 1887, however, permission was finally granted for tracks across the iron bridge to Wells Street. That same year C.L. Centlivre built his own street railway out Spy Run Avenue from the St. Mary's River to his brewery operation a mile north; but the county commissioners wouldn't let him run the service across the bridge. Centlivre also had a beer garden and park for patrons just beyond the brewery. In 1888 the Centlivre line was allowed across the bridge and connected with the other system.

A turntable was initially installed at Main and Calhoun streets so the cars could be turned around. The site was called Turntable Corner for a period, It was a cause of considerable delay and irritation, however, and was abandoned for better trackwork in 1888. After that the corner became known as the Transfer Corner. By 1891 there were twenty-eight cars in service. Tracks were extended over much of downtown and the outlaying areas of town. Disaster struck in 1890 when the east barns of the Street Rail Company burned on December 23. Located on Baker Street, the barns were large stables filled with straw that held the huge draft horses. Sixty animals died in the blaze before help could arrive.

The first electric car in Fort Wayne operated without a trolley, but employed battery power. Designed by Marmaduke Slattery of the Fort Wayne Electric Works, the streetcar's first run was on the night of November 11, 1891. It took the "Beltline" route, which became the principal core of the electric system for several generations — Calhoun, Main, Broadway, and Creighton loop. Forty-six people traveled that first trip at 12 miles per hour. The operators of the system found the Slattery streetcar expensive and unreliable, however, and returned to horses. Finally in 1892 the Fort Wayne Street Railway announced the spending of $100,000 to electrify the service.

The first trolley car in Fort Wayne ran along Main Street, Calhoun Street, and East Washington Boulevard on July 8, 1892. At the controls was M. Stanley Robison, manager of the Fort Wayne Street Railway. The service

Electric trolley cars and horse-drawn buggies were frequent sights on Clinton Street in 1892. Courtesy, Fort Wayne and Allen County Public Library.

Opposite
Top
The corner of Broadway and Jefferson streets in 1890. The streetcar driver is Frank Carall, nephew of Superintendent McNutt. Courtesy, Fort Wayne and Allen County Public Library.

Bottom
Main Street was a bustling business district in 1880. The Sam, Pete, and Max Star Clothing House once existed at the Calhoun intersection. Courtesy, Fort Wayne and Allen County Public Library.

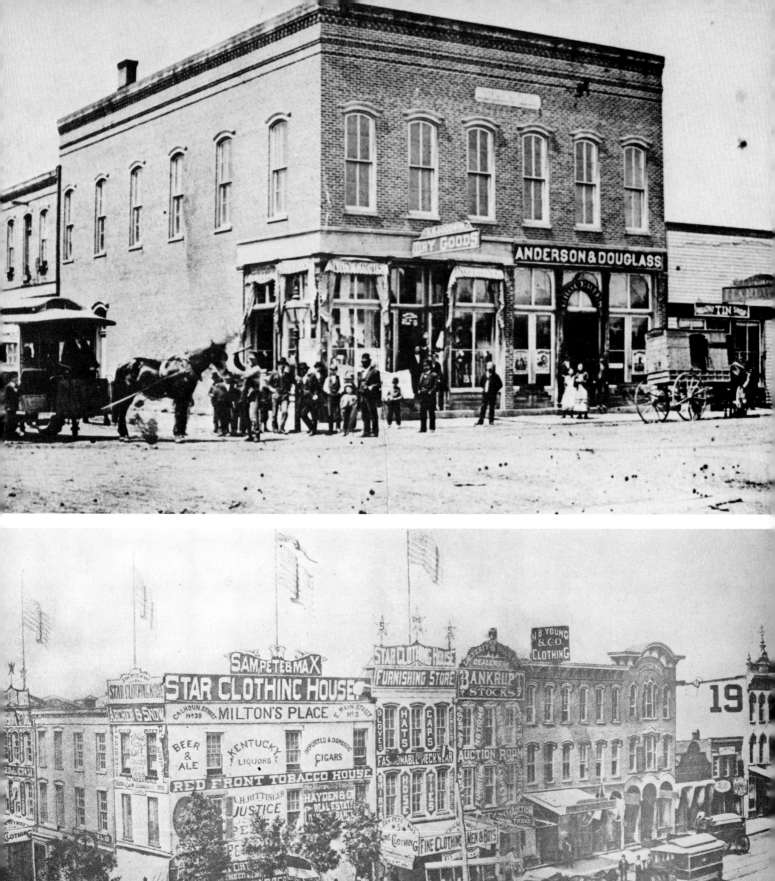
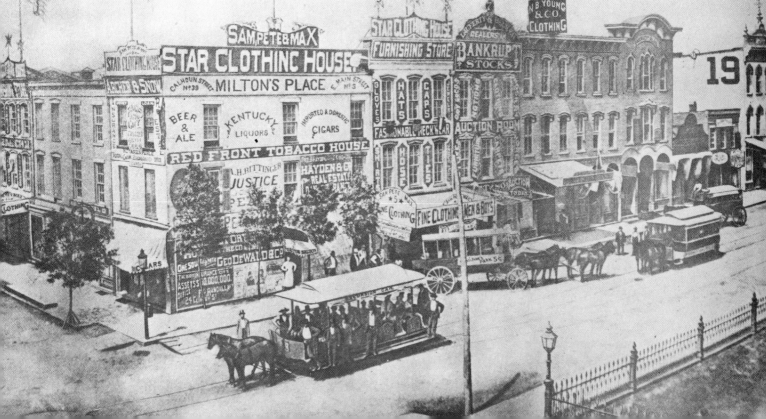

followed months of preparation, setting poles and stretching copper wire over various avenues. Power for the first electric run was furnished by Jenny Electric Light and Power. The first trolley cars were open coaches, with roofs and benches but no sides. By 1894 there were fifty-seven coaches operating on twenty miles of track. By that time the firm had been renamed Fort Wayne Electric Railway and all the horse-drawn cars retired.

In the era of bustles and derbies streetcar parties became a fad. Gay blades and ladies would gather with refreshments and food baskets to spend an afternoon in a noisy tour of the growing city. So popular was the festive habit that the Fort Wayne Consolidated Railway Company developed a major amusement park to exploit the rider and recreational potential. On May 30, 1896, the first run was made to Swift Park, seven miles north of the city on the west bank of the St. Joseph River. The park was located at the old canal feeder dam. The trolley firm bought 265 acres and ran out a double line from Spy Run Avenue, over the State Boulevard Bridge, out Parnell Avenue, and then along the river. The park included a large dance pavilion, a roller coaster, and many other amusements and attractions. Swift Park was mainly the creation of M. Stanley Robison, general manager of the trolley firm, and was renamed Robison Park after its first year of operation. The grand opening of the park on July 4, 1896, drew more than 35,000 people.

Opposite
Top
Robison Park, the community's entertainment center at the turn of the century, was linked to the city by streetcars. The amusement park was located seven miles northeast of town along the St. Joseph River. Courtesy, Fort Wayne and Allen County Public Library.

Opposite
Bottom
Louise Carnahan photographed these young men and women at Camp Larrimore on August 7, 1889. Courtesy, Fort Wayne and Allen County Public Library.

Below
A curious child wearing a conductor's hat stands in front of an electric streetcar put into service by the Fort Wayne Traction Company in 1900. Courtesy, Fort Wayne and Allen County Public Library.

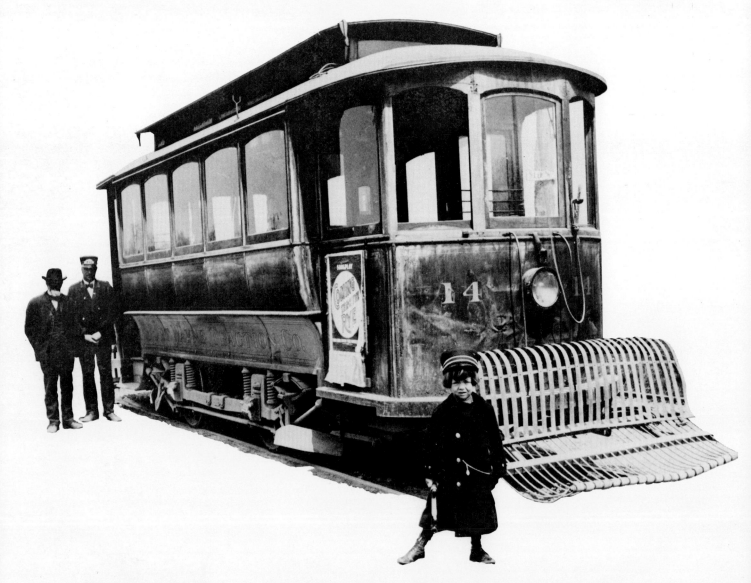

The Barr Street Market and City Hall, shortly after construction in 1893. Courtesy, Fort Wayne and Allen County Public Library

CHAPTER
VI

TURNING
THE
CENTURY

As the 19th century moved through its final decades, the urban style of the Gaslight Era replaced the more rustic habits of earlier days. Though the Fort Wayne Gaslight Company was established in 1855, it wasn't until almost the turn of the century that home use of gaslight became widespread. Local captains of industry were given to gaudy shows of wealth, and their Victorian-style mansions reflected their attitudes during the gaslight era. John Bass built a huge stone house surrounded by lakes and yards stocked with elk and buffalo. (This house and property along the Bass Road became the nucleus of St. Francis College when it was founded in 1942.) Ronald McDonald, the moving force behind Fort Wayne Electric, rented an entire train of the Jackson and Saginaw Railroad to celebrate the day he married Lillie Morse of Angola. Usually the rich businessmen of this period were Republican, while the Irish- and German-dominated Democrats controlled city politics. Franklin Randall, who served as mayor for five terms, including the Civil War years, was an exception, however. He was rich and a Democrat, and his mansion was a visiting place for many celebrities of the day.

When Lillie Langtry appeared on the Fort Wayne stage in January of 1883, her performances were accompanied by after-show parties at the various great houses, sleigh rides through the snowy city streets, and late suppers at the Nickel Plate Restaurant. Many of the noted performers of the time played in the city's theaters. "Prior to 1870 playgoing had been regarded as a pastime for the lower classes of the populace; but after 1870, more fashionable audiences attended," observes Fred Reynolds in a report on the era. Other luminaries who played locally included some of the most celebrated figures of the era. Lotta Crabtree, Joe Emmet, Julia Marlowe, Edwin Booth, Robert Downing, Mark Twain, Annie Oakley and Buffalo Bill, and Eddie Foy all came to Fort Wayne. Later Anna Pavlova, the Barrymores, John Drew, Otis Skinner, Frank James, and John L. Sullivan staged performances.

The city's first regular theater, Colerick's Opera House, opened on December 26, 1853, on East Columbia Street. P.T. Barnum's celebrated midget, Tom Thumb, appeared there in 1856. In that period circuses came to town by canal boat, then later by railroad. Other early theaters included the Hamilton Hall, the Olympic Theatre, the Rink (also known as the Academy of Music), and the Temple Theatre. The Temple, opened in 1884 at the northeast corner of Wayne and Clinton streets, seated 1,000 patrons and remained the main music hall for many years. It burned to the ground in an explosive fire the night of February 10, 1923. But by that time it was being outgrossed by the Majestic Theatre, a 1,600-seat house built on East Berry Street in 1904.

After nearly fifty years of wear, the original City Hall at the southeast corner of Berry and Barr streets was thought to be insufficient for a sophisticated urban center. Not only was its size a problem, but the onion-

This drawing by Bert Griswold depicts the Peoples Theatre as it looked in 1868. The theatre was located on West Main Street.

Opposite
Top
Brookside, the imposing residence of nineteenth-century industrialist John Bass, became a part of the St. Francis College campus. Courtesy, Fort Wayne and Allen County Public Library.

Bottom
This 1889 view from the top of Reservoir Hill shows Creighton Avenue in the foreground and the huge Bass mills in the distance. Courtesy, Fort Wayne and Allen County Public Library.

shaped bell tower and simple design were unsuitable to late Victorian tastes. So it was torn down, and in 1892 plans for a new city hall were furnished by local architects, J.F. Wing and W.S. Mahurin. The heavyweight sandstone edifice was completed the next year and the building dedicated on April 20, 1893. The second City Hall remained the political nerve center of the town until 1971, when the mayor's office and city council chambers were moved to the newly constructed City-County Building. By that time the City Hall, more commonly called the Police Station, was black with age and soot. After a number of years of disuse and indecision regarding whether to tear it down, the homely building had gained warmth in the hearts of the community. The Allen County-Fort Wayne Historical Society adopted the premises, moving their offices in and making renovations for a museum on January 1, 1980. The moving expenses alone cost more than the building had originally cost — $69,806 for construction and furnishings — in 1893.

A great day in public life occurred on November 17, 1897, when the cornerstone of the Allen County Courthouse was laid. The stone itself weighed eight tons and a large crowd gathered for the ceremonies in the public square. Governor James A. Mount represented the state of Indiana and Louis Peltier, the city's oldest citizen — he had been born in the Old Fort in 1813 — represented the city. The main building materials were blue Bedford stone, Vermont granite, and white marble. The length of the building was 270 feet, the width 134 feet, and the height from the sidewalk to the tip of the statue 225 feet. Miss Liberty, the rotating bronze figure on top, measured thirteen feet eight inches.

Two years of planning preceded the construction. There were arguments over whether to demolish the third courthouse, which had been built, mostly of brick, in 1861. But ambition prevailed and an imposing Greco-Roman building designed by Brentwood Tolan, a fortunate choice in architects, received the nod. The general contractor was James Stewart Company of St. Louis. The cost of the building was $817,553. Portions of the building were sufficiently completed in 1900 for occupancy. Other work continued, however, and the dedication of the courthouse occurred on September 23, 1902. It remains the centerpiece of Fort Wayne's downtown to this day.

The turn of the century found Fort Wayne a city of 45,115 and a rail and trading center of significance. Sixty-five saloons were located in a ten-block stretch of Calhoun Street, and on the north end of that street was a notorious string of brothels. Democratic presidential candidate William Jennings Bryan came to town in 1900 to deliver his famous "Cross of Gold" speech against the gold standard, and to criticize the bosses behind Republican William McKinley. Gentlemen were wearing derbies and talking machines were soon to be the rage. Even an occasional motor-machine appeared on city streets to scare the horses.

Right
The second Allen County Courthouse, built in 1860, was later rebuilt in 1897. Courtesy, Fort Wayne and Allen County Public Library.

Far Right
The Temple Theatre aflame the early morning of February 10, 1923. Explosives on the top floor added another dimension to the already spectacular event.

Bottom
East Berry Street, 1910. The open-air "Dome" is at left and the Majestic Theatre is located next to it. Courtesy, Fort Wayne and Allen County Public Library.

"Every spring and summer the ladies of the DAR [Daughters of the American Revolution] planted fresh flowers around the marble slab, and if there were a ceremony, I made sure I attended," said author Karl Detzer about Old Fort Park in the 1890s and early 1900s. The small sodded triangle with a cannon mounted was just north of the intersection of Main and Clay streets, where the second and third American Army forts were once located. The site of Anthony Wayne's fort built in 1794 was a little farther up the hill where the present streets of Berry and Clay intersect. The annual ritual at the old fort site had faded by the 1940s.

From the turn of the century until the late 1930s a network of electric trains called interurbans connected Fort Wayne with towns and centers throughout the Midwest. The interurbans flourished for a brief period, then quickly disappeared. Today little remains of even the memory of the once far-flung system of transportation.

Indianapolis, the state capital, was the busiest center in the nation for interurbans; and the states of Ohio, Indiana, and Illinois had the most trackage and the largest number of trains. By 1919 more than 400 runs daily were moving in and out of Indianapolis over fourteen lines. Five lines operated out of Fort Wayne, going south, southwest, east to Ohio, and north to Michigan communities. On December 12, 1901, the first regular electric train ran between Fort Wayne and Huntington. The route was over the old canal bed, which had not been used since 1880. The original company was named the Fort Wayne & Southwestern Traction Company.

The interurbans looked like oversize streetcars and made piercing screeching noises on the steel tracks as they rounded corners. Sometimes they operated cross-country as singles; other runs would be trains of two, three, or four cars. The interurbans carried both freight and passengers. A number of firms were organized into a system to operate through Fort Wayne. The system linked numerous small towns to neighboring cities. The great expansion occurred in the years before automobiles became the usual mode of travel; and prior to the building of paved highways to the extent of later times.

The turn of the century was also a peak period of immigration to Fort Wayne, as it was for much of the rest of the country. Among those migrating to Fort Wayne in the early 20th century were Macedonians, stimulated by the Illinden Insurrection of 1903 and the Balkan War of 1912-1913. Many were employed in the Bass foundries and other heavy industry. Numerous Macedonians eventually became prominent in the food industry and politics, and in later generations numbered about 5,000. Their cultural and religious heritage was more binding than most other immigrant groups. Bulgarian Orthodox services were held at Stolzenau Hall in the 1920s and 1930s. An Eastern Orthodox church, St. Nicholas, was dedicated in 1948 at Warsaw and Oxford streets. The first full-time pastor was the Reverend George Nedelkoff.

Top
The Allen County Courthouse framed between the Lincoln National Bank and the Fort Wayne National Bank by photographer William Willig. Courtesy, Fort Wayne and Allen County Public Library.

Right
This bronze Miss Liberty, almost fourteen feet tall, stands atop the courthouse and rotates with the wind direction.

Far Right
A decorative bronze lamp adorns the marble walls of the Allen County Courthouse. Courtesy, Fort Wayne and Allen County Public Library.

The early 1900s also saw the addition of families immigrating from Italy, adding their own dimension to Fort Wayne's cultural life. Most Italians found homes to the south of the Pennsylvania-Wabash railroad tracks or in the residential area just east of downtown. The majority were Catholic and joined either St. Patrick's or St. Mary's churches in those neighborhoods. A distinct shift in ethnic origin of the residents of those parts of town occurred, as early Irish and Germans were replaced by Italians and Eastern Europeans. Much later the same areas became increasingly inhabited by blacks, and immigrants from Mexico and Cuba.

Although immigrants from foreign countries usually came in large waves, the story of blacks in Fort Wayne is one of gradual assimilation from its earliest days. There was an occasional mention of a black visitor or resident in the days of Indian control of the area. When Isaac McCoy opened his missionary school in the old fort in 1820, one of the children was listed as Negro. The old city directories, which were first published during the 1850s, included a number of "colored" residents. Corinne Brooks, a Fort Wayne woman whose family came to the city in the early days of this century, recalled that a number of those black families had apparently been living in Fort Wayne for a long time.

The small black community was not segregated in a particular part of town as it was in later periods. Mrs. Brooks's father was a contractor, "one of the few independent things" a black person could be then, according to Mrs. Brooks.

"Dad often said, 'When I first came to town, blacks ate in most any restaurant they pleased.' And there were blacks living all over town at that time — Chestnut Street, Hoffman Street — I still have relatives on Bass Street. There were job opportunities with the railroads, the foundries — my grandfather was hired by the Bass Foundry."

Records show children of black families in the schools of various parts of the city, whether public or parochial. Discrimination undoubtedly existed, however, in jobs and professions; and this became increasingly a problem in the 1920s, 1930s, and 1940s. As the black population grew, mostly from Southern migration, segregation was instituted in theaters, restaurants, and housing. The two fanciest downtown theaters, the Emboyd and the Paramount, confined Negro patrons to the balconies. This situation continued until the World War II period, when soldiers stationed at Baer Field complained about the practice. Mrs. Brooks credits Roy Grimmer, Sr., of the Catholic Interracial Council, and Jim Henderson of the NAACP in getting Meyers Drugstores to drop racial discrimination at their soda bars. (The Meyers chain was the major drugstore chain from the 1920s through the 1950s in Fort Wayne.) Another barrier came down when a separate cafeteria for blacks was closed at the Wolf & Dessauer Department Store, the city's

Top
A large crowd gathered on November 17, 1897, for the laying of the cornerstone for the county courthouse. Indiana Governor James A. Mount was among the speakers of the day.

Right
The Indiana Department of the Grand Army of the Republic had its reunion parade down Calhoun Street in 1907. Here the parade approaches Wayne Street.

Far Right
Interurbans, looking like oversize streetcars, at the Main and Calhoun intersection, circa 1910. According to the clock on the Citizens Trust Building it is only five minutes before 10 A.M.

largest during the period, at the insistence of its then-president, G. Irving Latz. The most intractable problem remained in housing and real estate, which in turn was greatly responsible for the concentration of blacks in the central city area and the racial imbalance in the schools.

The city was governed for a crucial period of the new century by William H. Hosey, beginning with his election as mayor in 1905. A Democratic figure in local politics until well into the 1930s, Hosey ran on a platform of public ownership of the utilities. He resisted the move to transfer the water system (established in 1880 when the reservoir was built at Lafayette Street and Creighton Avenue) to private ownership, and promised to build a city-owned electric light plant. City Light came into being after Hosey submitted the question to voters in 1906. The referendum was overwhelmingly favorable and construction was begun the following year. Initially City Light furnished only street lights and municipal needs, but soon competed with the Fort Wayne & Wabash Valley Traction Company for commercial and residential business.

Also in the first decade, the community gained its first real public library building. The Greek-temple-like structure was built at the southwest corner of Wayne and Webster streets, and was completed in 1904. A library in the city first grew out of the efforts of D.N. Foster and R.S. Robertson in 1878. Though it was some years before councilmen could be convinced of appropriating funds for such "frivolous" purposes, a reading room was established in 1887 by Mrs. Emerine Hamilton and her three daughters on

Left
Paving the street in front of the Temple Theatre at Clinton and Wayne streets in 1911. These men worked for the Barber Asphalt Company. Courtesy, Fort Wayne and Allen County Public Library.

Bottom
A group of children stop to be photographed in 1926 near the Rolling Mill district on the west side of Fort Wayne.

Opposite
The Fort Wayne Public Library as it looked during the early 1940s. The building, at Wayne and Webster streets, was removed in the mid-1960s to make way for the new library building.

West Wayne Street. The first regular librarian was Margaret Colerick, who guided library affairs for the next thirty-six years.

Jesse Grice, a Republican in an era dominated by Democrats was elected mayor of Fort Wayne in 1909. A butcher and stock-trader, Grice when in the mayor's office began a great street and sidewalk-building program. More than 35 miles of brick paving were laid, plus 53 miles of sidewalks. More than anyone else, he changed Fort Wayne from a dirt-street community to a paved one; and much of the brick still sometimes seen on old street and walkway surfaces stem from this period. That progress, however, didn't save the Republicans from natural calamity. The spring thaws were joined by 4.75 inches of rain in the days of March 23-25 in 1913; and the Maumee River went to 26.1 feet — an all-time high. Breaks began to appear in the St. Joseph Boulevard dikes. Wide areas were swept by the flowing tide. An estimated 15,000 persons were made homeless. Six deaths, including four children who drowned in the St. Mary's River, were attributed to the 1913 flood. The mayor declared martial law to control food and prevent looting.

The flood and its handling led to a return of the Democrats to City Hall. Bill Hosey, a Democrat who had first been elected in 1905 returned from his job in the Pennsy Shops to reclaim the mayoralty. In what appears to be an anomaly in local party elections, a major party candidate came in fourth. Charles Buck, an Independent, came in second; third was William Boerger, on the Socialist ticket; and then came William La Tourrette, the Republican candidate.

The Indiana statehood centennial was celebrated with horseless carriages and flag-waving crowds in 1916. Courtesy, Fort Wayne and Allen County Public Library.

CHAPTER VII

OVER THERE
&
BACK HOME

"What this country needs is a good five-cent cigar," is one of those curious quotes, which for no particular reason has stood the test of time. But it distinguished the otherwise undistinguished political career of Thomas Marshall, one-time Fort Wayne schoolboy who was elected vice president under President Woodrow Wilson. Marshall claimed residence in nearby Columbia City when elected in 1916. A better-known Wilsonian slogan of that year was, "He kept us out of war." But despite the slogans, the usual propensity of the community to vote Democratic, and the vice-presidential candidate's local connection, a majority of Allen County uncharacteristically voted Republican — 10,082 votes went for Charles Evans Hughes, the Republican nominee, and 9,134 went for Wilson. Five months later, on April 6, the United States under the newly elected Wilson declared war on the Central Powers.

A wave of patriotic fervor swept the community. From the day of the declaration of war to the following June, 4,000 men from the community went to training camps — all enlistees. By the time the draft began on July 20, another 7,785 men were registered. But the fervor soon took on an unpleasant flavor in a city with a large population of German ancestry — especially one which prided itself on German culture and still used the language in common discourse and in parochial schools. There is little evidence of serious pro-German attitudes on the part of local German-extracted families; but that didn't stop zealots from suspecting it existed and pushing measures to stamp it out. "Enemy Alien" German-Americans could not cross the central city railroad tracks without a pass. Widespread registration of "enemy aliens" was required under threat of imprisonment. In one celebrated case, an aging blacksmith who had resided in town since before the Civil War refused to conform to the registry and was actually sentenced to a federal prison.

The resentment of German immigrants was exacerbated by the efforts of several federal officials and the vigilance of such "patriotic" organizations as the state-sponsored Council of Defense and the Liberty Guards. Numerous immigrants ran into legal difficulties because they had failed to follow through with final naturalization processes, but had been voting and otherwise participating in civic matters for decades. The schools and churches where the German tongue was commonly employed were the greatest targets of abuse. Pastors of Lutheran churches and teachers in some of their schools resisted the overt intrusions on the basis of language usage. There were even reports of spies sitting in on Lutheran services ready to report use of alien language. Records indicate the German-language churches did employ more English from that time, but retained a considerable amount of German for both church and school usage. German was also used in several Catholic schools as a second language with English. This practice was dropped, however, in 1917, but not without comment by Monsignor John Oechtering, who had been pastor of St. Mary's since 1880.

Oechtering, a native of Germany, was an author, a translator of classics into English, and spoke seven languages. He incurred the ire of the zealots by pointing out publicly the anti-intellectual nature of their purge. Many families of German ancestry felt inhibited to speak German when in public. One small financial institution, the German-American Bank, changed its name to the Lincoln National Bank in 1917; it eventually became the city's largest.

But the war ended successfully on November 11, 1918, with citywide parades, decorated horses, and celebrations. Records show that those with German surnames served in the effort in proportion with the population. And when World War II rolled around, there was no repeat of the persecution — not locally, anyway — though the country stood idly by as California Attorney General Earl Warren led something even worse against those of Japanese extraction. During World War I Allen County service deaths numbered 131. One hundred seventeen of the male casualties had served in the Army; ten in the Navy; and two in the Marines. Two women had worked with the Red Cross. Yet it is estimated that more people in Allen County died during the 1918 flu epidemic than in direct war casualties.

Cultural life, business, and industry underwent extraordinary changes in the post-World-War I period. The busiest commercial area of town moved several blocks to the south from the old Columbia-Main-Berry district to the Wayne-Washington-Jefferson area. Practically all shopping and entertainment were concentrated downtown. The main exceptions were corner groceries, drugstores, shoe repair shops, and bakery outlets which were scattered throughout the residential neighborhoods.

It was an era of family-owned businesses. Many provided home delivery — usually by bicycle, motorcycle, or horse-drawn wagons. People had iceboxes instead of refrigerators. Icemen worked their routes from horse-drawn wagons, carrying the chunks of ice into the homes of each customer, who indicated the size of the chunk wanted by a sign in the front window. The horses seemed to know the route and always stopped in front of the right houses. One of the many sights in that era that have disappeared forever was that of great clouds of sparrows (numbering in the millions) that were attracted by the leavings of horses on city streets.

The incursion of new industries changed the city's business climate. In the previous century furniture and fabric manufacturers, iron mills, and the electrical companies had been the principal employers. Change came in a number of ways. Some of the old concerns, such as the Wayne Knitting Mills Company, were sold, and industrial growth shifted, in large part, to the east end of town. In 1922 construction was begun on a plant for International Harvester Company, a manufacturer that would eventually employ more than

10,000 workers. The Greater Fort Wayne Development Corporation provided the energy and financing for International Harvester and other major new plant locations in the area of East Pontiac Street and Bueter Road. International Harvester produced trucks and farm machinery, which stimulated the Truck Engineering Company plant nearby to start making special parts for International Harvester trucks. In the same area, the Rea Magnet Wire Company was founded in 1927, and the Essex Wire Company moved here from Detroit.

Wire soon became identified with Fort Wayne. Eventually Fort Wayne would produce more than half of all the wire in the United States. By World War II an estimated 90 percent of the wire-die production in the world came from the city — mostly from the numerous small plants specializing in this diamond-related skill.

The wire industry led to a local concentration of electronics-related firms. Homer Capehart, a future United States senator, located the Capehart Company on East Pontiac Street in 1927. A maker of fine phonographs, the company floundered in the Depression, but the plant was taken over in 1938 by Philo T. Farnsworth, who brought his Farnsworth Television and Radio Corporation to Fort Wayne. Farnsworth had discovered in 1927 the system for transmitting and receiving electronic images in a vacuum tube that made television possible. The Farnsworth firm merged with International Telephone and Telegraph in 1949.

Magnavox, a small firm which originally made speakers and phonographs, moved to Fort Wayne in 1929 from California. The firm expanded into military detection equipment and television technology at its plant on Bueter Road. In later periods Magnavox added plants at the Interstate Industrial Park, north of the city, and moved its headquarters to a site west of town near Interstate 69. The local Magnavox payroll eventually exceeded 4,000 employees.

Theodore Zollner, a piston maker, was attracted to Fort Wayne from Duluth, Minneapolis, in 1931 — largely because of the International truck market and the Detroit industries some 150 miles to the northeast. Fred Zollner, one of his sons, later ran the firm and became a sports figure with the Zollner-Piston basketball and softball teams. In the meantime, a small pump maker, which had set up in a one-story building on Wabash Avenue, began expansions. This was Tokheim Oil Tank and Pump Company, incorporated in 1918. The moving force was Ralph F. Diserens, who had been general manager of Wayne Pump Company. In those days, Bowser Pump on Creighton Avenue and Wayne Pump on Tecumseh Avenue were major local industries. Tokheim would eventually eclipse them with its worldwide operations.

Central Soya, Incorporated, was established in 1934, having grown out of

Top
The Fort Wayne Zollner Pistons became the world's professional basketball champions at Chicago Stadium in 1946. From left in the front row are Bud Jeanette, Bob McDermott, and Curly Armstrong. In the second row are Jerry Bush, Chick Reiser, Bob Taugh, and Charlie Shipp. And in the back row are Carl Bennett, John Pelkington, Bob Kinney, Ed Sadowski, and Fred Zollner, the owner. Courtesy, Fort Wayne and Allen County Public Library.

Bottom
The iceman, a familiar figure around town, is pictured in the 1874 advertisement for Peter A. Moran, dealer in "pure crystal ice." Cut from the lakes and rivers during the winter, ice was delivered year-round by horse and wagon from the 1850s until as late as the 1930s.

McMillen Feed Mills. Dale W. McMillen initiated the firm in 1916 and by the mid-1920s, Wayne Feed Company, its subsidiary, was shipping 4,000 rail carloads of feed annually. McMillen, who lived to the age of ninety-one, was prominent in expanding the city park system (McMillen Park was named after him) and children's baseball leagues.

The building of the Fort Wayne Chamber of Commerce and the Fort Wayne Woman's Club at Wayne and Ewing streets was begun in 1926. It grew out of earlier organizations, the old Wayne Club, started in 1893, and the Commercial Club, begun in 1899, which were merged into the Chamber in 1917 with Samuel Foster as president.

Foster figured in two enterprises, the Lincoln National Life Insurance Company and the Lincoln National Bank & Trust Company, which remain large financial establishments. Both institutions built landmarks during the 1920s. The Lincoln National Life Insurance Company grew from a one-room office on Berry Street in 1905 to a new headquarters building on Harrison Street that featured the Lincoln Youth statue, created by sculptor Paul Manship, which was set in place in 1932. Lincoln Life got its start toward being one of the nation's ten largest insurance firms during World War I. Until that time the Germans had been the main activists in the reinsurance field. With the Germans out of the market, Lincoln became a main exploiter of this phase of the business. In 1928 the company began the Lincoln Library and Museum, which became the largest collection of literature and information ever assembled about one man, Biblical figures excepted. Dr. Louis Warren was the founding curator.

Samuel Foster's German-American Bank was founded in 1905. Anti-German sentiment inspired a name-change to the Lincoln National Bank & Trust Company, in 1917. In 1929 it broke ground for the Lincoln Tower, a twenty-two-floor structure that for years would remain Indiana's tallest building. Construction was launched just weeks prior to the stock-market crash of October 29, 1929; the Lincoln Bank would be one of only two local banks to survive the Depression. The other survivor was the Peoples Trust & Savings Company, founded in 1903 by Patrick J. McDonald and William L. Moellering.

The first bank in town, a branch of the State Bank of Indiana, had been founded in 1835. Its state-named directors were Allen Hamilton, Hugh Hanna, and William Rockhill. Hamilton founded the Hamilton National Bank in 1853. In later years the state branch bank became known as Old National Bank.

Few people in Fort Wayne had anticipated the disastrous events that began with the 1929 stock-market crash and led to the nation's largest depression. Nineteen twenty-nine seemed then to be the best of times. Fort Wayne had never seemed more prosperous. The rising inflation and gold

Above
The Lincoln Tower in full bloom. Courtesy, Fort Wayne and Allen County Public Library.

Opposite
Top
The United States Post Office was built in 1931. It was new when this photo was taken. Courtesy, Fort Wayne and Allen County Public Library.

Right
The Fort Wayne Chamber of Commerce building was constructed in 1926. Courtesy, Fort Wayne and Allen County Public Library.

Far Right
The Lincoln National Bank began construction of its twenty-two-story building on Berry Street just about the time of the 1929 stock market crash. Courtesy, Fort Wayne and Allen County Public Library.

hoarding didn't worry local citizens any more than it seemed to worry Herbert Hoover, the nation's engineer president.

But in just two years, 25 percent of the work force would be unemployed. Many of those still with jobs had shorter hours and less pay. A makeshift Hooverville, actually called a "shanty town" in those days, began springing up at the Jailhouse Flats between Clinton and Calhoun streets, north of Superior Street. Efforts to remove the homeless squatters were resisted. Lines of hungry people formed at the soup kitchens operated by the Wayne Township Trustee and several other charitable organizations. Shabbily dressed men could often be seen wandering along Fort Wayne's streets or shuffling down alleys to investigate the potential of garbage cans. There were thousands of hoboes in Fort Wayne during the early 1930s, due in part to the numerous railroads operating in the city. Freight trains, of which several hundred passed through the city daily, were the mode of travel for those who rode the rails.

The chugging, thumping, and clashing of the railroad switching yards could be heard around the clock in most parts of Fort Wayne through the 1930s. Hundreds of trains and thousands of cars were switched daily. Fly ash and soot created pollution and a peculiar odor, which gradually supplanted the earlier horse smell that had pervaded the urban vicinity. This may help explain why pictures taken in that period often seem to have a rather hazy quality. Most factories and homes still employed coal in the main; and the softer, cheaper, and dirtier grades were used as the Depression deepened.

Prohibition was in its final days, but raids on speakeasies and other illegal liquor operations still made daily news. On one night — July 10, 1931 — twenty-four operators of liquor and beer operations were arrested. On July 22 two federal agents were gunned down by an ex-convict named George Adams near the Stellhorn Bridge on the city's south edge. The agents, John Wilson and Walter Gilbert, both died, and local newspapers speculated that their liquor-running killer would get the electric chair. But the jury handed down a verdict of manslaughter, and Adams served only three years. Walter E. Helmke, the prosecutor, later questioned one of the jurors about the mild verdict. "I knew Prohibition was over," Helmke said, "when he answered, 'We should have given him a medal.' " Repeal of the Volstead Act in 1933 brought the return of the Centlivre and Berghoff breweries to full operations in Fort Wayne.

The Depression also had an unfortunate effect on Fort Wayne's population growth. From the 1900 census count of 45,115, the population grew to 63,933 in 1910, and to 86,549 in 1920. The figure moved up rapidly during the 1920s to an official figure of 114,946 in 1930. But hard times produced stagnation, and the city population only went to 118,410 by 1940 — the smallest gain since Fort Wayne had been formed.

Although times were hard during the Depression years, they were not

Top
As the depression grew worse, squatters built a shanty town or Hooverville between Clinton and Calhoun north of Superior Street. Painter Louis Bonsib captured the grim scene in oils in 1932. Courtesy, *News-Sentinel*.

Right
When World War II shut off the gasoline supply, the Berghoff Brewery trotted out some heavyweight horses to keep the town in brew. Courtesy, Fort Wayne and Allen County Public Library.

without diversion. Little Carol Jane Peters, born in Fort Wayne in 1908 on Rockhill Street, was on her way to becoming a reigning queen of the silver screen as Carole Lombard. Ole Olsen and Chic Johnson in 1936 began their *Hellzapoppin'* musical comedy review at the Palace Theatre on East Washington Boulevard, then moved on to New York for a record 1,040 performances on Broadway. Local moviegoers had two art-deco palaces for first-run films. Seats were 25¢ and 35¢ for adults, 10¢ for children. The Emboyd Theatre, built in 1927 in the 100 block of West Jefferson Street, seated 3,000 in red-glow splendor. The theater was later renamed the Embassy, and remained in 1980 as a civic music hall. The Paramount Theatre, built in 1930 in the 100 block of East Wayne Street, was its equal in pretention and appointments — it had cool, blue-green decor and bronze statuary. Both movie houses were operated by Clyde Quimby, who handled the Palace and the Jefferson Theatres, as well. The Jefferson was located on West Jefferson across the street from the Emboyd. The Paramount, which had been built on the site of Fort Wayne High School was razed in the 1960s.

Several anecdotes from the troubled period reveal how different personalities reacted to the stress. Henry Paul, chairman of the Old First National Bank, prided himself on being a self-made man. When an agent of the federal banking agency came in to instruct Paul on new regulations, Paul didn't take the matter lightly. According to Carl Dannenfelser, then secretary at the bank, Paul shouted that he was running the bank, picked up an ink well, and threw it at the federal official, who was, by this time, backing through the door. The harsh handling of the First National by the government might be attributed in part to this and similar experiences.

Another story about Paul confirms his reputation as a tightwad. The story, which may be apocryphal, had Paul riding a streetcar when he noticed a piece of rope on the side of the street. He reportedly jumped off, grabbed the item, and returned to his seat on the public conveyance. Another story, less amusing and equally open to question, concerns the bank panic. While Paul, then bank chairman, and Frank Cutshall, the bank president, told the public not to panic and to leave their money in the bank, both are said to have been secretly removing their own funds.

The wave of bank robberies that swept America in the 1930s touched Fort Wayne as well. George Kelly and his Chicago mob held up the Broadway State Bank at the corner of Broadway and Taylor Street on August 20, 1930. George W. Clark, the cashier, was pistol-whipped, and Theodore Ruby of Blue Lake, a customer, was wounded by shotgun pellets. The Kelly gang escaped with $5,912, but were later captured, returned for trial, and sentenced to fifteen years apiece.

The best-known bandit of the following years, however, was John Dillinger, who was in and out of Fort Wayne on numerous occasions, but for

Carol Jane Peters, who was born on Rockhill Street, already shows some of the charm of future movie star Carole Lombard.

Opposite
Top
Students painting at the Fort Wayne Art School on West Berry Street in 1931.

Right
During an evening meeting at the Wheatley Social Center in 1936, some women play table tennis while others prefer to observe. Courtesy, Fort Wayne and Allen County Public Library.

reasons never explained, he never robbed a Fort Wayne bank. Nor was he ever bothered by local law-enforcement agencies, despite his sweep of the surrounding towns. Dillinger's mob even raided Indiana police stations: Auburn on October 16, 1933; Peru on October 20, 1933, and Warsaw on April 13, 1934. His gang took an arsenal in machine guns, bulletproof vests, pistols, and shotguns.

Three men from Fort Wayne had connections with Dillinger. Clifford Mohler served time with Dillinger at the Michigan City prison before being released in the general amnesty of the spring of 1933 (Mohler had been convicted in the 1926 slaying of a Fort Wayne police officer). Bank robber Sam Goldstein and Homer Van Meter were the others. Homicidal Homer was Dillinger's most constant companion in the final wild months of 1934. Dillinger had reportedly talked Homer out of "drilling" Policeman Jud Pittinger at the Warsaw station raid in April. Homer had been a train robber at age nineteen; like Dillinger and Mohler, he was paroled in the ill-advised clemency movement of Governor Paul McNutt. He and Dillinger were at the Spider Lake, Wisconsin, shootout with federal agents in May, 1934, where two agents were killed and four wounded. A month after Dillinger was shot down by federal officers at the Biograph Theatre in Chicago, Van Meter himself, on August 23 in St. Paul, Minneapolis, was ambushed by police. His body was brought home to Fort Wayne for burial in an unusual empty-casket

Marilyn Maxwell, who ushered at the Rialto Theatre in the 1930s, is shown at a later date with Bob Hope.

Below
Fort Wayne's water filtration plant, built in 1930 at the head of the Maumee River, is shown behind the Columbia Avenue Bridge in 1949. Courtesy, Fort Wayne and Allen County Public Library.

episode. An empty casket was supposedly taken to Lindenwood Cemetery to thwart curiosity-seekers; three days later the family quietly went about the business of the actual burial.

It was during 1930 that work on the Filtration Plant at Three Rivers was started, including a dam and pumping station on the St. Joseph River. The plant, capable of processing twenty million gallons of water daily, cost $2.5 million. Mayor Hosey who had been elected to a five-year term in 1929, was 80 years old in 1934, but decided to run for reelection anyway. When the votes were counted the Democratic warhorse was a loser by a mere 587 votes. The winner, Republican Harry Baals, would carve out a career as mayor almost as long as Hosey's.

The 1930s also marked important strides for labor unions in America. Fort Wayne was the site of the birth of a major labor organization in 1936 — the United Electrical Workers Union (UE). Because of the location of General Electric plants and other similar companies related to the electrical industry, workers in Fort Wayne provided a significant power base. National organization representatives met in the Anthony Hotel. James Carey was named the first president of the UE, and later that year affiliated the union with a committee headed by John L. Lewis. Carey was named CIO secretary when Lewis founded the CIO in 1938. Among those organizing the UE that Depression year of 1936 was George Gould, long-time international

representative, who said he rode into town for the meeting on a freight car. In 1949 the Fort Wayne locals switched from the UE to a recently formed organization, the International Union of Electrical, Radio and Machine Workers (IUE). The new union was developed by mostly the same people who had formed the UE in Fort Wayne in 1936.

Union activities in the city had begun early in its history — going back to the railroad organizations of the 19th century. In 1887 twenty-four unions formed the Trades and Labor Council of Fort Wayne. In 1897 the council was granted a charter by the American Federation of Labor (AFL). Eugene V. Debs, a frequent visitor to the city, directed the great American Railroad Union Strike of 1894, which was a watershed in labor battles. What would eventually be the largest local in Fort Wayne, Local 57 of the United Auto Workers, was formed in the auto-industry strife of the 1930s. The UAW local represented workers at International Harvester.

People had less money to travel, so local music, theater, and other diversions prospered. The Fort Wayne Community Concert Association was formed in 1931, and thereafter brought many of the world's orchestras and opera figures to local stages. It was initially headed by J. Ross McCulloch, Mrs. Isabelle Peltier, and Mrs. John Moring. In 1933 the Fort Wayne Civic Symphony was founded out of a nucleus of local talent first put together during the 1920s by George and Gaston Bailhe. The Civic Symphony led to the eventual development of Fort Wayne Philharmonic Orchestra in 1944 and 1945. The first conductor was German-born Hans Schwieger, who was succeeded in 1948 by Russian-born Igor Buketoff. During that period Fort Wayne had the foremost concert orchestra of any city of its size in the nation. It usually filled the Scottish Rite Auditorium on West Berry Street for its performances.

The Old Fort Players, a stage group founded in 1931, leased the Majestic Theatre from 1933 to 1940. The Majestic was located on East Berry Street, on the south side just beyond Clinton Street. Hundreds of men and women with stage aspirations, plus thousands of patrons, enjoyed these productions during the Depression. The Old Fort Players died as a separate group in 1940 with the purchase of the Majestic by the Civic Theatre organization, which had been more recently formed. The Civic focused on theater education and began a Children's Theatre. It also organized its own orchestra. The Civic Theatre remained in the Majestic until it was razed in 1957 to make way for the new Wolf & Dessauer department store. When the Civic moved from the Majestic to the Palace Theatre in the 100 block of East Washington, it was like moving uptown. Plush, with loge boxes and balcony, the Palace seated 2,000. During the 1930s it doubled as a movie theater and music hall for swing bands and traveling magicians.

Right
Members of the United Auto Workers Union went on strike at International Harvester plants in November 1979.

Center
The cast of the Civic Youtheatre in the 1936 production of *The Steadfast Tin Soldier* at the old Majestic Theatre.

Bottom
A 1936-37 season ticket for the Old Fort Players at the Majestic Theatre.

Calhoun Street looking north, the morning after Thanksgiving, 1954. Before shopping centers took away most of the retail trade from midtown, this was a familiar scene.

CHAPTER
VIII

MODERN
TIMES:
1940-1980

By the end of the 1930s another war was on and employment in local plants moved up apace. On December 11, 1940, the site of a major Army Air Corps base was announced. Within months, this became Baer Field on the city's south fringe west of State Road 1. By October of 1941 the base covered 907 acres. Quarters for 2,000 men were provided. The base became active on December 6, 1941, with the arrival of crack fighter squadrons — pilots and their Airacobras of the 31st Pursuit Group. The new military activity received wide local publicity, but it was cut short in twenty-four hours when Pearl Harbor dropped a shroud of secrecy around Baer Field. Months later another military installation was mobilized for Fort Wayne. This was Camp Scott, built between Wayne Trace and the Pennsylvania Railroad on May 8, 1942. The 130th Railroad Battalion trained men in rail operations and maintenance. Toward the end of the war, it became a camp for German prisoners. Barbed wire and guard towers were erected. It was the only known instance of foreign prisoners of war being held at Fort Wayne — at least since the days of the first forts when a few British or Canadian captives were at the stockade.

Women in war plants and numerous soldiers on the streets changed Fort Wayne as much, if not more, than did the rationing of gasoline, food, and shoes. The downtown area became particularly active. Gambling, which had been rather loosely controlled anyway, became more open. Fort Wayne was considered "a good liberty town." Another sign of the times came on May 14, 1942, with the arrival of the cherry blossoms. The Japanese Gardens in West Swinney Park were renamed Jaenicke Gardens. This served to honor Adolph Jaenicke, who had created the gardens in 1927, and to insult the enemy Japan. In the meantime, the Tokheim and Wayne Pump plants had switched to the making of bombs. International Harvester built military trucks. General Electric constructed a huge plant on Taylor Street for production of aircraft superchargers. Magnavox made submarine detection devices and electronic gear.

High-school kids became experts at siphoning gasoline to combat gasoline ration stamps, which weren't issued to them. But there were few serious problems locally with the draft. As the war dragged on, it became a choice only between enlisting in the service of one's preference while still seventeen or being drafted into the army soon after.

From the European theater of World War II came word of the exploits of Captain Walker (Bud) Mahurin. America's leading air ace at the time, Mahurin shot down three German planes over Berlin on March 8, 1944, bringing the total to twenty enemy planes hit with his Republic Thunderbolt. Later in March, however, he was shot down over France, but was rescued by French underground partisans. Soon he was back in Fort Wayne to promote war-bond sales.

The war ended shortly after the atomic age was introduced with the

Top Left
When World War II broke out, an honor roll of those Fort Wayne residents serving in the armed forces was established at the courthouse. This shot of the dedication was taken on Armistice Eve, November 10, 1942. Courtesy, Fort Wayne and Allen County Public Library.

Top Right
The factory district at Anthony and New Haven looked grim in February 1945. While war plants were busy, two miles away at Camp Scott German prisoners-of-war were held behind barbed wire and machine-gun towers. Courtesy, Fort Wayne and Allen County Public Library.

Bottom
Many women joined men at work in war plants during the Second World War. Here, workers are changing shifts at the General Electric Company plant on Broadway in 1944. War plants operated around the clock seven days a week. Courtesy, Fort Wayne and Allen County Public Library.

dropping of bombs over Hiroshima and Nagasaki. Victory Day was September 2, 1945. Jubilation and snake dances down Calhoun Street were followed by parades, the ringing of church bells, and services of thanksgiving. By that date the Allen County war dead, in all branches of services, totalled 361. Harry Baals was still mayor of Fort Wayne, having defeated Democratic challenger Harry Gottschalk in both 1938 and 1942. He would then serve a five-year term — an arrangement to put city elections back on the off-year schedule that was disrupted in 1929. In the 1947 elections Henry Branning, a Democrat, defeated Republican Otto Adams. The main issue that year was a federally financed proposal to build parklike expressways through the center of the city. Adams was associated with the expressway proposal. In the voting, however, a majority went against Adams and the expressway referendum. In the sports arenas Fort Wayne had a lot to cheer about: the Zollner-Piston basketball team won the world professional championship twice, in 1945 and again in 1946, both times in a playoff tourney at Chicago Stadium.

Post-War Breeze

The second World War changed Fort Wayne, as it changed America. Though the old downtown continued as the center of business and entertainment, the rapid buildup of residential sections in the fringe areas forecast the shopping centers which would be built in the next decade in the suburbs. New industries, such as Dana Corporation and North American Van Lines, broadened the economic base. Socially the single largest gathering in town was for the *News-Sentinel* fireworks display on the Fourth of July. About 100,000 persons from the city and area communities would attend. It was held at Foster Park in the 1930s, then switched to McMillen Park in 1948, and changed to Johnny Appleseed Park in 1972. Gambling had mostly disappeared as the community moved into the 1950s, and some of the more tawdry saloons along Calhoun Street were closed.

The Allen County Memorial Coliseum was completed and dedicated in 1952. It had an arena with a capacity of over 10,000 seats and an exhibition hall on the lower level. The Coliseum housed Fort Wayne's two professional sports teams. It was the home floor of the Fort Wayne Pistons until that pro basketball team moved to Detroit in 1957. The Fort Wayne Komets, an ice hockey team, began play there in 1952. The Coliseum also hosts the annual Christ Child Festival. as well as other events.

It was a time when television was new in the city. The first station, WKJG-TV began broadcasting on November 1, 1953. The second station, originally with the call letters of WIN-T, but later changed to WANE-TV. began regular broadcasts on September 26, 1954. The third outlet was WPTA with transmissions starting September 17, 1957.

The face of downtown, which had stayed more or less the same since the

The voting down of the Anthony Wayne Parkway plans in 1947 deprived the city of a major expressway network through the middle of town and was considered a mistake for years thereafter. *News-Sentinel* cartoonist Bill Sandeson later showed this mistake as a skeleton in Fort Wayne's closet. Courtesy, *News-Sentinel*.

Opposite
Top Left
Americans sold war bonds almost everywhere, even in city trolley coaches. The women in this 1944 photo are selling savings stamps. Courtesy, Fort Wayne and Allen County Public Library.

Top Right
Mayor Harry Baals and Congressman E. Ross Adair, to the right of the hostess, welcome home television comedian Herb Shriner. Shriner is wearing the dark sport coat in this 1952 photo. Courtesy, Fort Wayne and Allen County Public Library.

Bottom
Washington Boulevard at the Wolf and Dessauer stop near Calhoun in 1945. In the distance to the right can be seen the Palace Theatre, the Masonic Temple, and the YMCA. Courtesy, Fort Wayne and Allen County Public Library.

early part of the century, changed in the 1950s and early 1960s. The stone-supported Barr Street Market pavilion was torn down in 1958. It had been a landmark building since its completion in 1910; the site had been a farmer's market since 1855, when the original city hall and market buildings were erected. Three spectacular fires made further alterations. In the last week of December 1958, the 101-year-old MacDougal Building at the northwest corner of Berry and Calhoun streets burned. The Fort Wayne Waste Paper Company, at 301 East Columbia Street, which also went back to the canal days, burned on May 13, 1958. Then on February 10, 1962, fire gutted nearly a block of downtown along Washington Boulevard between Clinton and Calhoun streets. Five buildings used by the Wolf & Dessauer department store were gutted. Fire and smoke attracted such a large crowd that Fire Chief Howard Blanton warned it was hampering the firefighters. The blaze, which raged out of control for ten hours, threatened the entire vicinity, but was eventually contained. The combination of 3,800,000 gallons of water used in the effort and the freezing temperatures created an eerie and treacherous scene. The site, which became known as "The Hole" for years thereafter, eventually became the location of the high-rise Summit Square in 1980.

The flight of retail trade from downtown began as a trickle during the 1950s and turned into a flood in the 1960s. First small shopping centers such as Quimby Village on the Bluffton Road, the South Anthony Plaza, and the Rudisill Boulevard developments were erected. Then in 1955 the Southgate Shopping Center north of Pettit Avenue provided a score of outlets and 2,500 parking spaces. This was followed by the Northcrest Center on eighty acres along Coliseum Boulevard built in 1958, and the Skyline Plaza on Goshen Road in 1959. Fort Wayne's major shopping malls came a few years later. The Glenbrook Mall, begun in 1965 on Coliseum Boulevard with seventy stores and an investment of $7 million, was continuously expanded thereafter and by 1980 construction was nearly tripled in size. Major stores included L.S. Ayres, Sears, Penneys, and under way in 1980, J.L. Hudson. Some retail reports indicated that Glenbrook Mall became the highest volume retail center in the state. The Southtown Mall, of similar size and investment, was begun in 1967 at Tillman Road and U.S. 27 south. The Georgetown Shopping Center on East State Boulevard broke ground in 1967 with almost continuous expansions thereafter, being in the community's fastest-growing residential area. A mile to the north at State Road 37 and Maplecrest Road, the Maplewood Center enjoyed similar progress. The Canterbury Green Shopping Center and nearby Canterbury Apartments (with a resident population of some 4,000) was built at St. Joe and St. Joe Center roads. On the southwest end of town, the Time Corners Shopping, at one time an almost-rural market, was greatly expanded into an urban retailing center in the 1960s and 1970s.

Of Fort Wayne's five accredited colleges, the largest by far is the Fort

Top
"Five and Ten Cent Stores" dominated this block of Calhoun near Main Street in 1946. The high-rise Fort Wayne National Bank building now stands at this location. Courtesy, Fort Wayne and Allen County Public Library.

Left
The last customer at the Barr Street Market before it was razed in 1958. Courtesy, Fort Wayne and Allen County Public Library.

Center
The Barr Street Market was a gathering place for farmer vendors and town shoppers in 1949.

Right
The anchor from the battleship USS *Indiana* stands on the Allen County Memorial Coliseum grounds. Courtesy, Fort Wayne and Allen County Public Library.

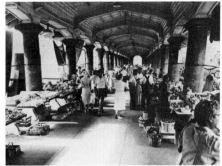

Wayne campus of Indiana and Purdue Universities at Coliseum Boulevard along the St. Joseph River. The campus, originally 120 acres when purchased in 1958, was subsequently expanded to 412 acres. Buildings at the site were started in 1962 and in ten years the student enrollment was about 5,000. Toward the end of the 1970s, the student population had doubled that figure.

The joint Indiana-Purdue venture had its beginning in 1957 with a proposal of A.W. Kettler and Walter E. Helmke, Purdue and I.U. trustees, and the support of industrialist Walter Walb and others in the city. Unification of the administrative was approved in 1973. The university, begun with largely two-year programs, was expanded into regular four-year academics. It remained a commuter program for area students with extensive buildings designed for degree work, but no on-campus residences. The I.U.-Purdue University at Fort Wayne grew out of much earlier but separate programs in midtown.

The Fort Wayne Extension of Indiana University was founded in 1917, and over the years was variously located in old Central High School, the Dime Trust Bank at Wayne and Clinton streets, and from 1939 to 1964 in the former building of the Lutheran Institute on Barr Street. Purdue first began operations in the city in 1941 as a wartime technical training institute. It consolidated in the Transfer Building at the northwest corner of Main and Calhoun streets in 1946; but in 1947 it moved to the large brick structure at the southwest corner of Jefferson and Barr streets, formerly the Catholic Community Center. By the time of the 1964 move to the new campus Purdue had 1,462 students. At that date the I.U. local student body numbered 1,335.

In the spring of 1944 the old Bass estate on the Bass Road, two small lakes and all, became the campus of St. Francis College. The Sisters of St. Francis moved the college from Lafayette to Fort Wayne. The student body grew from forty-four the first term to more than 1,700 in the next thirty years. A graduate school was formed in 1960.

The Fort Wayne Bible College became a state-accredited school in 1955, together with a building program at its campus along West Rudisill Boulevard. It was earlier known as the Fort Wayne Bible Training School and had been founded by the Missionary Church Association in Fort Wayne in 1904.

The Indiana Institute of Technology, which had been known as Indiana Technical College when located on East Washington Boulevard for many years after its founding in 1930, moved to its present campus in 1957. The location on Maumee Avenue was formerly the site of Concordia College.

In 1957 Concordia Senior College moved onto one of the more interesting campuses in the nation. Designed by architect Eero Saarinen, the college lies west of the St. Joseph River, southeast of North Clinton Street. Saarinen designed the landscape and buildings to reflect a pastoral environment. The architect even designed the diamond-shaped bricks and unique roofing, the

Top
Downtown Fort Wayne in 1960. Many of the buildings in the five-block foregound area have been razed. Courtesy, Fort Wayne and Allen County Public Library.

Left
The Wolf and Dessauer fire of February 10, 1962, threatened a city block and drew thousands of onlookers to East Washington Boulevard. It took ten hours and three million gallons of water to control it. Courtesy, Fort Wayne and Allen County Public Library.

Center
Shoppers crowd the sidewalks during the Christmas rush at Wayne and Calhoun streets, 1954.

Right
The Fort Wayne Extension of Indiana University once occupied the White National Bank building at the northwest corner of Wayne and Clinton streets. Later, the Dime Bank was located here. Courtesy, Fort Wayne and Allen County Public Library.

latter still known as "Concordia roof" wherever it is used. The initial building program, directed by Dr. Martin Neeb and Dr. Herbert Bredemeier, cost about $8 million. The campus, designed for a relatively small number of live-in students, consists of 186 acres.

The Crosier House of Studies, just north of Fort Wayne on the Wallen Road, is a relatively new educational institution, but has deep roots in European history. The present building was constructed in 1957 with expansion in 1963. The Crosier fathers, who operate the school for seminary students, were originally founded in Europe during the 13th century. The property the order occupies at Fort Wayne was once known as The Academie by the French settlers who established the school in 1840. Beginning in 1912, a Catholic girls' school named the Sacred Heart Academy occupied the old building. It closed in 1934, and it was this building, since razed, which the Crosiers first occupied in 1939.

The *News-Sentinel* moved into a newly constructed building at 600 West Main Street in 1958. The newspaper's former home at Barr Street and Washington Boulevard, built in 1926, became the Foellinger Center for United Community Services. The morning *Journal-Gazette,* which had been located at the southeast corner of Clinton and Main streets, also moved into the new building of the News Publishing Company. At that time an agency corporation named Fort Wayne Newspapers, Inc., began providing production, advertising, and circulation services for both newspapers. The *News-Sentinel,* which stemmed from the city's first newspaper, the *Sentinel* (founded in 1833) was published by Oscar Foellinger from 1920 until his death in 1936 and by Helene Foellinger thereafter. At the time of the 1958 move, Clifford B. Ward was *News-Sentinel* editor, and upon retirement in 1965, was succeeded by Ernest E. Williams. At the *Journal-Gazette,* Miller Ellingham was succeeded as editor by Frank Roberts, who in turn was succeeded by Larry Allen. On February 20, 1980, the sale of the *News-Sentinel* to Knight-Ridder Newspapers, Inc., was announced. Helene R. Foellinger remained publisher of the *News-Sentinel.* Phil deMontmollin was named president of Fort Wayne Newspapers, Inc., and Richard G. Inskeep, publisher of the *Journal-Gazette,* was named chairman of Fort Wayne Newspapers, Inc. Also in 1980, the Radio Station WGL was sold by the News Publishing Company to Patten Communication Corporation. WGL, a pioneer station, which began commercial radio in 1924 with the call-letters WHBJ, was operated by Chester Keen. The next station, WOWO, started by Keen in 1925, was sold to Frederick Zeig in 1928.

Once known as the "City of Churches" — and saloons — Fort Wayne has become a city of parks and festivals in recent decades. Fort Wayne's early parks were tiny affairs designed merely to commemorate historical events, while later parks were generous in size and activities built with recreation in

Top
Franke Park, a beautiful place to enjoy the good old summertime. Courtesy, Harry Grabner, Board of Park Commissioners.

Bottom
Two clowns entertain visitors at the Franke Park Children's Zoo. Courtesy, *Journal-Gazette.*

mind. Henry M. Williams was the moving spirit behind the town's first park — Old Fort Park purchased in 1863 next to the canal at East Main Street where the old fort had once stood. Williams later gave the city Williams Park at Creighton and Hoagland avenues, but it was modified in the 1890s into a residential development. North Side Park was purchased by the city for use as a State Fair Grounds in 1866. This park, between North Clinton Street and Spy Run Avenue, was in 1899 renamed Lawton Park after General Henry Lawton, medal of honor recipient in the Civil War, the man who captured Geronimo the Apache, and who was killed in the Philippine campaign following the Spanish-American War. Lakeside Park, at Lake Avenue and Forest Park Boulevard, was acquired in 1908 and became the site of the celebrated rose gardens. The two Delta Lakes were carved out so that the earth could be used for the levies along the Maumee and St. Joseph rivers, which had been flooding the vicinity.

The larger parks, which figure so prominently in the city's festivals, are of more recent vintage. David N. and Sam Foster donated Foster Park in 1912. It extends for two miles along the St. Mary's River and, with later additions, includes 218 acres. The municipal golf course and numerous tennis courts are located there. Swinney Park, on either side of the St. Mary's River near downtown, was expanded in 1918, though a portion of the park near the old Swinney homestead was purchased by the city as early as 1869. It is a picnic and tennis center. At one time West Swinney was called Trier's Park because of the amusement concessions located there by George Trier. The amusements included a roller coaster brought from Robison Park when it was closed in 1919, a dance hall, and various rides and fun houses, which were all closed in 1953 after decline in attendance and fires. Memorial Park, a thirty-five-acre tract on the east end, was purchased in 1918 and dedicated to the men and women in the service during World War I. Each tree planted there is a living memorial for someone who died in the conflict.

On the north end of Sherman Boulevard lies the Fort Wayne Children's Zoo, opened in 1965 and expanded in 1975 with the "African Veldt" exhibit. The site is Franke Park, which originally started with an eighty-acre gift in 1921 by John B. Franke. Expanded to many times that size, it includes Shoaff Lake, a nature preserve; the Foellinger Outdoor Theatre; the Diehm Museum of Natural History; a miniature steam-engine train; a toboggan slide; and a soap-box-derby track. McMillen Park, made possible by the donations of Mr. and Mrs. Dale McMillen in 1937, is a 168-acre park just west of Hessen Cassel Road that includes two football fields, a swimming pool, an eighteen-hole golf course with night lights, and an artificially iced skating rink. The Fred B. Shoaffs donated funding for Shoaff Park, a 169-acre playground along the St. Joseph River north of the city. It has boat ramps, lighted ball diamonds, a fishing pond for children, and an eighteen-hole golf course. A county park

Top
During the winter, the Soap Box Derby track at Franke Park is used as a toboggan slide. Courtesy, *News-Sentinel.*

Bottom
The rock band *Crossfire* entertained at the McMillen Park Ice Arena in the spring of 1979. Photo by Harry Grabner.

department was started in 1965 — a move that led to the purchase of 381 acres southwest of the city known as the Fox Island Nature Preserve.

The equestrian statue of Anthony Wayne, a massive bronze created in 1916 by George Ganiere, was moved from Hayden Park to Freimann Park at Main and Clinton streets in 1973. Freimann Park, made possible by a bequest of Frank Freimann, long-time president of Magnavox, was designed as a formal midtown park between the City-County building and the Theatre for the Performing Arts, which was designed by architect Louis Kahn and completed in 1973.

The Performing Arts Center was a project of the Fine Arts Foundation established in 1956. It was formed to provide broad support for the Philharmonic Orchestra, the Civic Theatre, the Art School and Museum, the Fort Wayne Ballet, and the Community Concerts series. The Ballet was established that same year. Both the Civic Theatre and the ballet troup used the Performing Arts Theatre. Other theatre groups were linked with the First Presbyterian Church, the Arena Theatre at the Chamber of Commerce, and the PIT Theatre at Indiana-Purdue University Center. In the spring of 1973, the PIT group took a remarkably entertaining musical comedy, *Dames At Sea*, to full-house performances at the Kennedy Center in Washington, D.C. The Fort Wayne Light Opera Festival, launched in 1945 and known as the Festival Music Theater since 1955, performed in the 2,500-seat Foellinger Outdoor

Opposite
Top Left
Young Fort Wayne ballet dancers practicing for a performance.

Top Right
Two very young violinists following instructions at the Performing Arts Center during the summer of 1978.

Bottom
The Fort Wayne Philharmonic Orchestra performing at the Foellinger Theatre at Franke Park on September 23, 1979. The music director, Ronald Ondrejka, was conducting the orchestra in its 36th season.

Below
Entertainment may be found at Freimann Park almost any summer day. In 1978, Kathleen Hill and the ensemble performed at the park.

Theatre at Franke Park.

A new trend in population statistics was noted between 1950 and 1960. While the city population increased 10 percent to 161,000 by 1960, the Allen County population was going up more than 20 percent to 232,196. Because the farm population was actually declining, practically all the gain can be attributed to suburban growth around the city. Census figures show the same trend through the 1960s. The city population only went to 178,021 by 1970, yet the county population expanded to 280,455. The situation indicated a failure in the city's annexation programs and made widespread the tax advantages of locating outside city limits, even though the suburbs were a part of the same general urban community. It was a condition that became more pronounced in the 1970s when more than 80 percent of the building in the county was begun outside the city limits.

In 1965 Edward H. White, III — a member of an old Fort Wayne family — became the first man to step into space when he ventured outside a Gemini 4 capsule for his celebrated space walk. Astronaut White was the great-grandson of Civil War Captain James White, who was a prominent merchant in Fort Wayne. The astronaut's grandfather was a local banker and his father was Air Force General Edward White, II. His mother, Mary Haller, was at one time a teacher in the Fort Wayne public schools. Ed White perished in 1967 during an Apollo I moon countdown at Cape Kennedy, Florida. Astronauts Roger

Left
George Ganiere's bronze statue of General Anthony Wayne was originally placed along Maumee Avenue in 1916. In 1973 the statue was moved to its present location in Freimann Square.

Opposite
Top Left
The horizontal line of dancers on a Freimann Park bench offers a counterpoint to the vertical sweep of the Fort Wayne National Bank in the background. Courtesy, *News-Sentinel*.

Top Right
A Fort Wayne Civic Theatre program for the presentation of *Mrs. Bumpstead Leigh* in 1937.

Bottom
Members of the Fort Wayne Dance Collective in motion at the Performing Arts Center.

The DRAMALOG
CIVIC THEATRE MAGAZINE
FORT WAYNE · · INDIANA

Presenting

"Mrs. Bumpstead Leigh"
By Harry James Smith

April 29, 30, May 1, 1937

OLD FORT PLAYERS, Inc

Chaffee and Virgil Grissom died in the same flash fire in the spacecraft.

Urban renewal, which was a catch phrase of the 1960s as cities vied for federal funds, has had rather mixed results in Fort Wayne. The Fort Wayne Redevelopment Commission launched the Hanna-Creighton Project in 1964 with disastrous results. A 112-acre area south of the Pennsylvania Elevation and east of Hanna Street was cleared of 532 buildings, most of them private residences. The inhabitants — mostly black families who, for the most part, owned their own homes — were displaced and a virtual wasteland created that lasted for years. A few government-supported apartment projects and commercial ventures appeared but the city had little else to show for its $5.5-million effort.

The Main Street Project was more successful. The Redevelopment Commission cleared land in most of eight blocks in the old section of downtown, including decaying stores and warehouses associated with the canal era. Most of old Columbia Street disappeared, with one block west of Calhoun Street, renamed The Landing, remaining after the other demolition. The Landing was spruced up with gas lamps and old-town character. Razed were the buildings north of Main Street from Calhoun Street to the Maumee River. The Three Rivers Apartments, started in 1964 at the confluence of the

Opposite
Top Left
The Landing, a preserved block of old Columbia Street. Courtesy, Fort Wayne and Allen County Public Library. Photo by Robin Steury.

Top Right
A 1977 presentation of *My Fair Lady* at the Fort Wayne Civic Theatre. Photo by Gabriel R. Delobbe.

Center
The 1980s began with three downtown city blocks of open space in the initial stages of development. Photo by Gabriel R. Delobbe.

Below
Mute buildings in the 200 block of East Columbia Street. Courtesy, Fort Wayne and Allen County Public Library.

St. Mary's and the Maumee rivers, was the first construction project. Ground was broken in 1968 for the City-County Building. The $9.1 million government structure at Main and Calhoun was dedicated September 25, 1971. To the east, on the other side of Clinton Street, came Freimann Park, and beyond that the Performing Arts Theatre, dedicated on October 5, 1973. On the east side of Lafayette Street at Main Street, the Central Fire Station was built in 1971.

The Main Street renewal had the effect of moving the focus of the central city several blocks north. The government and financial interests supplanted in great part the earlier commercial activity downtown. Main Street was made into a parkway from Clay Street to Calhoun Street. The widening of Main Street was continued two blocks west in 1979 with the demolition of aging structures on the north side of the street. On the south side of Main, in the block extending along Calhoun Street to Berry Street, most of the land was cleared by private sources to make way for a new Fort Wayne National Bank Building. A major razing job was done on the old Anthony Hotel at the corner of Berry and Harrison Street. On January 13, 1974, a controlled series of explosions brought the hotel down in a spectacular show. The thirteen-story Keenan Hotel at the southwest corner of Washington Boulevard and Harrison Street was brought down on October 20 of the same year.

Travelers are often more aware of the unusual public library collection of Fort Wayne than are many of the local residents. In the area of genealogy, the Fort Wayne collection is among the top three in the nation (the other two being in Washington, D.C., and Salt Lake City, Utah). The present library building at Webster Street between Wayne Street and Washington Boulevard was dedicated August 21, 1968. Its 173,000 square feet of floor area provided space for 222,000 volumes in open shelves and 1,278,000 volumes in closed stacks. Much of the collection was expanded, beginning in the 1930s, through the efforts of head librarians Rex Potterf and Fred J. Reynolds. A gallery for fine arts, reading and study space for 600 persons, microfilm equipment and records, research facilities, and a publishing department were provided in the building. In 1979 and 1980 a major extension of the library complex was being built along Wayne Street.

The Three Rivers Festival, which was destined to become the city's most popular week-long event, attracting more than a half million people from near and far in the past decade, was begun in 1969. The July festival has parades, music, races, crafts, dancing around the clock at parks, downtown, theaters, and in the streets. The crowd for the clownish raft races down the St. Joseph River alone usually attracts as many as 100,000 people along the river banks. Each year the event has expanded and the participating groups grown in terms of color, distance, and creativity from a three-state area. A giant parade on July 4, 1976, for the United States Bicentennial observance nearly overlapped

Top Left
Fred Reynolds, head Fort Wayne librarian, stands between the busts of earlier librarians Rex Potterf and Margaret Colerick in 1970. Courtesy, Fort Wayne and Allen County Public Library. *News-Sentinel* photo.

Top Right
Sidewalk artist John Sheets, along old Columbia Street, attracts passersby during the Three Rivers Festival in July of 1970. Courtesy, Fort Wayne and Allen County Public Library. *News-Sentinel* photo.

Bottom
The Anthony Hotel, at Berry and Harrison, crumbled in this 1975 demolition blast. Courtesy, *News-Sentinel*

the festival, which began the following week, but only added to the festive mood that seemed to pervade the community that year.

The replica of Old Fort Wayne got underway in 1975 at a site between the St. Mary's River and Spy Run Avenue. The location was chosen because of its proximity to the original fort built by Anthony Wayne in 1794 just across the river from the new stockade. The site chosen was actually the location of a Miami Indian village for generations prior to the coming of the Europeans. The program to reconstruct the fort was originally outlined in 1966 by the Allen County-Fort Wayne Historical Society. The cost was in excess of $1 million and the reconstruction took more than two years to complete.

The Old Fort was built with the actual plans drawn by Major John Whistler for the third American fort at Three Rivers erected in 1815; copies of the plans were acquired from the archives of the War (now Defense) Department in Washington. A foot bridge across the St. Mary's River was constructed to provide access from the parking facilities and a visitor's center. In 1976 a large bronze statue of Little Turtle was unveiled on the western side of the river. It was the work of sculptor Hector Garcia. A feature of the fort operation is a corps of volunteers who act out in costume the characters of soldiers, pioneer women and children, and others of the fort period, so that modern visitors can get a glimpse of life in those faraway days.

The Johnny Appleseed Festival grew out of the Bicentennial celebration and became an autumn event on its own in 1977. It expanded in proportion to the growing interest in American and Indiana heritage, especially in the old crafts and the spirit of the pioneers. Weaving demonstrations, cider mills, blacksmithing, Indian dances, music, and visual arts all enhance the weekend festival. The location was established at Johnny Appleseed Park near the St. Joseph River and Coliseum Boulevard. The grave of Johnny Appleseed and the Allen County Memorial Coliseum are at the site.

The population of Fort Wayne, officially at 177,738 in 1970, actually declined slightly during the following decade. The Allen County population, often termed the metropolitan figure, went from 280,455 in 1970 to estimates ranging from 293,300 (the State Board of Health count) to projections as high as 313,000 by other agencies for 1980. The period from 1970 to 1980 was not spectacular in Fort Wayne's history, but a few events are worth noting.

The sale of the City Light Utility to Indiana & Michigan Electric Company followed a referendum in the May, 1974, primary. The vote was 17,589 votes in favor of a thirty-five-year lease of the municipal operation and 10,386 against. On September 13, 1974, Mayor Lebamoff signed the lease with Robert M. Kopper of I&M. At that time the sixty-six-year-old city utility had 35,000 customers, but purchased most of its power from Indiana & Michigan. The old generating plant, located along Spy Run Creek at Lawton Park, was

Top Left
Soldiers raise the flag on the parade grounds inside Old Fort Wayne.

Top Right
Sculptor Hector Garcia at work on his massive statue of the great Miami warchief Little Turtle. The statue was cast in bronze in 1976. Courtesy, Fort Wayne and Allen County Public Library.

Bottom Left
The Old Fort Settlers reassemble a log house at Swinney Park in 1979. The 130-year-old building was originally located at Huntington, some miles southwest of Fort Wayne.

Bottom Right
At the 1976 Johnny Appleseed Festival, Mildred Ellingwood spins while Ed Greven watches. Courtesy, Fort Wayne and Allen County Public Library.

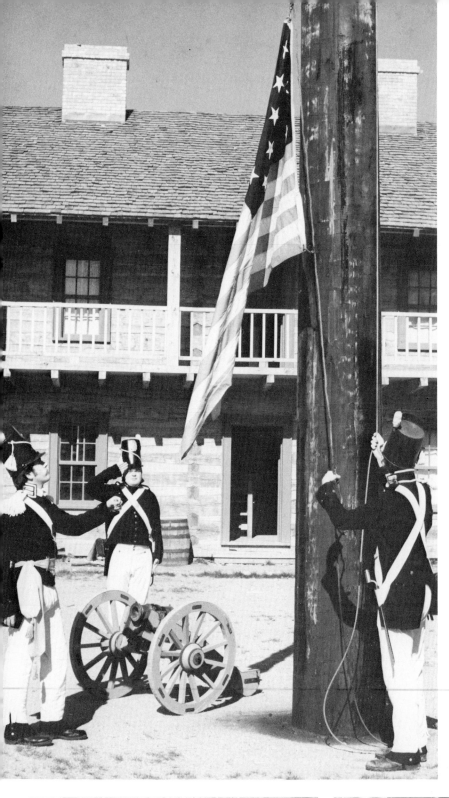

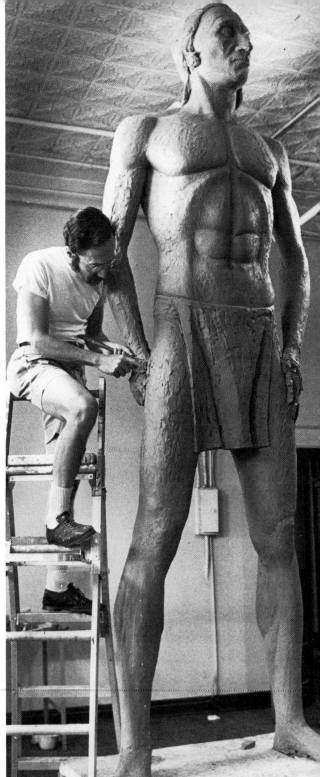

shut down.

On the night of February 3, 1975, fire started by arson gutted two venerable buildings at The Landing. One was the Rosemarie Hotel, built in 1887. Presidents Benjamin Harrison, James Garfield, and Rutherford B. Hayes had stayed in the four-story Victorian structure. The Bash Building across the street, also destroyed, had been built on the site of the canal turnaround landing sometime after the canal was abandoned and turned into a railroad bed in 1880. No serious injuries were reported in either of the fires.

Fort Wayne's Matt Vogel won two gold medals in the 1976 Summer Olympics at Montreal. Vogel took first in the 100-meter butterfly, then picked up a second gold for his part in the winning American effort in the 400-meter medley swimming relay. The son of Dr. and Mrs. Lloyd Vogel, he was a graduate of Snider High School and a nineteen-year-old student of the University of Tennessee. Eight years earlier, in the 1968 Olympics in Mexico City, another Fort Wayne swimmer became the first local resident to win Olympic gold. She was sixteen-year-old Sharon Wichman, who took first in the 200-meter breast stroke. Wichman also won a bronze medal for a third-place finish in the 100-meter breast stroke. Sharon, at the time of her victories, was a junior at Snider High and trained at Club Olympia on the city's northwest side.

One of the worst blizzards in the history of Fort Wayne struck during the last four days of January, 1978. Within a twenty-four-hour period seventeen inches of snow were recorded, with four or five more inches in the following days. Wind whipped drifts up to eight feet. All traffic was stalled. Travelers along the highways were isolated — and though eventually rescued, some were desperate or even unconscious due to cold and exposure. One family of five on the way from Michigan to Arkansas was found just north of the city on Interstate 69. When they later awoke at the medical center, they were surprised to find they were still alive. Schools and businesses were closed; grocery-store shelves were soon emptied by people walking in on skis and snow shoes. Beer, milk, and bread were the first to go. President Jimmy Carter declared the vicinity a disaster area. The big clean-up took some time on the part of public and private crews. Then came one more problem: on March 23, the Maumee rose 8.6 feet above flood stage, inundating a quarter of the city and forcing more than 1,000 people from their homes.

A major fight developed in 1978 over the sale of five suburban utilities to a private investment group instead of to the city of Fort Wayne. The utilities in question had entered bankruptcy reorganization under the supervision of the U.S. District Court in 1968. The major creditors were the Lincoln National Bank in Fort Wayne and several financial institutions outside the city. The owning creditors agreed to sell the properties to a group of private investors at the time when the city was also offering to buy them for the $4

Top
Matt Vogel, Olympic gold medal-winning swimmer, waves to hometown fans during a parade held in his honor in 1976. Courtesy, Fort Wayne and Allen County Public Library.

Bottom Left
A lone figure, on usually busy Calhoun Street, the morning of the great blizzard of January 26, 1978. About 19 inches of snow fell during the storm. Photo by Greg Dorsett.

Bottom Right
Fire fighters battle the Rosemarie Hotel blaze of February 3, 1975. A relic of nineteenth-century highlife on Columbia Street, the hotel was completely gutted, but no lives were lost. Courtesy, News-Sentinel.

million sale price or slightly more.

A bank stockholder suit was filed in federal court contending conflicts of interest on the part of several officers or former officers of the Lincoln Bank. Something of a power struggle within the bank board also developed as several probes of the transaction were pursued. Robert A. Morrow, Sr., board chairman and chief executive officer of Lincoln, resigned on January 29, 1979. He was succeeded by Carl Gunkler, Jr. The Inbalco utilities, as the buying interest was called, included Diversified, Puritan, Clearwater, SUI, and Maplewood Park sewer and water companies. Stockholders charged Morrow, his son, and a former bank employee with conflict of interest involving bank funds. Numerous investments and companies were named, Inbalco one of them. No criminal action was taken against Morrow.

Five blocks in the central business district were the subject of mass razing and beginnings of buildup as 1979 turned into 1980. The property had once been the major 20th-century shopping district of Fort Wayne. Use of the streets for heavy through traffic and shortages of parking space hurried the demise. The five-block area extended from Wayne Street on the north to Douglas Street on the south, and from Harrison Street to Clinton Street. Among the few properties in the area retained in the general renewal were Cathedral Square, the Embassy Theater on Jefferson Street, and stores west of Calhoun Street between Wayne Street and Washington Boulevard.

The catalytic force in the five-block redevelopment project is Summit Square, the name given by the Peoples Trust Bank and Indiana & Michigan Electric Company for their twenty-six-story structure between Wayne and Washington, east of Calhoun Street. The development grew out of years of planning and hinged in part on the sale of the City Light Utility to I & M. Construction began in 1979 and was due for completion within three years. Donnelly P. McDonald, Jr., bank chairman, and Jack Stark, vice president of I & M, reported that the building would provide shopper and convenience facilities in addition to office space for the major tenants. Financing was arranged through private resources.

The Civic Center in the block bound by Calhoun, Jefferson, Harrison, and Washington is the centerpiece of Fort Wayne's downtown renewal. Estimated to cost about $6.5 million, the triangular-shaped building was planned for 81,000 square feet of exhibition space, meeting rooms, and banquet halls. Completion was scheduled for late 1981. In the same block with the Civic Center, but facing onto Calhoun Street, a $23-million hotel which will have 351 rooms with restaurants and small shops, will be built. Redevelopment Commission efforts and federal funding provided land for the Civic Center, which was largely financed by room taxes on local inns and hostelries.

To give the downtown a new dimension, a botanical gardens and plant conservatory was in the planning stages in 1980 for a two-block area bound

Below
Ralph Farrington dancing at the Embassy Theatre in 1979. The Embassy, an art deco movie palace built in 1927 as the Emboyd Theatre, was restored as a 3,000-seat music hall in the 1970s. It was made a part of the downtown Civic Center development in 1980.

Bottom
Early construction of Summit Square, home of the Indiana and Michigan Electric Company and the Peoples Trust Bank, in June of 1979. Photo by Gabriel R. Delobbe.

Opposite
Though the Fort Wayne Museum of Art was just a model in early 1980, the project of the Fine Arts Foundation was due to be constructed at Lafayette Street, just east of the Performing Arts Center.

by Calhoun, Douglas, Harrison and Jefferson streets. A section of Lewis Street will be closed to make way for the series of sun-absorbing structures and walkways. The idea for the gardens was originally suggested by Mrs. Oscar Foellinger, and the development, to cost an estimated $8 million, was backed by the Foellinger Foundation and the Freimann Charitable Trust. The Lincoln National Life Insurance Company, whose headquarters lies just to the south, agreed to contribute $750,000 for maintenance. The conservatory will be linked to the Civic Center by a bridge spanning Jefferson Street.

On January 1, 1980, the Allen County-Fort Wayne Historical Society moved into new offices and began a new museum. The place was Old City Hall, a Victorian stone building at the southeast corner of Berry and Barr streets, which had been completed in 1893. The building was restored in keeping with its original character. The museum was designed to display the development of Fort Wayne in a manner appealing to citizens and tourists, and to be a major repository for historical materials. The Historical Society had been founded in 1921 and had occupied the Swinney Homestead in Swinney Park since 1926.

Later in January of 1980, the Fine Arts Foundation gave its approval for a Fort Wayne Museum of Art at Main and Lafayette streets, just east of the Performing Arts Center. The building, expected to cost about $3 million, will provide 30,000 square feet for permanent collections, visiting exhibits, and art education purposes. The arts center will be within walking distance of the Performing Arts Theatre, the Old City Hall Historical Museum, and the reconstructed Old Fort. Already under construction in early 1980 was a long-planned bridge across the St. Mary's River at the north foot of Fairfield Avenue. A $2,095,000 county bond issue provided funds for the span, which will connect the Wells Street district with the midtown area. The old iron-truss Wells Street Bridge, built in 1860, has been retained for pedestrian use. It was the city's earliest iron bridge, and the only one still in use in 1980.

Fort Wayne's future, in the eyes of many people, rests with the annexation of wide suburban areas and the resurgence of midtown as a center for cultural and financial activities. Retail shopping seemed to be the permanent element of a ring around the former city districts. But while residential growth continued in the fringe areas, there was renewed interest in old in-city neighborhoods and in reclaiming what had been decaying 19th-century mansions. Unlike some cities where downtown flight was almost complete, in Fort Wayne the principal denominational churches continued to flourish in the core area. The festivals, the art groups, and government continue to build and use downtown as a focus for activities and buildings. All these things tend to make Fort Wayne not only a place, but a place with a soul — one with a fascinating and colorful history, only the highlights of which have been mentioned here.

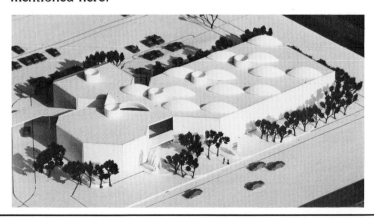

CHAPTER
IX
COLOR
PLATES

Major John Whistler designed Fort Wayne so that the buildings opened onto a parade ground inside the stockade walls. Note the period mortar. Photo by Alan Vandever.

Right
The grave of Johnny Appleseed lies on the north side of Fort Wayne a short distance from the St. Joseph River. The site, once the Archer family cemetery, is now called Johnny Appleseed Park. Photo by Alan Vandever.

Below
With black leather seats and open-air comfort, this buggy sits idle on a Grabill street. In Amish country, the horse and buggy remains a common sight. Photo by Alan Vandever.

Left
The Number 3 Engine House, built in 1893, is now a museum for fire-fighting equipment of bygone eras. Complete with watchtower and hayloft, the station is located on West Washington Boulevard near the public library. Photo by Alan Vandever.

Below
Shining red engines and nickel-plated bells fill the Number 3 Engine House museum. Photo by Alan Vandever.

Above
A Currier & Ives scene published in 1870 shows rural life as it was near Fort Wayne in the 1830s.

Left
This Fort Wayne woman, dressed in colonial garb, works the spinning wheel at the Johnny Appleseed Festival. Photo by Alan Vandever.

Above Left
This wooden washtub was used in the Fort Wayne area in the 1880s. Photo by Alan Vandever.

Left
Trinity Episcopal Church, built in 1865, stands along West Berry Street. Photo by Alan Vandever

Above
Wheels from the past and tools hammered by a forgotten blacksmith are on display at the Souder Museum at Grabill, Indiana. Photo by Alan Vandever.

Above Right
A sentinel, in the uniform of the 1812 era, stands at the gate of Old Fort Wayne near downtown. Volunteers from the city act as soldiers. Photo by Alan Vandever.

Right
Old Fort Wayne City Hall, abandoned in 1971, became the Historical Museum in 1980. The nerve center of local government since its completion in 1893, City Hall was usually called "the police station." Photo by Alan Vandever.

Above
Horses carry their weight and
then some during harvest time in
Allen County Amish farm
country. Photo by Alan Vandever.

Left
Iron coffee grinders such as this
one were standard pieces of
equipment in Fort Wayne grocery
stores in the last century. Photo
by Alan Vandever

Top
The Lakeside Park Rose Garden.
Photo by Alan Vandever.

Above
The Swinney Homestead. Photo
by Alan Vandever.

Opposite
Top
A C.L. Centlivre Brewing
Company advertisement.

Bottom
The Forest Park residential
section. Photo by Alan Vandever.

Right
Victorian America is alive today
in the Swinney Homestead
Museum. Photo by Alan Vandever.

160 Color Plates

Above
The Richardsonian period of architecture is preserved in the gables and turrets of a house at Broadway and Wayne streets. Photo by Alan Vandever.

Above Right
An old well marks the location of the first American fort — built by Anthony Wayne in 1794 — at the present corner of Main and Clay streets. The site was also the city's first park alongside the Wabash-Erie Canal. Photo by Alan Vandever.

Right
The burial plot of Philip Ostrander of the United States 1st Army who died in 1813 at Fort Wayne. Photo by Alan Vandever.

This Eastlake-style house was
erected about 1880 at the corner
of Berry and Jackson streets.
Photo by Alan Vandever.

Above
This Italianate-style home on West Wayne Street was built in the 1870s for a banking family. It currently houses the office of Joel Salon, M.D. Photo by Alan Vandever.

Left
This 1860 iron truss bridge across the St. Mary's River at Wells Street was the first and remains the last of Fort Wayne's old iron bridges. During the campaign of 1860, supporters of Stephen Douglas tossed an effigy of Abraham Lincoln off this bridge. Photo by Alan Vandever.

Opposite
Top
Alfred Timler designed this stained glass window depicting General Wayne at the Battle of Fallen Timbers. It decorates the south wall of the City Glass Building. Courtesy, City Glass. Photo provided by the News-Sentinel.

Bottom
Built in 1852, the stone Canal House served as a warehouse for trade on the nearby Wabash-Erie Canal. Photo by Alan Vandever.

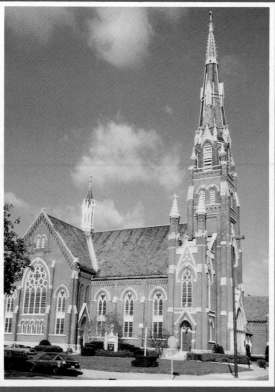

Above
The facade of the Allen County courthouse includes the busts of Anthony Wayne and John Allen over the entrance. Photo by Alan Vandever.

Far Left
This marker shows the location of the first French fort, called Fort St. Philippe and later Fort Miami, along the St. Mary's River in 1721. Photo by Alan Vandever.

Left
The St. Paul Lutheran Church, home of a congregation dating to 1839, stands majestically along Barr Street. Photo by Alan Vandever.

Right
A magnificent stained-glass dome highlights the interior of the courthouse.

Workmen install new streetcar tracks on Calhoun Street, south of Main, on June 30, 1920. Courtesy, Fort Wayne and Allen County Public Library.

CHAPTER
XI

PARTNERS
IN
PROGRESS

Dreams, diversity, development. Just as Fort Wayne's three rivers have shaped the geography of the city, so have these three ideas shaped the city's commercial history. In Fort Wayne's early days, the settlers' dreams of commercial prosperity carved a pulsing business center out of the marsh-laden Indiana frontier. The pioneers journeyed from the East, a steady flow of modest traders, farmers, clerks, and builders, united by the ambition of starting a new, independent life where the St. Joseph, St. Mary, and Maumee Rivers crossed to form the small Indian village of Kekionga.

From their dreams and toil grew a small business community. With the area's vast natural deposits of clay and limestone, builders constructed homes, factories, and office buildings. The physical growth of the town, in turn, attracted more business and stimulated the construction of hospitals, schools, and churches to serve the growing population.

By the end of the nineteenth century, the descendants of the original settlers had transformed Fort Wayne into a manufacturing city and enhanced its traditional reputation as a convenient commercial hub on the major transportation arteries of the Midwest. Fort Wayne factories were soon producing magnet wire, wire dies, and, later, radio systems for the burgeoning electronics industry. Fort Wayne entrepreneurs invented ore-mining equipment for the local and national construction industry. As the automobile gained acceptance and popularity, Fort Wayne manufacturers turned out axles, pistons, and gasoline pumps.

Gradually, in the early twentieth century, Fort Wayne's economic base widened, and this diversity in production served to shelter it from the devastating depression of the 1930s. During this period, civic leaders sensed the importance of a wide-ranging economy and began an organized attempt to attract new business. The Greater Fort Wayne Development Corporation, sponsored by the Fort Wayne Chamber of Commerce, was instrumental in attracting Magnavox, International Harvester, and Zollner to open new plants in the Fort Wayne area. This emphasis on industrial development continues today, both in attracting outside interests and revitalizing local businesses.

Although Fort Wayne's natural resources, skilled labor force, and transportation network have made progress inevitable, it has not been easy. As the following pages graphically illustrate, the success of turning dreams into development could only come with one other vital Fort Wayne asset — determination.

ALLEN COUNTY BANK AND TRUST COMPANY

Allen County Bank and Trust Company, headquartered in Leo, is the county's smallest bank and the first bank founded in Allen County, Indiana, in the past thirty years. It opened its doors in a temporary bank facility in a modified mobile home in October 1971, after applying for and receiving authority to do business from the state of Indiana. The bank was formed by electrician John Boley and Fort Wayne attorney F. Walter Riebenack after residents of Leo expressed a strong desire to have a bank in their community. The original board of directors reflected the bank's local concerns: besides Riebenack and Boley, members included Eugene Lindley, president of the bank; Roderick Bergstedt, a Magnovox engineer; John Bollinger, a life insurance underwriter from Leo; Ronald L. Reinking, a certified public accountant; and Galen Acra, owner of Leo Builders Supply.

As Allen County Bank and Trust Co. has strengthened its loan portfolio and established a regular clientele, it has grown rapidly, from its original staff of five to its present staff of twenty-nine full- and part-time employees. The bank's management is accessible to customers, and the bank has generated more accounts than financial institutions twice its size. The management believes that a small staff encourages effective performance and good customer relations. Allen County Bank offers its customers a people-oriented bank, open five full days a week, plus Saturdays from 9 a.m. to noon.

The prominent feature of Allen County Bank and Trust is a strong base of personal service which it provides to its more than 300 shareholders, most of whom are individual citizens rather than large corporations. This personalized banking style, widely sought after by other communities, has been instrumental in the organization's growth.

Allen County Bank and Trust Co. is flourishing, with three branches in Allen County; it remains small in scale, though expansive in vision. In October 1972, the bank moved to its current Leo building on Amstutz Road. It opened a branch at Georgetown Square in Fort Wayne in December 1974, and at Huntertown in December 1978. Today, the bank is seeking additional branch locations. Its three offices maintain a high capital base (for example, its capital-deposit ratio is never lower than 10 percent, when other banks' dip as low as 6 to 8 percent) so that it can branch out successfully. At the end of 1979, the bank claimed assets of $13,210,676, with $11,696,752 on deposit.

The current board of directors is composed of Riebenack; Acra; Boley; Bollinger; Levon Bender, a plumbing and heating contractor from the Leo area; Martin Torborg, a Fort Wayne attorney; Vincent Hansen, executive vice-president and chief executive officer; Gilbert Bierman, a Fort Wayne orthopedic surgeon; and Wallace Scheffel, president of Eagle Pitcher

Eugene Lindley, F. Walter Reibenack, Ronald L. Sowers, John L. Bollinger, Roderick Bergstedt, Galen H. Acra, and John Boley served as the bank's original directors.

Fort Wayne attorney F. Walter Reibenack was one of the founders of Allen County Bank and Trust Co., the first bank established in Indiana in thirty years.

Plastics near Grabill.

Reflecting their concern for public service, each of the bank's directors is actively involved in community affairs. Riebenack is on the board of Saint Francis College. Torborg serves many civic organizations, has been on the local school board, and is active in the Allen County Bar Association. Hansen, who came to Leo from Fort Wayne to join the bank in 1973, is a founding member of the Leo-Cedarville Regional Sewer District, a factor in northeastern Allen County's rapid growth.

BROTHERHOOD MUTUAL INSURANCE

The first policy issued by the aid association that grew into Brotherhood Mutual Insurance Company cited a verse from Galatians: "Bear ye one another's burdens and so fulfill the law of Christ." Every policy issued since 1917 has carried the same message, a constant reminder of the company's dedication to the Christian ideal of service.

In 1916, Albert Neuenschwander of Grabill realized that people of his Evangelical Mennonite Church Conference needed fire and windstorm protection. He took the matter up with his pastor, the Reverend Aaron Souder, and together the men suggested the formation of an aid association at the annual conference. The plan was approved, bylaws were drawn up, and the Brotherhood Aid Association was organized. Along with Mr. Neuenschwander and other laymen, the Reverend Souder was a director and served as secretary for a short time until his death in 1918. Mr. Neuenschwander then became secretary and manager, a post he held until his death in 1959.

The association was formed as an assessable mutual, meaning it paid claims through the year and then assessed each member his share of the losses at year's end. It became a nonassessable mutual in 1959, charging policyholders a premium at the beginning of the year and relying on surplus funds in the event of a deficiency after losses and expenses were paid.

By 1935, the aid association had grown to the extent that its directors incorporated it as Brotherhood Mutual Insurance Company and it became independent of any church affiliation. The offices were in Grabill until March 1, 1939, when the first Fort Wayne office was opened to meet the need for larger quarters. The company moved into the old Hoffman home, 634 West Wayne at Broadway, as co-owner with the Central Agency Company, and offices were shared with newly organized Brotherhood Mutual Life Insurance Company. After two other moves, the company built and occupied offices at 1615 Vance Avenue in 1959.

Early on, the association began insuring the properties, primarily farms and homes, of members of those church denominations opposed to smoking. Today, the company's specialty (45 per-

Above
M.L. Klopfenstein served as president of the firm from 1966 to 1971.

Above left
In 1917, Albert Neuenschwander made a suggestion to the Reverend Aaron Souder that led to the formation of the Brotherhood Mutual Insurance Company.

cent of its business) is insuring churches: property coverages, liability, workers' compensation, bonds, and church buses.

Neuenschwander's assistant manager, M.L. Klopfenstein, took over as manager in 1959. A Grabill native, he was president from 1966 until he retired in 1971, and Paul A. Steiner, who joined the company in 1964 and had served as its home office representative, director of claims, and treasurer, then became president. In 1974, he accepted the position of chairman of the board.

Under Steiner, growth has continued, and the company plans to move into a new 45,000-square-foot home office on Route I-69 on the north edge of Fort Wayne by the fall of 1980. Brotherhood Mutual issues policies in nineteen states, the top five in premium volume being Indiana, Florida, Illinois, Ohio, and Michigan.

C. MILLER & SONS, INC./CMS ROOFING

Roofing, sheet metal, and the Miller family have been synonymous in Fort Wayne since 1913, when Christ Miller, his son Waldo, Carl V. Miller, and George C. Miller, Sr., formed C. Miller & Sons. The father, three brothers, and one employee repaired tin porch roofs and metal milk cans for the local Eskay Dairy, now a part of Meadowgold, at their shop at 1107 Broadway. Shingle work and built-up roofing was also done.

Built-up roofs, consisting of layers of hot asphalt and paper to waterproof flat roofs, became an increasingly important part of Miller's business through the 1920s and 1930s. Today, job descriptions range from the smallest home roof installation and repair to commercial and industrial jobs as large as the North American Van Lines roof. C. Miller & Sons' crews cover the tri-state area and parts of Illinois and Kentucky.

Growth is equally apparent in the sheet metal end of the business. Those early milk can repairs have been replaced by jobs as extensive as the engineering, formation, and installation of several miles of duct-work, ventilation, and air conditioning in Three Rivers Apartments, and the many miles of process pipe, duct-work, and air conditioning at the B.F. Goodrich plant in New Haven.

As the business expanded, property was purchased in 1920 at 1115-1117 Broadway, where the company erected a building in 1924, the same year it opened a hardware store. Two warehouses were added in later years.

In 1960, the company left its Broadway location to move into the old Bass Foundry building at Wallace and Hanna Streets. And in 1970, an existing building at 4136 West Washington Center Road met growing demands, and the company relocated. But the thriving business necessitated additions until the sheet metal plant alone covers 20,000 square feet and houses forty metal fabrication employees. The roofing and engineering department staffs bring the employee total to an average of 100, depending on the jobs in progress.

Waldo Miller died at a young age, leaving his father, who died in 1943, at eighty-four, and two brothers to carry on the business through its second generation of Millers. The third generation has been in charge since George C. Miller, Sr., died in 1960. They are George C. Miller, Jr., president; Stanley W. Miller, secretary; and K. James Miller, treasurer.

Another family-oriented business has emanated from this company — CMS Roofing, Inc., which specializes in commercial and industrial roofing. It allows for further expansion of roofing interests.

Christ Miller established C. Miller & Sons in 1913.

George C. Miller, Sr. (second from left); Christ Miller, founder; and Carl V. Miller repaired many milk cans in the early days of the firm.

CONTAINER CORPORATION OF AMERICA

Although Container Corporation of America (CCA) has been located in Fort Wayne since 1956, when it bought the Wayne Paper Box and Printing Corporation, the firm's roots are deep in Fort Wayne's commercial history.

Andrew G. Burry, founder of Wayne Paper Box and Printing Corporation, moved to Fort Wayne after graduating from Oberlin College. In 1895, while he and his associate, Joel Welty, were operating the Fort Wayne Book Bindery, they learned that the Fort Wayne Electric Works needed thirty-six cloth-covered, pigeon-hole desk boxes.

Although Burry's bindery was not equipped to manufacture boxes, he agreed to do the job and subsequently devoted nearly a week of after-hours work to complete the task. The electric company was pleased with the boxes and later referred Mr. Fox, a candy manufacturer, to the bindery. Fox placed an order with Burry for several hundred boxes in assorted sizes (an order that could not be completed through handmade production processes).

Because Burry needed machinery to complete the job, he consulted with Theodore Thieme, manager of the Wayne Knitting Mills. As a result of his discussions with Thieme, Burry purchased the necessary machinery from a Chicago-based box manufacturer in the fall of 1897.

Burry and Welty, unfamiliar with operating box-making machinery, hired Joe Ligett, an experienced Chicago box-maker and set up the new machines in a small space adjoining the bindery. Materials for manufacturing the boxes were purchased from Thieme, who then agreed to give all his box business to Burry and Welty. As a result, Wayne Knitting Mills was first on a long list of businesses in Fort Wayne that used millions of boxes manufactured by Burry's business.

The bindery was sold in the spring of 1898, and on July 11 the Fort Wayne Paper Box Company was incorporated with a paid-up capital of $6,000. Messrs. Joel Welty, Andrew G. Burry, Howell C. Rockhill, Henry C. Paul, and Samuel M. Foster were the incorpora-

tors. Welty managed the firm until his health failed and Burry took over in February 1903.

Burry managed the company for nearly forty years until Ermin P. Ruf took charge and Burry became chairman of the board. Ruf joined the company in 1908, and, after advancing to sales manager in 1926, was elected to the board after the death of Howell C. Rockhill.

In 1936, the Fort Wayne Paper Box and Printing Company had five departments including postcards and calendars, set up boxes (gift boxes produced until 1970), folding cartons, commercial printing (which became Didier Printing in 1948), and stationery (dropped in the late 1940s).

Today, as Container Corporation of America, the company is in the business of paperboard packaging. The Fort

Above
Employees Walter Smith, Dick Shively, and Lloyd Cox prepared to roll out their trucks in this late 1950s photograph.

Top
Wayne Paper Box Company moved into this brick and wood building at 102 West Superior Street in 1910. Today, after five additions, the structure still houses Container Corporation of America's local offices.

Wayne CCA carton plant not only specializes in folding cartons but also is the company's only custom packaging operation — handling new product introductions, test market programs, and special promotions.

CCA/Fort Wayne produces a wide range of paperboard packaging for customers in the Indiana and Michigan areas. The company has 180 employees, including production and office personnel and drivers who transport the products in CCA trucks to markets within a 300 miles radius of Fort Wayne.

COUNTY LINE CHEESE COMPANY

When Fred Marolf established his cheese-making business on the Allen-DeKalb county line in 1913 and called it, appropriately enough, "County Line Cheese," he did not know the company would grow from a one-man operation to the second largest manufacturer of branded, natural cheese in the nation.

Marolf came to Fort Wayne from Berne, Switzerland, in 1912, sponsored by a Swiss immigrant who manufactured cheese in Leo in northern Allen County. Marolf soon founded his own business. He purchased 2,000 pounds of milk each day from local farmers, which made 200 pounds of cheese. He manufactured cheese only eight months of the year, shutting down in the winter months when the cows, not heavily bred for year-round milk production, stopped giving milk until their calves were born in the spring.

Today, the County Line plant north of Fort Wayne and its two sister plants in Wisconsin take in 1.2 million pounds of milk each day and turn it into 120,000 pounds of cheese. A fleet of milk tanker trucks gathers the milk from local farmers, some of whom have sold milk to County Line for more than forty years. Refrigerated trucks carry packages of cheese to the major supermarkets of the midwestern, eastern, and southern United States.

The company still makes Longhorn Colby cheese in the 12-pound cylinders that were a familiar sight in Fort Wayne in the early 1900s. County Line also produces, packages, and distributes

Cheddar, Swiss, Monterey Jack, and a variety of unsalted and low-fat cheeses.

The Auburn plant consumes all of its own by-products and disposes of all of its own wastes through a sewage treatment facility big enough to serve a small town. County Line built the North Osborn Cheese Company in Seymour, Wisconsin, in 1968 and acquired the Green Valley Cheese Company in Cecil, Wisconsin, in 1979. Both plants are responsible for County Line's Swiss and Cheddar cheeses. And the firm runs a milk receiving station in Shipshewana, Indiana.

The company was a sole proprietorship until 1946, when Fred Marolf, Jr., who had been in the business since his graduation from the University of Wisconsin's dairy school in 1939, became a partner. The company, incorporated in 1949, was one of several Fort Wayne food companies acquired by Beatrice Foods Company in 1971.

Fred Marolf, Sr., retired in 1955. Fred Marolf, Jr., who had been president of County Line, is now a divisional president of Beatrice. The third-generation Marolf, Fred Jr.'s son, Michael, was with the company but left to operate his own Dakota Farms Cheese Company in Rapid City, South Dakota. Since the merger with Beatrice, County Line Cheese has almost doubled production and the size of its market, but continues to make the same high-quality cheeses that have been its hallmark for almost seventy years.

Above
County Line Cheese Company employee Mark Steffen captured a prize, as well as a little girl's delight, when he took this photograph for parent company Beatrice Foods' "shoot-out '77" contest with the theme of "Beatrice people serving people around the world."
Top left
In the firm's early days, horses and wagons transported milk to the factory and then carried the cheese to Fort Wayne markets.
Top right
With the arrival of motorized conveyances, County Line's products were shipped the modern way, but the farmhouse where it all started was always visible. Recent additions to the plant and offices now obscure the original site.

DANA CORPORATION

The company's history began in New York in 1902 when the popularity of the steam engine was at its peak. Clarence Winfred Spicer, a student of mechanical engineering at Cornell University, knew that it was standard practice to transmit the power to the rear axle by using sprockets and a chain. However, he realized that chains were noisy, difficult to lubricate, and in constant need of repair. So he adopted the idea of a drive shaft, which is a piece of tubing with a couple of universal joints on it to replace the chain and sprocket, and the following year built an experimental car.

The next spring, in 1903, Spicer began manufacturing and marketing universal joints in Plainfield, New Jersey. He soon went on the road in an effort to convince automakers to support his idea, and by 1905, his sales efforts were producing more than the organization could handle.

Gradually, the plant enlarged and ten years later all operations moved to a new plant in South Plainfield.

Spicer was a good engineer. He was persistent, industrious, and ambitious. Nevertheless, by 1913, competition had

brought on financial difficulties. Charles A. Dana, a prosecuting attorney from New York City, became interested in the firm in 1914. Within two years he had successfully reorganized the company, a feat that won him honor thirty years later when the firm was renamed the Dana Corporation.

The motor truck was showing increasing promise as a commercial vehicle as the century progressed; by the end of World War I, trucking operations

had multiplied tenfold. This, of course, meant a greater demand for Spicer universal joints.

Confident that the firm's future lay in the acquisition of related product lines and the development of existing facilities, Dana began to add companies and products to meet the needs of a rapidly growing car and truck industry. One such acquisition was the Salisbury Axle Company of Jamestown, New York.

In the late 1920s, the center of the vehicle manufacturing business had moved westward with the development of the great auto companies in Detroit and the surrounding areas. Spicer Manufacturing Corporation moved to Toledo in 1929 to be closer to its business interests.

The 1930s were difficult for most people, especially businessmen. However, Dana continued to anticipate a better future. He not only added companies and new products during this period but also encouraged a positive attitude among his employees.

As the company entered the new decade, the board of directors decided business volume justified a second plant specifically for axles. After much investigation, the parent company selected a site in Fort Wayne and approved construction contracts for a plant on West State Boulevard. Complete axles were coming off the assembly lines by April 1946, with production since then reaching volumes of more than 120,000 axles monthly.

The original plant has been expanded to 1.14 million square feet of work space under one roof, plus an additional 182,000 square feet of warehousing in an adjacent building. Today, with two miles of overhead and five miles of gravity feed conveyors on their assembly lines, Dana Corporation's Spicer Axle Division is among the world's most complete light truck axle production plants.

Top
Charles A. Dana revived the struggling Spicer Manufacturing Company in 1916 and was recognized in 1946 when the firm's directors renamed the business in his honor.
Left
Dana Corporation's Fort Wayne Spicer Axle Division plant covers 26.5 acres.

DEISTER MACHINE COMPANY, INC.

Taggart's *Handbook of Ore Dressing,* the official textbook at many mining schools, lists the name Deister in its index forty times. The name refers to Fort Wayne's Emil Deister, who invented, patented, and began manufacturing ore separating tables in Fort Wayne in the first decade of this century.

Deister's differential motion ore separating table, which has riffles attached to its surface that collect the heavier ore particles and convey them one direction toward a collector while water washing across the riffles carries the lighter impurities away, is praised in the textbook as the first serious competition to the only other kind of ore separating table which was available at the time.

Emil Deister was born in Germany in 1872 and moved to the United States with his parents as a youth. He grew up in Woodburn, Indiana, and took his first job as a lathe operator at the Bass Foundry and Machine Company in Fort Wayne in 1893. By 1905, he had become a draftsman and erecting engineer for Bass, and he had also taken up the study of ore separation, starting with a centrifugal separator to extract gold from mercury amalgam and moving on to ore separating tables. Deister built his first separating table in his basement on Baker Street by the Pennsylvania Railroad Station and took it to Arizona, where he begged space from mill owners and demonstrated his invention. Armed with orders, he came home to set up business. The first tables were manufactured in Louis Sipes's machine shop on Superior Street, with woodwork done in a barn nearby. In 1906, he founded the Deister Concentrator Company (which still exists today, though Deister was bought out by the company's directors in 1912) and established Deister Machine Company at its current location, 1933 East Wayne Street.

Deister's first innovation in the mining industry was not his last. In 1926, the company developed a line of vibrating screens for the separation of crushed stone, sand, gravel, coal, coke, and ore according to particle size, a process needed to meet state, federal, and industrial specifications. It introduced a special screen for sizing the aggregate used in hot-mix asphalt plants in 1933. In recent years, it has added vibrating grizzly feeders and foundry equipment, including shakeouts, compaction tables, reclaimers, and oscillating conveyors.

Deister was still active as president and general manager of his company when he died in 1961 at eighty-eight years of age. His sons and grandsons now run the business: Emil Deister, chairman of the board; Irwin F. Deister, president; Irwin F. Deister, Jr., vice president of marketing and comptroller;

Above
Emil Deister invented ore separating equipment that is used today in mines around the world.

Top
Founder Emil Deister posed with a group of employees outside of the company's original plant at 1933 East Wayne Street.

and Mark Deister, vice president of manufacturing and treasurer.

Today, Deister Machine Company is the leader in its field, producing equipment used in mines all over the world. The firm continues its tradition of providing safe, reliable, innovative machinery for the mining industry.

DILGARD FOODS COMPANY

Dilgard Foods Company is Fort Wayne's only home-owned, full-service food distributor. The many local competitors specialize in serving either institutional food services or retail stores, and few are independently owned.

The company's unique approach to food distribution started soon after it was founded in 1924 by Howard Dilgard, who originally distributed margarine and malt exclusively. Later, in 1937, when Birds Eye frozen foods were placed on the market, Dilgard was selected to be their only Indiana distributor. He supplied grocers with frozen food cabinets and built large storage freezers in his own warehouse at 2111 South Calhoun Street. His business developed into one of the largest frozen food distribution operations in the state, and today the company is the oldest independently owned Birds Eye distributor in the country.

Dilgard and his wife, Faye, ran the company until 1960, when it was purchased by a group of local investors. At that time, the company had eleven employees; today, fifty employees account for twelve times the business done in that year.

In 1963, the company built and moved into its present quarters at 830 Hayden Street, where the first refrigerated truck dock in Indiana holds orders to be loaded and delivered by the company's fleet of refrigerated trucks. Dilgard now has more than 1,700 customers and its market area has grown from a 50-mile radius around Fort Wayne to a 65-mile radius. The firm delivers twice a week throughout most of its market area, once a week to a few cities, and daily in Fort Wayne if its customers so desire. The company tailors its shipments and schedules to the customer's needs.

In addition to Birds Eye, Dilgard carries the product lines of General Foods, Nifda, Blue Water, Ore-Ida, Heinz, Campbell-Swanson, and Harriss. Produce, added to the product line in 1964, is bought directly from the area where it was grown. Meat, added in 1968, is shipped directly to the company's own USDA-Inspected processing plant on Hayden Street to be cut and packaged. Dilgard is the only full-line distributor with its own meat processing plant. From July 1973 to October 1979, Dilgard was the exclusive Kraft Food Service distributor for the Fort Wayne area. In 1974, it acquired Allen County Foods from John and Max Schmitz.

The company's officers are Howard J. Couch, president and chief executive officer; Robert W. Smith, Jr., vice president, sales-marketing; Edward P. Woehnker, vice president, purchasing-merchandising; David G. Anderson, vice president, operations-comptroller; and Ronald D. Blue, vice president, meat division.

The company's director-owners are J. Thomas O'Reilly, Robert Kinney, Lawrence Kinsey, James Houlihan, Howard J. Couch, and George Kiproff.

Dilgard Frozen Foods, Inc., operates out of this building on Hayden Street, the first location in Indiana to have a refrigerated truck dock.

ESSEX GROUP OF UNITED TECHNOLOGIES

From fifty employees in one vacated wire mill building in the winter of 1936, Essex Wire Corporation's Fort Wayne operation has become the headquarters of the Essex Group of United Technologies with twenty-seven plants organized into five divisions employing more than 7,500 persons. Essex, a member of United Technologies' Electronics Group, is one of the largest manufacturers of electrical wire products in the world.

Organized as Essex Wire Corporation in 1930 in Detroit, the basis for the company's move to Fort Wayne is rooted in earlier city history. George Jacobs, who had married W.E. Mossman's daughter, was an up-and-coming figure in the Sherwin-Williams Paint Company in Cleveland, Ohio, when he devised the first practical enamel for coating fine wire, producing the first small-gauge magnet wire in 1910. Jacobs formed a partnership in 1911 with his father-in-law and brother-in-law, B. Paul Mossman, and named the new company after his hometown of Dudley, Massachusetts. To lure Jacobs to Fort Wayne, where the rest of the family lived, the elder Mossman built a small, barnlike building on Wall Street

to replace the rented quarters in Cleveland that the Dudlo Manufacturing Company was quickly outgrowing. Mossman's scheme worked, and the firm moved to Fort Wayne in July 1912.

Dudlo's growth as the world's major producer of magnet wire was stimulated by Henry Ford's need for reliable coils for his Model-T ignition. Dudlo produced millions of coils for Ford: four for each Model-T, plus frequent replacements.

Ford Motor Company also figures prominently in the early history of Essex. Ford established its own wire and cable division in 1924 to produce internal wire assemblies. In February 1930, Addison E. Holton, backed by a group of his friends, concluded an agreement with Ford whereby he would acquire the assets of the wire and cable division and would manufacture auto wire for Ford. His newly incorporated Essex Wire Corporation leased a corner of the sprawling Highland Park plant near Detroit and began production.

Soon afterward, Holton acquired not only RBM Manufacturing of Logansport, Indiana, which made automotive switches, but also Chicago

Transformer Company. Another early acquisition was the Indiana Rubber and Insulated Wire Company, founded in 1890. The plant in Jonesboro, near Marion, Indiana, noted in the construction industry for its Paranite brand of wires and cables, had been idle. A judge presiding over the fate of the plant accepted Holton's offer because the executive had assured the judge that he wanted wire, not just equipment, and would reactivate the factory.

In 1936, Holton found another idle wire mill, Dudlo, closed in 1933 by General Cable Corporation, which had taken it over in 1927. Its enameled magnet wire facilities were just exactly what Holton had been seeking. Holton's Highland Park operation had included some magnet wire equipment that could produce more wire than the automaker needed. Holton started selling the wire, which is used to create a magnetic field, to electric motor manufacturers and found a greater demand than the Highland Park plant could fill. So Essex acquired not only 38,000 square feet of the abandoned Dudlo plant but also wire manufacturing equipment. Eventually Essex would occupy the entire plant along Phenie and Wall Streets.

After the company acquired the Fort Wayne facilities, Essex found itself producing coils, complete electrical wire assemblies, small transformers, general purpose wire, and power cords for electrical equipment manufacturers. By the early 1940s, Essex had twelve plants and was solidly established as a producer of automotive electrical systems, building wire and cable for the construction industry, magnet wire and lead wire for electrical motors and transformers. World War II brought urgent needs for thousands of miles of field wire for the U.S. Army Signal Corps, millions of transformers for communications equipment, and wire assemblies for B-24 bombers, plus wire and cable needed by other defense plants and priority domestic needs.

In the late 1940s, the company's expansion accelerated in response to the skyrocketing demand for electrical wires, circuitry, switches, controls, and systems for the postwar boom in electric appliances. The general prosperity of the 1950s also encouraged expansion by auto designers, whose advances required more sophisticated wiring systems. The company also began to manufacture electrical insulating materials and electrical and electromagnetic controls and systems.

In 1959, Walter Probst succeeded Holton as Essex president; Holton continued as chairman and chief executive officer. Probst instituted procedures organizing and consolidating Essex, preparing it for still greater growth through the 1960s. Under Probst, Fort Wayne became the company's headquarters. In 1962, Holton retired and Probst was elected chairman and chief executive officer. Three years later, Essex became a publicly held corporation, its shares listed on the New York Stock Exchange. Sales that year were about $354 million and net earnings were about $17 million. Paul W. O'Malley was elected president in 1966. Probst retained his posts as chairman and chief executive officer.

O'Malley established new plants in the United States and abroad and diversification came at a rapid pace at Essex, which changed its name to Essex International, Inc., in 1968. By 1972, sales were $696.4 million with net income of $37.1 million. Essex employed some 28,000 persons in ten divisions with over 100 plants in seventeen states, the United Kingdom, Spain, Canada, and Mexico, with thirty-eight warehouses in twenty-two states and Canada by 1974.

Essex merged with United Aircraft Corporation (changed to United Technologies Corp., UTC, in 1975) on February 5, 1974. Later in the year, upon the retirement of Probst, O'Malley became chairman and chief executive. In 1976, the company changed its name to Essex Group, Inc., and in 1978, Peter L. Scott, at that time president of UTC's Norden Systems Division, succeeded O'Malley as president and chief executive of Essex, with former Essex presidents Probst and O'Malley continuing to serve UTC as members of United's board of directors.

After reorganization in 1979, Essex Group became part of UTC's Electronics Group with Scott heading the newly formed group as UTC executive vice president. James A. O'Connor, an Essex veteran since 1949 and former vice president-general manager of the Essex Magnet Wire & Insulation Division, succeeded Scott as president of Essex Group in December of 1979.

Headquartered at Fort Wayne, Essex today consists of five multiplant divisions reflecting the company's 50-year heritage of leadership and supplying magnet wires and electrical wires and cables to the appliance, electrical equipment, construction, telecommunications, utility, and mining industries.

Above
This building along Wall Street, the birthplace of the magnet wire industry, is now part of Essex Group's headquarters, though its exterior has been substantially remodeled since this scene was photographed in June 1920.

Left
A myriad of disciplines and applied technology is evident in the diversity of electrical conductors made by Essex Group, covering insulated magnet wires finer than spider's silk to large high-voltage power cables, underground communications cables, construction wires, cables, and appliance wires.

Far left
In 1930, Essex Wire Corporation began constructing automotive wire harnesses in a leased corner of Ford Motor Company's Highland Park factory. By the 1970s, every U.S.-built car included at least one Essex product.

FRANKE PLATING WORKS, INC.

Harry L. Franke took his father's advice in the late 1920s and opened a metal-coating shop in Fort Wayne. Harry had been a pattern maker for metal castings at Flint & Walling Manufacturing Company in Kendallville, Indiana, when he took the big step into being an independent businessman. His father, William J. Franke, who was superintendent of Flint & Walling at the time, helped by keeping the books for the one-man shop.

Harry started with galvanizing, but he soon decided the emerging electroplating process held more promise for metal protection. So he converted his equipment, founding Franke Plating Works in 1930. The process is basically the dipping of a piece of iron or steel into a vat where zinc galvanically coats the part to keep it from rusting. Electroplating offers a greater flexibility of coatings; the parts are put into a plating metal solution — usually cadmium, zinc, gold, or other metal. A current is passed through the solution to bind the metal to the part.

Franke Plating Works provided Fort Wayne's diverse industrial roster with a source of corrosion-proofing for its wide variety of metal parts. A few of the first companies to send Franke parts to be plated were Tokheim, Bowser, Wayne Pump, Horton Manufacturing Company, and the Capehart Company — among the world's leading manufacturers of such products as gasoline pumps, washing machines, and fine phonographs.

The need for this type of flexibility in protective plating services challenged Franke and his employees to stay in the forefront of the industry. Electroplaters deal not with easily visible products but with component parts for manufacturers. The plating works has put coating finishes on subassembly parts by the thousands, from the tiniest fasteners, to any type of motor, fan housings, or chassis.

Business grew steadily with additions to the original plant at 2109 East Washington Boulevard, capped by an addition in 1969 that doubled the size of the building, including space leased to a commercial laboratory.

In the early 1940s, Franke made Ward S. Hubbard his partner. From the late 1940s until his death in 1963, Hubbard was president and general manager; in 1963, William J. Franke, Harry's son who joined the company in the early 1950s, became president and general manager.

Today, six electronically programmed hoist lines carry parts to the plating tanks. Franke's capabilities include electroplating with copper, nickel, chrome, cadmium, zinc, silver, and gold, along with phosphating, black oxidizing, polishing, dry filming, and vibratory tumbling. The company has numerous different accounts ranging in size from the largest industries to small tool and die shops. The firm's clients are spread across an area 200 miles in diameter.

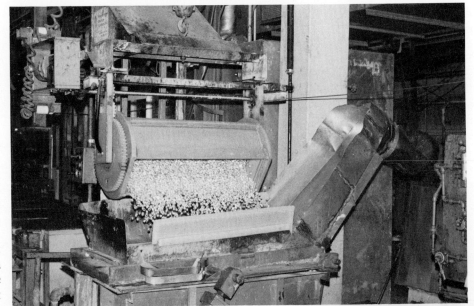

Above
Because many plating solutions contain cyanide, proper waste treatment procedures are vital to the industry. Franke Plating holds a patent in this area.

Top
Electronically programmed hoist lines deposit parts to be plated in a vat holding a metal solution. After the current has plated the metal parts, the line carries them to a bin from which they are tested and shipped.

FORT WAYNE NATIONAL BANK

From humble beginnings in the darkest days of the Great Depression, Fort Wayne National Bank has become one of northeastern Indiana's major financial institutions. Established by community leaders Fred B. Shoaff, James M. Barrett, Jr., L.H. Moore, Gaylord Leslie, Edward M. Wilson, H.J. Bowerfind, and Walter S. Goll, the new bank first opened its doors at 123 West Berry Street on October 30, 1933.

With the year's bank panics barely eight months behind them, organizers moved to ease depositors' fears by choosing a respected non-banker, Fred S. Hunting, retired head of General Electric's Fort Wayne operation, to lead the new institution. Mr. Hunting served as president of Fort Wayne National Bank for eight years and continued as chairman of the board until 1948, when Wendell Laycock assumed the bank's top management position. Russell Daane succeeded Laycock in 1963. Today, Paul E. Shaffer is president and chairman, positions he has held since 1969.

The bank's resources have risen steadily, from $5,584,422 in 1933 to $43,718,795 in 1943, to $130,767,701 in 1965, to more than $498,753,-000 in June 1979. A full-service bank, Fort Wayne National operates fourteen offices, among them four that feature automated teller machines, the city's first when introduced in 1972. The bank also maintains an international banking department that aids area companies engaged in business in foreign countries.

Especially during the past decade when so much has been achieved, the bank, through its employees and directors, has been significantly involved in virtually every one of those major downtown improvements already accomplished or presently planned. In other areas, the bank is particularly proud and supportive of its many employees who are unusually active in our community's affairs.

In 1970, the bank relocated to spacious new headquarters in a 26-story glass and concrete skyscraper at the northwest corner of Calhoun and Berry Streets. The building, which is featured in bank advertising, is the tallest structure in the Fort Wayne area and second tallest in the state. It serves as a towering launching pad for the annual Three Rivers Festival fireworks display. Comprised of approximately 215,000 square feet of rental space, the bank building claims several major tenants, including Central Soya Co., Inc.; the brokerage house of Merrill Lynch, Pierce, Fenner & Smith; attorneys Shoaff, Keegan, Baird & Simon; and the accounting firm of Ernst & Whinney.

Paul E. Shaffer, James M. Barrett III, George B. Farnsworth, Douglas G. Fleming, Donald B. Grissom, Joseph J. Guidrey, Frederick H. Holt, Bob F. Jesse, Lynn A. Koehlinger, G. Irving Latz II, Jackson R. Lehman, Kenneth W. Maxfield, Dale W. McMillen, Jr., Carl W. Moellering, Amy B. Morrill, James A. O'Connor, Jack W. Schrey, Max P. Shambaugh, Thomas M. Shoaff, Alfred F. VanRanst, Richard D. Waterfield, and Don A. Wolf are directors of the Fort Wayne National Bank.

Below left
Fred S. Hunting came out of retirement to lead the Fort Wayne National Bank as president and chairman of the board. During his tenure, the bank safeguarded the records of the Honolulu Finance & Thrift Co., Ltd., whose facility was threatened by the 1941 bombing of Pearl Harbor.
Below
The current portion of Fort Wayne's ongoing downtown redevelopment began with the construction and occupancy of the Fort Wayne National Bank building in May 1970.

GREATER FORT WAYNE CHAMBER OF COMMERCE

Left
Noted architect Guy Mahurin designed the city's Chamber of Commerce building, erected at the northwest corner of Ewing and West Wayne Streets in 1926 at a cost of $350,000.

Right
"Fort Wayne with might and main" was a motto of the Fort Wayne Commercial Club, a forerunner of the Greater Fort Wayne Chamber of Commerce. Photos courtesy of the *News-Sentinel.*

On the night of August 28, 1875, a small group of young, enterprising Fort Wayne businessmen gathered at the Agricultural Hall to consider the feasibility of forming a chamber of commerce. The group agreed to organize a chamber and selected the first officers: John M. Coombs, president; John Orff, vice president; S.W. Ellsworth, treasurer; and William Lyne, secretary. By the end of the year, seventy businessmen were members. Today, the more than 2,800 members represent more than 1,800 firms.

In its early years, the Chamber was not often a strong force in the community, though among the first of its fifty-five presidents were James B. White, father of the department store, and Samuel M. Foster. In 1893, Robertson J. Fisher led a new group named the Wayne Club, and six years later another group, the Fort Wayne Commercial Club, began to meet in a building at the northeast corner of Wayne and Harrison Streets. In 1910, the two clubs merged and reorganized as the modern Chamber of Commerce.

Soon after the reorganization, Louis Fox bequeathed $10,000 to be applied to a new Chamber of Commerce building. Plans for the new building slowly evolved when Guy Mahurin was chosen as architect in 1925. A successful five-day fund-raising campaign netted $40,000 over the goal of $250,000 on the second day. Meanwhile, the Fort Wayne Women's Club agreed to pay for an extra story on the building for their meeting rooms. In May 1926, the present site at the northwest corner of West Wayne and Ewing Streets was purchased for $50,000.

Some of the Chamber's best early projects took shape at the same time the Chamber building took shape. Chamber leaders formed the Greater Fort Wayne Development Corporation in response to the requirements that International Harvester set forth before establishing its truck factory in Fort Wayne in 1922. The Development Corporation was also responsible for enticing Magnavox Corporation to relocate from California, along with several other East End industries that increased Fort Wayne's industrial output 747 percent in the fifteen years before 1930. Thanks to this growing, diversified economic base, Fort Wayne came to be reputed as "depression-proof" during the 1930s.

Today's Chamber, officially renamed the Greater Fort Wayne Chamber of Commerce in 1973, offers four types of service: (1) information to individuals and industries; (2) educational programs and other public service events; (3) research on business-related topics; and (4) services to specific groups through such innovations as Business-in-Education Day, fleet safety contests, or home-planners institute. The Chamber's members serve on twenty-two different committees, ranging from Good Roads and Air Service committees to Rural Affairs and World Trade committees.

Fort Wayne's Chamber facilities are distinguished by its restaurants and bar, operating without subsidy from the dues. Not only is it the only one in the nation to own its own food service, but the Chamber's Arena Dinner Theater is unique among similar organizations. One of the rooms of the refurbished building was recently renamed the Madison Room to honor Harrison Madison, who has been serving the community's business leaders their cocktails for more than forty years.

Today's Chamber is led by Edwin C. Metcalfe, president; Paul E. Seybert, president-elect; Fred Prange, treasurer; Richard J. Galli, secretary; Alen G. Wyss, past president; and D.J. Petrucelli, executive vice president.

FORT WAYNE SAFETY CAB CORPORATION

Haskell B. Schultz drove his first cab, his brother's Model-T, on his eighteenth birthday, July 1, 1926, in his native Rochester, New York. When his brother moved to Dayton, Ohio, to establish a taxicab business, Haskell followed him. The Dayton venture fared poorly, however, and the Schultzes moved on to Fort Wayne, where they started a new cab company just before the stock market's 1929 plunge.

The firm's first decade was difficult. Underwriters were reluctant to insure a taxi fleet. Unscrupulous companies would agree to take the risk, but they often collected the premiums and then dissolved, leaving the cab company with no protection, no authority to satisfy claims. Obtaining affordable insurance proved to be a constant battle for the fledgling business.

The Schultzes initially bought reconditioned Yellow cabs from Chicago, but they shifted their operating method in 1930 — each driver would own his own car. At the time, the rate for a cross-town trip was fifty cents, twenty-five cents to go downtown. To stimulate

business, Schultz initiated a 25-cent flat fee to go anywhere in town. When that charge was eventually lowered to fifteen cents, the local streetcar company objected. At that rate, Schultz's Safety Cab Company could undercut their business.

The Indiana Service Corporation arranged a meeting of state public service commission officials and city councilmen in February 1933 to lower streetcar rates and to suggest putting Fort Wayne taxis under city regulation. By April, streetcar operators were threatening to abandon Fort Wayne's miles of track unless the cabs were metered, licensed at fifteen dollars per cab, and bonded. Ensuing restrictions prohibited passenger pickups at streetcar stops, and taxi drivers were forbidden to own their own cabs. The city set rates at twenty-five cents per mile for the first mile, ten cents per half-mile thereafter.

Cab companies fell rapidly during the depression years — Red Top Cab, State Cab, Yellow Cab, and a predecessor to Schultz's firm, Safety Cab Company. Some of the competitors went out of

business; others were acquired by Schultz's company.

In 1936, the failure of the company's two insurers forced Schultz to accept a $1,000 deductible rate and set him on a course that would emphasize the *Safety* in Safety Cab. Haskell Schultz decided to study driving habits, and by 1945, he had written *Design for Safe Driving*, a book that became the model for a training film he has sold to numerous cab firms and still uses in his own company. Last revised in 1968, it has served as the driver's education text for Central Catholic High School. With royalties from the sale of his safety educational materials, Schultz formed a traffic safety foundation to continue to promote safety behind the wheel and on the road.

Today, fifty years after Schultz and two brothers founded Safety Cab Company, the firm makes 67,000 runs per month (804,000 per year) with an average 1.5 passengers per run. The corporation, located at 436 East Washington Boulevard, operates forty cars, most of them Checker cabs.

Above
In October 1951, Fort Wayne Safety Cab honored nine 30-year employees.

Left
Founder and president Haskell Schultz stands near a Checker cab, one of several taxi models used by the firm in its 51-year history.

HAGERMAN CONSTRUCTION CORPORATION

Above
In February 1980, the firm moved into its new office building.

Top
In 1969, the firm built Fort Wayne's nine-story City-County Building.

Hagerman Construction Corporation has never lacked projects to point to with pride, but its current mark of distinction is particularly meaningful to a Fort Wayne struggling to redevelop and enliven its downtown area. Hagerman construction teams built what is referred to in the office as "The Triangle," whose sides are formed by lines joining the Performing Arts Center, Freimann Square, and the City-County Building on Main Street and Lincoln Tower on Berry Street.

William C. Hagerman and Frederick C. Buesching, brothers-in-law, founded Buesching-Hagerman Construction in 1908. William Hagerman had come to Fort Wayne in 1891 as a boy of twelve to join his sister, Johanna (Hagerman) Buesching. Theodore H. Buesching, son of Frederick, joined the firm but left in 1937 to form his own construction company.

The original firm became Hagerman Construction Corporation that same year when William's sons, Ted, an engineer educated at Purdue, and William O. (Pete), a business administration graduate of Valparaiso University, entered the business. Ted became president and treasurer following the elder Hagerman's demise in 1944. Pete served as vice president and secretary, directing all field activities. William L. Kerr, who joined the firm in 1957, became secretary upon Pete's retirement in 1978. Ted became chairman of the board and his son, Mark F., became president. Ted's other son, Kenton L., became vice president along with James A. Schafenacker.

Hagerman Construction Corporation ranks among the top five construction companies in Indiana and the top 400 in the nation. Hospital work is Hagerman's self-proclaimed specialty. The firm has been responsible for hospital construction, with additions totaling well over $100 million. The corporation recently moved to a new office building at 510 West Washington Boulevard.

Hagerman's major local construction projects include the City-County Building, Freimann Square, Fine Arts Building, Memorial Coliseum, Parkview Hospital, Lutheran Hospital, Magnavox Consumer Products office building and Government Sections Plant and new Lab buildings, Perfection Biscuit Company, Concordia Senior College buildings, Indiana-Purdue building complex, in addition to Trinity English Lutheran Church, Wayne Street Methodist Church, St. Francis Science and Administration buildings, Wolf & Dessauer Department Store, S.S. Kresge Warehouse, and Potlatch Manufacturing Plant. Shopping centers built by the firm include Southtown Mall, Northcrest Shopping Center, East State Plaza, Washington Square, and New Haven Shopping Plaza.

Much of Hagerman's work has been undertaken outside of Fort Wayne. Some of these major projects are Indiana University buildings, Ball State buildings, and Valparaiso University and Purdue University buildings. The company also completed construction of warehouse facilities for Hardware Wholesalers, Inc., in Illinois, Ohio, Missouri, and Texas as well as Indiana University Hospital and Marion County Hospital additions in Indianapolis, City-County Building South Bend, and hospital additions in Logansport, Wabash, Peru, Angola, Decatur, Richmond, and Frankfort, Indiana. Department stores have been built for Sears, Roebuck and Co. in Indianapolis-Castleton and in Fort Wayne, Indiana.

HALL'S RESTAURANTS, INC.

Ironically, it was his father's sudden death in 1936 that catapulted Don D. Hall into business. A former All-City tackle from South Side High School, Hall went to Indiana University at Bloomington on a football scholarship. During Christmas vacation of Hall's junior year his father died, and Hall stayed home to provide for his mother and two sisters. He soon added five meat markets and two frozen food locker plants to his father's original shop at 1800 South Calhoun Street.

During World War II, Hall would make the rounds of area packing companies for the meat markets. On his way to the Ossian Packing Company, he would cross the Oakdale Bridge to Bluffton Road, where he often passed a man selling produce out of a pickup truck, a scene that impressed him. Fort Wayne businessmen doubted people would cross the bridge to shop, so the land just across the river from a thriving residential area remained undeveloped. Hall decided to put a drive-in restaurant there as soon as the war ended.

He bought the land from the bridge to Brooklyn Avenue, selling two-thirds of it to finance his new venture. Hall broke ground for the drive-in in the spring of 1946 and opened for business the day after Thanksgiving. He doubled as manager and meat processor.

In 1950, Hall opened a barbecue restaurant and bakery next door to the drive-in and shortly afterward converted a meat market at 4009 South Wayne Avenue to Hall's Prime Rib Number One. Prime Rib Number Two opened in 1953 at 2005 East State Boulevard, followed in subsequent years by Hall's Hollywood restaurant on State Road 3, a much-needed commissary, and Stockyards restaurant on Maumee Avenue, and a smorgasbord restaurant on New Haven Avenue.

Hall's successful catering of a company picnic for 14,000 in September of 1954 led to the establishment of a catering business. In 1970, Hall built Lester's Party Room, named in honor of his longtime friend and associate, Les Price, who has headed the firm's large catering operation since its inception.

In 1955, Hall embarked on another seemingly hopeless venture, the Gas House Restaurant, formerly Fort Wayne's original Gas Company, located at 305 East Superior. Extraneous sheds had to be demolished and a huge storage tank filled with oil sludge had to be drained and removed to provide parking space. The Gas House, one of few restaurants within walking distance of downtown offices, quickly gained popularity and has proven to be the geographic hub of the later-coming Performing Arts and Convention Centers, Three Rivers Apartments, and the Old Fort.

Hall died unexpectedly July 29, 1972, at the age of fifty-seven, and was survived by his wife, Dorothy, four sons, and three daughters. His oldest son, Don Hall II (Bud), took over management of the business. The Factory on Coldwater Road opened a few days after Hall's death, and was managed by a second son, Sam.

Restaurants at South Anthony and Paulding opened in 1976; in the Georgetown shopping district on East State in 1977; and in 1978, the upstairs meeting rooms of the Gas House were converted into a Japanese-style restaurant, the Takaoka, honoring Fort Wayne's sister city in Japan. A new commissary (under the management of a third son, Scott) and restaurant on U.S. Highway 30 in New Haven opened in 1979. A twelfth Hall's restaurant, the Orchard House, has opened in the Glenbrook Shopping Center. There are also plans for additional operations at the old historic Cass Street Railroad Depot and in the Times Corners area.

Left
Hall's caterers borrowed the champagne fountain principle to provide cold lemonade for 14,000 at a 1954 birthday party for Fort Wayne businessman Dale "Mr. Mac" McMillen. Girl Scouts served the Central Soya Company's guests.

Below
Don Hall, who knew little about restaurants before he opened one in 1946, developed a chain of varied eating establishments, as well as a catering operation.

HARDWARE WHOLESALERS, INC.

Independent retail hardware, lumber, and home center stores were finding it increasingly more difficult to compete with high-volume operators, especially mushrooming chain stores, when Arnold Gerberding, a Fort Wayne businessman, proposed an alliance of shopkeepers to secure name-brand products at bulk-rate prices. Working from an office in his home in 1945, he laid the groundwork for a dealer-owned distributorship that would do nearly $427 million in sales by 1979, serving 2,500 retailers in twenty-five states as Hardware Wholesalers, Inc. (HWI).

At the organization's first annual meeting, there were ninety-six subscribers. The board of directors consisted of John Suelzer, president; Harold Rosser, vice president; Howard Travis, secretary; Paul McGill, treasurer; and Warner Gelzer, Vere Calvin, Clair Reed, Harold Main, and C.A.E. Rinker, members. Gerberding served as general manager.

The firm's initial order of merchandise arrived in Fort Wayne in March of 1946. Lacking a proper storage facility or corporate offices — Gerberding still maintained an office at his residence — HWI arranged to use space provided by a local real estate agent and rented warehouse accommodations at special monthly rates from Fort Wayne Storage Company on Haydon Street. Plans to erect a 30,000-square-foot office/warehouse on a nine-acre Nelson Road site purchased in February were disrupted by the mandates of the war-spawned Civilian Production Administration, which controlled industrial construction at the time. Prospects of postwar shortages also limited contractors' bids.

Four separate efforts to gain government approval finally yielded results,

boosted by the aid of a Fort Wayne real estate firm and the area's chamber of commerce. An autonomous HWI Building Corporation financed the construction project, and the firm's thirteen employees and merchandise holdings occupied corporate headquarters in the spring of 1948.

Growth of the company has necessitated numerous expansions. Today, the Fort Wayne facility includes 350,000 square feet of warehouse and 53,000 square feet of office space. HWI also maintains a total of 1,430,000 square feet of space at warehouses in Cape Girardean, Missouri; Dixon, Illinois; Medina, Ohio; and Waco, Texas.

Gerberding retired in 1967, passing the reins of HWI management to Don Wolf. The corporation, which now boasts a work force of 650 people, organizes merchandise shows for its dealers and offers expertise in advertising, store management, store layout and decor, inventory control, financial management, and retail merchandising, in addition to providing in-bulk buying power.

Left
Hardware Wholesalers, Inc., the brainchild of Arnold Gerberding, has grown to nearly one-half billion dollars in sales.

Below
The firm's Nelson Road headquarters, opened in 1948, now provides 350,000 square feet of warehouse space and 53,000 square feet of office space.

HEFNER CHEVROLET, INC.

When William J. Hefner took over Bueter Chevrolet on February 28, 1955, it was the smallest of Fort Wayne's three Chevrolet dealerships. In the ensuing twenty-five years, Hefner Chevrolet became the largest Chevy dealership in Indiana. During that time, Hefner Chevrolet became so dominant in its sales area that today over 50 percent of all Chevrolet cars and trucks sold in Allen County come from Hefner.

Still located at its original site at 500 East State Boulevard, across from North Side High School, Hefner Chevrolet originally employed thirty people. The showroom was so small that a single car had to be jacked up to fit on the display floor. Hefner's service department could handle only five cars at a time that first year, and the firm operated a single tow truck.

It was during that first year that Bill Hefner formulated a marketing plan that was to become his trademark: volume selling, an exciting atmosphere, and concern for the customer. In the mid-1950s, price cutting was unheard of in the auto industry. In a business where the philosophy was to make as much on each unit as possible, Hefner quickly established a policy of discounting, a policy that triggered a dramatic and immediate sales increase. In addition, Bill quickly parlayed the natural excitement of new car showing time into one of the most talked-about annual events in Fort Wayne. By bringing in headline entertainers (at a cost exceeding the previous owner's yearly advertising budget), tens of thousands of prospective customers flocked to Hefner's for the Hefner Show. Headliners included the Crosby Brothers, the Kim Sisters, and even an unknown singer named Elvis Presley. Tuxedo-clad salesmen helped introduce these would-be car buyers to the "Wonderful World of Wheels" at Hefner's. The shows quickly captured Detroit's eye, and the promotion won several national awards. The notoriety helped gain extra shipments of "hot" models from Detroit, which, in turn, aided Hefner's big volume image.

Today, after major expansions, Hefner still occupies its original, but vastly enlarged, location. The showroom is still at the original site, with an additional solar-heated sales facility across the street. The service area contains sixty-four stalls with a self-contained eighteen-stall body shop. The dealership, which now employs 157 people, sold over 7,000 vehicles in 1979. Today, Hefner operates a fleet of tow trucks twenty-four hours a day from a Cass Street location.

Bill Hefner remains active in the dealership as chairman of the board. He also devotes a great deal of time and energy to numerous civic endeavors and has been instrumental in Fort Wayne's industrial development — all part of his master plan to return to the community

Above
The precursor of Hefner Chevrolet, the smallest car dealership in Allen County when this 1955 aerial shot was taken, has grown under Hefner's leadership into the largest automobile marketplace in Indiana.

Top
Hefner employees spent the day before the premiere of the 1958 models decorating the firm's service department.

a measure of the success that he has received.

His loyalty to his customers can best be summed up in an actual written policy in Hefner Chevrolet's employee manual: "Every employee is bound to stop and help any disabled car with the Hefner-trademark 'Number 1' license plate on the front. Failure to comply could mean immediate termination of employment."

INDIANA & MICHIGAN ELECTRIC COMPANY

Indiana & Michigan Electric Company (I&M), Fort Wayne's supplier of electrical power, evolved from a long line of utility services dating back to the Citizens Street Railway Company. Citizens, incorporated September 8, 1871, established a horse-powered streetcar line on Calhoun Street running from Main and Calhoun to the Pennsylvania Railroad tracks in 1872. Fifteen years later, Fort Wayne Streetcar Company acquired the firm. The horses and mules were put out to pasture in 1892,

when the streetcar company was reorganized as the Fort Wayne Electric Railway Company.

Numerous additional mergers created the Fort Wayne & Northern Indiana Traction Company, an entity that eventually became the Indiana Service Corporation (ISC) in January 1920. Not only did the firm operate the city's streetcars but it also functioned as a utility company. ISC was preceded by more than twenty-five companies, including the previously mentioned

Citizen Street Railway Company and Fort Wayne Streetcar Company, as well as Jenney Electric Light & Power, founded in 1883, and the Fort Wayne Electric Light & Power Company, founded in 1902. Fort Wayne Mayor Harry Baals led an attempt to force an ISC linkup with City Light in 1944, but the voters rejected the referendum by a margin of four to one.

In September 1945, the Securities and Exchange Commission (SEC) conditionally approved the purchase of a major block of stock in Midlands Utility Company, ISC's parent firm, by American Gas & Electric of New York. The New York firm was a utility holding company that already owned I&M, an electric company established in South Bend in April 1904. I&M's service area included lower southwest Michigan and northern Indiana. Final approval of the stock transfer hinged on ISC's divestiture of transportation, gas, and water properties and an SEC-mandated merger of ISC and I&M, which was completed in September 1948.

ISC and I&M were serving contiguous areas, in some cases even sharing facilities, at the time of the merger, so the formation of the new power company, which kept the I&M banner, was greatly eased. The company set up headquarters at the former ISC complex at 2101 Spy Run Avenue, Fort Wayne.

Today, I&M is part of American Electric Power (formerly American Gas & Electric Company), a network of eight operating and eight coal-mining subsidiaries. In addition to two coal-fired plants, I&M operates the Donald C. Cook nuclear generating plant near Bridgman, Michigan. A third coal-fired facility is under construction near Rockport, Indiana. In 1979, the AEP system supplied 2,006,399 customers with 95.5 billion kilowatthours of electricity. AEP operates 1,400 miles of 765,000-volt transmission lines.

Top left
Fort Wayne's trolleys were a source of transportation in the late 1800s and early 1900s.

Left
By 1929, the crew that serviced Indiana Service Corporation's power lines could boast of this "modern" electric service truck.

INDIANA BANK AND TRUST COMPANY

Above
The original Dime Savings and Trust Company building opened for business on March 18, 1922.
Above left
Present principal downtown offices of Indiana Bank and Trust Company are located at the corner of Washington and Clinton Streets.

Building upon a foundation of leadership continuity, the 58-year-old Indiana Bank has become a dynamic member of northeastern Indiana's financial community. Established as the Dime Savings and Trust Company on March 18, 1922, the bank opened its offices at the northeast corner of Court and Berry Streets. Founding officers were Harry G. Hogan, president; Charles A. Spanley, Oscar A. Fox, and W. Clyde Quimby, vice presidents; James E. Ruhl, secretary; and W.H. Schafer, auditor. In 1927 the bank moved to the northwest corner of East Wayne and Clinton Streets.

Hogan, a Fort Wayne native who practiced law for twenty years before embarking on his banking career, managed the bank with a solid and conservative judgment for thirty-four years. He guided it through the panic of the depression years, making it one of the only three out of twelve area banks to survive the early 1930s without total reorganization.

In August 1956, a group of Fort Wayne business and professional men acquired approximately 75 percent of the bank's stock. The buying group included Dean F. Cutshall, Haywood M. Davis, Richard T. Doermer, brothers Sidney and David Hutner, Richard G. Nill, brothers Sol and Dr. Maurice Rothberg, F. Ed Schouweiler, and Gerald Zent. On the day of the purchase, the bank had total deposits of $9.8 million. Shortly thereafter, Doermer was named president.

The ensuing twenty years brought great growth to the banking industry and dramatic events for the bank. In November 1958, wryly noting that "the ten-cent dime isn't exactly what it used to be," the bank announced "a new name better suited to the age: Indiana Bank and Trust Company." It launched a wide range of customer computer services then unique to banking, among them payroll preparation, accounting for business accounts receivable, inventory control, physician billing, and personal cash-flow accounting through its copyrighted Recap-O-Matic bank statement. It moved, in 1961, into colorful new offices at the northeast corner of Washington and Clinton Streets, providing convenient under-roof, drive-up teller and parking facilities for its customers. Three additional floors were added to the building in 1966.

During this period the bank opened ten new branches, issued thousands of retail charge cards, and, through its "Check Plus" plan, consolidated checking, regular savings, and an open line of credit into a single monthly statement. It frequently sold stock to the public to increase its capital base, enlarging to over 1,900 the number of bank shareholders residing largely in Allen County. Deposits, assets, loans, and bank earnings surged during this period; and the bank emerged as a force of statewide significance among the over 400 banking institutions operating in Indiana.

Much of its growth, according to President Doermer, has been attributable to the bank's emphasis on staff involvement in the community. It employs 330 people. "We seek to employ only those who genuinely like people and who want to help people," Doermer notes. This guiding philosophy has had a dramatic and continuing impact on the bank's development since the mid-1950s.

The bank will celebrate the sixtieth anniversary of its organization in March 1982.

INDIANA VOCATIONAL TECHNICAL COLLEGE

Ivy Tech, a nonbaccalaureate, post-high school vocational technical educational institution created in 1963 by the Indiana General Assembly, is the by-product of a two-year study of Indiana's employment environment that found a critical shortage of skilled, technically trained workers to meet the needs of a rapidly expanding economy. The Fort Wayne branch, serving Region 3, the state's nine northeastern counties, opened its doors in 1969.

The college's first home was on the first floor of the former Concordia High School building at Anthony Boulevard and Maumee Avenue. Three programs — drafting technology, engineering technology, and secretarial technology — constituted the college's initial curriculum. Soon the entire building had to be leased from its owner, the Indiana Institute of Technology, to accommodate the technical college's growth.

Electronics, accounting, and data processing courses were added in the winter quarter of 1969. Fall 1970 brought management technology and auto body repair programs, the latter requiring the lease of additional work space. More faculty members were hired as enrollment climbed to 447 credit students in the fall of 1971. A second building was acquired, and an automotive service program was added.

By 1973, the Fort Wayne college recognized the need to abandon some of its leased facilities in favor of a new, central campus. The Indiana-Purdue Foundation at Fort Wayne deeded land to Ivy Tech for this purpose, and Region 3's first building on the site at North Anthony Boulevard and the U.S. 30 Bypass opened in the fall of 1976. Although it had been hoped that the entire college could be located in the new building, growth had been so dramatic that several leased buildings were still required. The Zollner Corporation donated acreage adjacent to the new campus, clearing the way for a second building, set to open in late 1980.

Today, Ivy Tech's Region 3 campus has over 2,000 students enrolled in twenty-three program areas and individual courses. The college is proud of its high placement record for its graduates becoming employed in their chosen fields. In addition to its on-campus programs, Ivy Tech offers special workshops and classes for area businesses and industrial concerns. Training sessions are conducted in factories, local high schools, and other community facilities.

Indiana Vocational Technical College is accredited by the North Central Association of Colleges and Schools. The institution is authorized to grant the associate of applied science degree.

Above
Today, the northeastern branch of the state's vocational technical college is located at North Anthony Boulevard and the U.S. 30 Bypass.

Top
Ivy Tech occupied the former home of Concordia High School from 1969 to 1976.

INDIANA WIRE DIE COMPANY, INC.

Although it was June, the furnace in Otis and Violet Ferrier's basement on Barr Street was going full force. As their small son watched, they put metal into the firebox, heated it, and then poured the molten metal into molds of sand to cast parts for the machine that would be the heart of Ferrier's new die cutting company.

Ferrier had been a diemaker in the diamond diemaking department of the Dudlo Manufacturing Company. After the company closed in 1930, he managed the Detroit Wire Die Company in Fort Wayne, which employed virtually all of the Dudlo diamond die department. Ten years later, "the old gang" of craftsmen started to form their own companies; today there are nine members of the American Diamond Die Manufacturer's Association, all located in Fort Wayne or the New York City area.

Ferrier found a storefront building at the corner of Holton Avenue and East Creighton Avenue to use as the headquarters for his new company, the Indiana Wire Die Company. Only a few years later, a serious fire forced the company into temporary quarters on Oxford Street; the new headquarters were opened at 314 East Wallace in the late 1940s.

The business was a family affair. Violet, who had been a coil winder at Dudlo and Otis's secret wife (because factory policy prohibited employing couples), and Otis's son, Dale, who tagged along to the factory after school and on weekends, both worked in the business. Ferrier not only owned the company, having bought out his partner, a bookkeeper named Velma Rideout, after the first year, he also managed the 30-employee firm and served as salesman for several years. Dale, who took over the firm after his father's stroke in 1960, recalls his father's whirlwind sales trips to the East Coast, when he came home after his usual 6 a.m. to 6 p.m. workday, packed the family into a car, and headed for New York.

Once a craft that traced its origins to crude, wooden, Phoenician dies to shape round strips of metal, wire die

Top
Following a disastrous fire that necessitated a move to temporary quarters, Indiana Wire Die Company settled into this building at 314 East Wallace in the late 1940s. Today, the firm occupies about a third of the block.

Above
Multiple-lead, electrically powered precision drilling, shaping, and polishing machines brought diamond dies into their own by the early 1950s.

manufacturing has evolved into a precise science. Lasers can drill through commerical and synthetic diamonds in less than a half hour instead of the five to eight days required by earlier equipment. Such a high degree of precision is now possible that Indiana Wire Die Company has drilled a hole through a diamond estimated at .000075 inch and awaits certification as the world's smallest diamond hole.

Thanks to automation in the firm's two buildings at the southwest corner of Wallace and Lafayette Streets, Indiana Wire Die employees produce dies for all ranges of wire and diamond powder, first for the company's own use and now as a product. The firm also sells artificial gemstones, including cubic zirconia, microscopes, wire pullers, and die cleaners, and does microscopic drilling for the other industries.

JOE GOLDSTINE & SON, INC.

A great deal of Fort Wayne's twentieth-century economic history has involved Joe Goldstine & Son, Inc., commercial and industrial Realtors. The company's history has followed the changing development trends of Fort Wayne and Allen County since it was founded in 1910 by Hyman Goldstine, grandfather of current president Robert Goldstine.

Hyman sold farms and homes throughout his career, but when his son, Joe, joined the business in 1915, the firm changed its emphasis to commercial sales. Along with groups of businessmen that he organized or joined, Joe had a hand in developing nearly every block of downtown Fort Wayne. Among his major contributions to the downtown landscape were bringing the first Walgreen's drugstore to Fort Wayne, negotiating the long-term lease for the property which was to become the Strauss Building, and placing the Murphy's department store on the corner of Calhoun and Wayne Streets, where it still operates today.

Not all the deals worked out, of course. On Joe's behest, the Marshall Field organization was prepared to develop the southeast corner of Calhoun and Washington Streets, but the year was 1929, and the ensuing depression caused local investors to lose the property.

After the Great Depression, Goldstine, Inc., was the first firm in America to sell a property taken over by the Federal Reconstruction Finance Corporation to a private investor. The deal put the first Walgreen's on the southwest corner of Berry and Calhoun Streets.

The end of World War II saw the company's arena of activity change from Calhoun Street to shopping centers on the outskirts of Fort Wayne. Goldstine developed the Rudisill Center (in its day one of the first outlying commercial centers), Gateway Plaza, Maplewood Plaza (of which Robert is secretary-treasurer), and Time Corners Shopping Center. Some years prior, Joe was active in the Greater Fort Wayne Development Corporation, which brought important industries like International Harvester to town.

When the shopping center market began to wane, Goldstine became active in the industrial realty market. The company found warehouses for General Electric, International Harvester, and Magnavox and sold old inner-city factories to new concerns. One of the first "recycled factory" sales after World War II was the sale of the old American Fork and Hoe Company on East Berry Street to the Wayne Candy Company.

Goldstine, Inc., has been a developer and agent for many small industrial parks. The firm has done much work for oil companies, both in acquiring properties to develop service stations and, recently, in reselling the properties as stations close down.

Recently, the company has handled the acquisition of the site for the new Summit Square Office Tower, to which it will move its offices from the Strauss Building, and for the new Lincoln National Life Insurance Building on Clinton Street.

Robert Goldstine has been a leader in community service for many years. From 1971 to 1979, he was the first president of the Embassy Theater Foundation, which saved the historic old theater with a $250,000 fund drive and began its operation as a concert hall, theater, and meeting place. Robert has also served on boards of the Fort Wayne Philharmonic, Saint Francis College, Historic Fort Wayne, Salvation Army, and Downtown Improvement Association and is a past president of the Fort Wayne Jewish Federation. He was named the Man of the Year in 1976 by the Chamber of Commerce.

Above
In the early 1900s, Hyman Goldstine maintained an office in the Tri-State Building (now the Strauss Building).

Right
Hyman Goldstine concentrated on the sale of farms and homes until his death in 1939. His son, Joe, introduced the company to the commercial realty business.

JOHN DEHNER, INC.

In 1930, John Dehner (standing second from left) posed with one of his pipe-laying crews.

John G. Dehner, born in Kentland April 21, 1887, seemed destined for success. After moving from his family's Yoder Road farm to Fort Wayne, he discovered that the construction sites where he was selling International Harvester trucks especially appealed to him. In 1927, he incorporated his own contracting business and remained active in it until his death fifty years later.

An old building at 1206 Clark Street, which has housed the company since 1932, has been remodeled so extensively to meet the demands of the thriving business that the original structure is no longer recognizable. From its initial ten employees, the company now keeps as many as 125 persons busy during its peak construction season in July.

Dehner's 1927 payroll amounted to a mere $500 per week, which consisted of an hourly wage of fifty cents for laborers, and seventy-five cents for heavy equipment operators. Although the nature of the work has not changed over the years, except to include more extensive drainage and sewer work, in addition to ditch-digging and heavy excavation, salaries have risen sharply. Today's workers earn sixteen dollars an hour, plus fringe benefits, resulting in a payroll of $1.6 million in 1979. Payroll for a week of peak construction came to $25,563.

The company's steady expansion has corresponded to Fort Wayne's fastest growth, influenced by increasingly more complex government regulations affecting water and sewage treatment. John Dehner, Inc., recently completed Fort Wayne's new pollution control holding ponds at the sewage treatment plant on Lake Avenue Extended and installed a sewage facility in Huntington. The firm is currently building a sewage system for Hamilton, Indiana.

A longtime active member of Kiwanis, Elks, and the Knights of Columbus, John Dehner was known for his civic involvement. He once served as president of the Allen County Historical Society; a wing of the original Diehm Museum of Natural History bears his name. A director of the Memorial Coliseum from its founding until his death, Dehner also was president of the Indiana Highway Contractors.

Dehner's sons, Gerald G. and Edward L., now run the business as president and secretary, respectively. William L. Winling is treasurer. Greg Dehner, Gerald's son, is vice president and the third generation of Dehners to enter the business. Richard Ensley is presently the office manager, and his assistants are Roger Carpenter and Chris Tevitt.

Important jobs now emanate from Environmental Protection Agency grants, among them the Fort Wayne and Huntington sewage projects. But most

John G. Dehner founded his business thirty years before this photograph was taken in 1957, by which time the firm was well established and he was involved in many community organizations.

of Dehner's jobs are won by submitting low bids after analyzing plans and specifications, visiting job sites, making test borings, getting material cost quotes from suppliers, and estimating cost of labor, materials, equipment, overhead, and bonds. The firm's years of experience provide an edge in this realm. Major clients include International Harvester and Dana Corporation.

KELTSCH BROTHERS, INC.

Arvid Polster established a small apothecary shop at the corner of Wells and Third Streets in Fort Wayne's Bloomingdale section in 1892. He sold the business in 1910 to Carl Albersmeyer, who had among his five employees Joe Humbrecht and Carl Keltsch, the first of a line of Keltsches who would transform the modest, little pharmacy into the largest locally owned chain of drugstores in Fort Wayne.

Keltsch and Humbrecht bought the store in 1925 and managed it together for twenty-three years. Don Keltsch, Carl's oldest son and a professional pharmacist, joined the firm as a partner in 1948, bringing with him new ideas and ambitious plans. He suggested remodeling the shop's storefront, a change that gave the drugstore one of the most modern-looking appearances of the day. The company became Keltsch Pharmacy when Humbrecht left the firm in 1950, the same year Carl's second pharmacist-son, Maurice, entered the business.

Ten years later, Don and Maurice opened a second Keltsch drugstore, this one on West State Street, a larger facility that incorporated many of the modern techniques of pharmacy retailing, including the self-service concept. The business flourished, and new outlets were established quickly: the North Anthony store in 1963; the South Anthony store in 1965; and the Georgetown store, the chain's largest, featuring more floor space and a wider line of products, in 1968. All the new stores followed the West State Street model; they were located in suburban shopping centers with supermarkets next door.

The business continued to grow with the addition of the Auburn store in 1971 and the Washington Square and South Calhoun stores in 1972. The original Wells Street store was torn down in 1969, and the business moved to a new building next door, the basement of which served as the Keltsch warehouse. In 1975, the business relocated to new offices and warehouse space in the former Stillman Department Store warehouse on North Clinton, and the South Calhoun store took over larger quarters at an adjoining site.

The Keltsches diversified their business with the 1974 opening of Keltsch Mediservices, the brainchild of Clyde Leedy, and the 1975 acquisition of the University Park Medical Center Pharmacy.

The founder retired in 1965, and Keltsch Brothers, Inc., was formed. As the 1970s ended, the firm had ten outlets ranging from another edition of the Wells Street store to the newest store in Ossian. Future expansion is planned. Today, the business's stockholder-directors are Don Keltsch, president; Maurice Keltsch, vice president and secretary; Clyde Leedy, treasurer; Lee Theobald; John Woehnker; David Brennan; Bob Fahrenbach; and Richard Keltsch, Don's son and the third generation of Keltsches to join the family business, which now employs 214 people.

Top
Carl Keltsch was fourteen years old when he posed for this photograph with co-worker Joe Humbrecht. The pair purchased the C.H. Albersmeyer Drug Store in 1925.
Left
The Keltsch brothers opened their largest store in 1968 in the Georgetown Shopping Center on East State Boulevard.

KORTE PAPER COMPANY, INC.

Fred C. Korte took the $1,500 he had saved selling wholesale paper for twenty-five years and established his own paper business at 127 East Columbia Street in 1940. Starting with only a rolltop desk, he handled all of the fledgling firm's activities except billing and mailing, which his wife and daughter did from their home. As the business grew, Korte purchased one of Fort Wayne's oldest hotels, located at 128 East Columbia Street, and set up an office and warehouse. Within a year, he was able to hire a warehouse manager and a man to staff the office.

At first, Korte made his living by buying rail carloads and truckloads of paper goods and reselling them in smaller lots to local business and industries. Interna-

Fred C. Korte managed the wholesale paper business he founded until his death in 1968.

Right
Korte Paper Company's second home was the 128 East Columbia Street location once occupied by one of Fort Wayne's oldest hotels.

tional Harvester, Tokheim, Wayne Pump Company, Wolf & Dessauer Department Store, Zollner, and dry cleaning companies like Hitzeman, Swiss, Peerless, and others were early customers.

To protect himself in the face of war-induced paper shortages, Korte visited paper mills in New York, Alabama, and Arkansas and secured assurances of credit and supplies to meet his firm's burgeoning needs. Even as other wholesale paper operations experienced difficulty obtaining products, the Korte Paper Company maintained a steady flow of business. Korte's close contacts

with paper mill managers proved advantageous throughout his career.

Korte developed such a fine reputation in the business that distributors often sought his advice and opinions regarding the state of the industry. When plastic began to replace paper dry cleaning bags, he added plastics to his line of products, along with containers used by food-service operations, and later included janitor supplies.

Mildred Roese, Korte's daughter, who had worked with the business from the beginning, joined the firm after graduation from the Luther Institute, a business school, and some study at Franklin College. In 1956, when the company incorporated, she became vice president and secretary.

Plans for Fort Wayne's new city-county building forced the corporation

out of its Columbia Street offices in 1964. Korte and some associates formed the Nebraska Realty Corporation and bought the former Eckert Packing Company building at 1825 West Main Street, and the Korte Paper Company and its nine employees moved in. Ten years later, the firm opened a cash-and-carry shop next door. Today, that retail outlet is five times its original size.

Korte died October 12, 1968, and Mildred assumed the presidency of the corporation, taking her rightful place behind her father's old rolltop desk. Her husband, F. Richard Roese, a doctor of chiropractic, is secretary. Their daughter, Gloria Nash, vice president and bookkeeper, also handles the payroll for the firm's twenty-eight employees. Gloria's husband, Jim, is sales manager.

THE LUTHERAN HOSPITAL OF FORT WAYNE, INC.

The same philosophy that today guides the men and women of the Lutheran Hospital of Fort Wayne, "A Christian Commitment to Care," was the motivation for the men and women who founded the hospital in the early years of this century.

As early as 1878, Lutherans living in the Fort Wayne area bought property for a hospital in the Village of South Wayne, only two blocks south of today's location. Years later, the Lutherans took up active hospital work through the Fort Wayne City Hospital at the corner of East Washington Boulevard and Barr Street. They sold their vacant lots on South Wayne and Packard Avenues to use the money for the benefit of Hope Hospital, as it was renamed in 1891.

The Lutherans, however, still longed for the opportunity to put their Christian convictions into action in a hospital of their own and were convinced that the south side of the city needed a hospital. Allen County's first infirmary had been located on the Indianapolis plank road in South Wayne before the Civil War. When Hope needed enlargement, the Lutherans resolved to build their new hospital. At a meeting on December 15, 1901, they formed a tentative hospital association with the Reverend Philip Wambsganss as its director. Pastor Wambsganss and many others from the city's Lutheran congregations worked on behalf of a new hospital and, on May 11, 1903, formally organized the Lutheran Hospital Association of Fort Wayne. The Reverend Wambsganss was elected its first president.

In the summer of that year, the association selected a site for the hospital — a 21-room farmhouse on Fairfield Avenue known as the Ninde Homestead. The purchase price was $10,000 but repairs and refurnishing cost an additional $9,617. By Thanksgiving in 1904, the building was ready. It contained twenty-five patient beds, an operating room, a reception room, a kitchen, and a dining room, and provided a room for the matron and her daughter and a room for an intern.

On March 10, 1905, only three months later, the association realized

space was needed and agreed to borrow funds for a $60,000 expansion. The addition, which gave the hospital a total of seventy-five rooms, was dedicated on August 25, 1906. The original building served as the nurses' residence until 1913, when the Judge S.R. Alden home adjacent to the hospital property was purchased for $15,000.

By the mid-1920s, the need for more space was answered with a new wing along Wildwood Avenue which brought the adult bed capacity to 215 and included a modern obstetrics department with two delivery rooms and a nursery, as well as a new kitchen with four separate dining rooms.

Construction began in the fall of 1953 on a $3 million project to replace the original building with a five-story tower to house new facilities and 105 additional beds. When the new building was dedicated in April of 1956, it housed a new pharmacy, a physiotherapy department, nine operating rooms, a fracture room, a cystoscopic room, a post-anesthesia recovery room, a new kitchen, and the Chapel of Mercy. Another remodeling in November 1957 brought the hospital's total capacity up to 385 beds.

The next twenty years were characterized by a flurry of expansions, including four more floors, an eight-story lateral extension on the North wing, and the construction of the Northeast Quadrant.

The facility marked its seventy-fifth anniversary in 1979 — it had come a long way from that 21-room homestead on the edge of the city. During that time, the hospital has had only three chief executive officers since the administrative title was adopted: E.C. Moeller from 1929 to 1959; Edgar C. Kruse, 1959 to 1977; and Robert H. Reedy, 1977 to the present. Reincorporated in 1972 as the Lutheran Hospital of Fort Wayne, Inc., it is operated under a Board of Control of some 170 delegates from area Lutheran congregations.

Today, the 589-bed hospital offers the most modern of services, providing a full range of cardiac-stroke care and rehabilitation. The Renal Dialysis program includes both chronic and acute inpatient care, as well as a Home Dialysis Center which teaches patients and their partners to use artificial kidney machines at home. The hospital also operates a mobile intensive care unit for inter-hospital transportation of the critically ill. Its newly remodeled emergency department includes three major trauma rooms for the critically ill, two general emergency rooms, a six-bed treatment area, and a large cast room. The department's 24-hour physician coverage policy was a Fort Wayne first in 1971. Lutheran's radiology department employs the latest in technologies, including a CAT full-body scanner and a linear accelerator for cancer treatment. Obstetrical care is centralized in the North wing with patient rooms, an intensive care-intermediate care nursery, and the newborn nursery.

Education is also a prime concern of Lutheran Hospital, which offers residency programs in both orthopedic surgery and family practice, and supports schools of nursing, medical technology, surgical technology, and radiologic technology. It also provides clinical training for a number of medical courses at other area schools, plus specialized seminars for regional medical groups, in-service education, and patient-family teaching programs.

Some 360 physicians practice at Lutheran, 123 of whom serve on its active medical staff. More than 1,900 employees fill 200 job classifications, and 700 volunteers contribute more than 87,000 hours each year.

Opposite Top
The Old Ninde Homestead, a 21-room farmhouse on the outskirts of Fort Wayne, was dedicated as the 25-bed Lutheran Hospital on Thanksgiving Day, 1904.

Opposite left
Barely three months after the hospital opened, space requirements necessitated expansion. The Reverend Philip Wambsganss led a prayer at the ground-breaking ceremony May 23, 1905.

Left
By 1927, overcrowded conditions were forcing the hospital to turn patients away. Four new stories and seventy-five new rooms were completed by the summer of 1928, raising patient capacity to 215.

Below
The Northeast Quadrant, a 63,300-square-foot, four-level addition tucked into Lutheran Hospital's L-shaped main building, was completed in 1977.

LINCOLN NATIONAL BANK AND TRUST COMPANY

Fort Wayne's population jumped from 45,115 in 1900 to 63,933 by 1910. In 1905, in the midst of this time of expansion, Theodore Wentz and Samuel Foster founded a bank — the ninth in town and the fifth national bank. Its office was located on Court Street.

Wentz and Foster were undeterred by all the competition because they had an idea that would set their bank apart. Fort Wayne banks had been either commercial banks devoted to the needs of businesses or savings banks devoted to the needs of individuals. The new bank, originally named the German-American National Bank, would offer the security of a national bank with a full range of services for both businesses and individuals.

By the end of its first day of business, May 20, 1905, Fort Wayne had responded to their idea with 800 new accounts totaling more than $100,000 (total liabilities and resources of the bank at that time were $218,960.75). Seventy-five years later, the bank's holding company balance sheet shows assets, liabilities, and stockholders' equity at more than $720.5 million.

On April 12, 1912, the bank established a branch office at Calhoun and Brackenridge, described in the bank's 1930 Silver Anniversary annual report as the largest and oldest branch office in Indiana. In 1914, the stockholders of the growing bank organized the Lincoln Trust Company. Anti-German sentiment, prevalent when the United States entered World War I, prompted the bank to change its name to Lincoln National Bank in 1918. Ten years later, in 1928, Lincoln National Bank absorbed the trust company and formed Lincoln National Bank and Trust Company.

Even without the stock market collapse in October 1929, the year would figure prominently in the bank's history. In January, Charles Buesching, who began his career with Lincoln as a teenage messenger, was elected president — a post he held for twenty-nine years. And in October, construction began on the Lincoln Bank Tower, a 312-foot, gilt-crowned art-deco structure which reigned for many years as the

Lincoln National Bank and Trust Company introduced drive-up banking to Fort Wayne in the 1950s.

The Lincoln Bank Tower on Berry Street was designed by A.M. Strauss of Fort Wayne and Walker & Weeks of Cleveland, with Buesching & Hagerman as general contractors. Construction began in October 1929 and ended in November 1930. Old City Hall, now a museum, is visible in the left foreground.

state's tallest building. The tower quickly became a symbol of the bank's strength, particularly after Lincoln Bank was able to ride out the rash of bank failures in the city in 1933, emerging as the largest bank in northern Indiana.

By 1930, the bank had instituted a popular loan department to enable "the small borrower to obtain funds quickly for taxes, furniture, hospital bills, and other emergencies," with regular weekly or monthly payment schedules. In addition to its innovative branch office, Lincoln sponsored two "affiliate banks" for a short period of time in the early 1930s: North Side State Bank, 1615 Wells Street, and East Side State Bank, 1201 Maumee Avenue. In the 1950s, Lincoln introduced drive-up banking to Fort Wayne.

Today, Lincoln is a full-service bank with twelve offices, 730 employees in six divisions, and the area's first non-credit card computer teller. Lincoln Financial Corporation has more than 1.1 million shares of common stock outstanding and a total stockholders' equity of more than $47.9 million.

MASOLITE CONCRETE PRODUCTS, INC.

Founded in 1929 as General Dredging Company, Masolite Concrete Products specialized in dredging, road grading, bridge building, and sewer work. With offices located at 2511 Taylor Street, F.W. Hitzeman became the firm's first president, Walter W. Walb its secretary-treasurer.

In 1931, the company won the Big Pipe Creek project, which involved more than fifty miles of main ditch, plus tributary ditches, in Grant County. State and local governments generated most of the firm's contracts during the 1930s, because public agencies were among the few entities with cash to pay contractors during the Great Depression.

Clyde A. Walb, Sr., assumed the presidency in 1935; his son, Walter, continued as secretary-treasurer. Another son, Ralph W., had joined the company in 1932. Clyde Walb had helped shepherd the Professional Engineers Registration Law through the Indiana legislature. Both younger Walbs were Purdue University graduates who became registered professional engineers. The Walbs were also instrumental in founding the Indiana Society of Professional Engineers.

The firm continued excavation, grading, and bridge work until World War II temporarily shifted the company into packing and shipping disassembled bolted steel barges, tools, and other items for export to the Corps of Engineers. Ralph Walb became vice president, secretary, and general manager in 1942, succeeding his father as president upon the elder's death October 1945. Walter remained as treasurer and director while two professional engineers, Paul C. Spears and Daniel H. Stouffer, became vice president and a director with a special interest in design matters, respectively.

In 1944, General Dredging purchased several acres of undeveloped land from the Wabash Railroad at 2200 Lafontain Street and built new offices and a large general operations building. When the war work ended, company officials pondered what to do with the property. When a staff engineer suggested a concrete joist business, the Walbs visited several concrete products plants in the Midwest and discovered that blocks were much more in demand than joists, so they ordered the machine and equipment to go into the concrete block business. The Masolite Division of General Dredging Company, formed in 1946, produced its first concrete block in June 1947. By 1950, the division was ready to produce concrete joists.

The company came to a crossroads in 1954 when both the contracting and concrete products divisions needed new equipment. Management opted to retain their "sideline" business, selling off their road contracting equipment.

The next five years brought improvements in the block-making facilities and a new building for production of prestressed structural slabs. Later the company began to make architectural precast panels. The Fort Wayne-Allen County Public Library, the IBM office building, Snider High School, buildings at the Indiana-Purdue regional campus, and the Magnavox corporate offices on Route 14 are among Fort Wayne structures featuring Masolite panels. The company also markets precast stadiums like those at Northrop and Wayne High Schools.

Since 1962, Masolite has acquired Lakeview Concrete Products in North Webster, Auburn Concrete Products in Auburn, and two block plants — one in Fort Wayne and one in Muncie — purchased from Old Fort Industries. The company name was changed to Masolite Concrete Products, Inc., in 1970.

Interrad International, Inc., bought the company in June 1978, and Ralph Walb retired to become a management consultant. William G. Kriesel, like his predecessors a Purdue graduate and a professional engineer, became the new president.

Below left
After the firm became fully engaged in the manufacture of concrete blocks and precast concrete products in the years following 1960, the Masolite workyard looked like this.

Below right
One of five General Dredging Company crews posed with Grant County officials during work on the Pipe Creek drainage project in 1931. Pictured are Elmer Simmons; Bill Martin; Clyde A. Walb, who later became company president; Judge Van Atta, who supervised the project; Ancil Ratliff, county commissioner; Harold Waldeck; and Joe Whitely, county commissioner.

MAGNAVOX GOVERNMENT AND INDUSTRIAL ELECTRONICS COMPANY

Magnavox Government and Industrial Electronics Company, located in Fort Wayne's Interstate Industrial Park, is heir to a 70-year tradition of electronic breakthroughs: from the first anti-noise microphone that enabled pioneer aviators to communicate with each other and their ground crews to the solid-state UHF radio family that is today's standard Air Force communications system; from the first practical underwater microphone system to detect submarines to the complex airborne data processors used by the U.S. Navy today.

The company began in 1911 in a small building in Napa, California. With capital of $2,500 and their newly developed "electrodynamic telephone," Edwin Pridham, Peter Jensen, and Richard E. O'Connor founded the Commercial Wireless and Development Company. Before Pridham and associates, the telephone was a scratchy-sounding instrument, using much the same principle as the cup-and-string telephones youngsters rig up to link garages to secret clubhouses. The new company's magnetic diaphragm devices put electrical power to work amplifying the voice.

By 1915, the company had developed the electrodynamic loudspeaker (the first public address system) and the amplified phonograph. In 1916, they announced the development of a completely electric phonograph. The next year, 1917, the firm merged with Sonora Phonograph Distributing Company of San Francisco to become the Magnavox Company.

World War I brought the company's first development project specifically for the military — the anti-noise microphone for aviators. Before the new communications system, pilots could only attempt to shout over the din of the engine or try to communicate by hand signals. With the new specially equipped helmets, flyers could contact other planes or units on the ground from altitudes of up to 10,000 feet. The system worked so well that it was also installed on more than 1,250 naval and merchant marine vessels and was employed on virtually every aircraft

using the wireless telephone.

After the war, the company introduced the first single-dial radio, which simplified tuning and led directly to radio's booming popularity during the next decades.

The year 1930 was a pivotal time for both Magnavox and Fort Wayne. By 1930, Fort Wayne was one of the country's major centers for the budding electrical industry: the home of Dudlo, one of the foremost manufacturers of magnet wire; the Capehart Company, producers of fine phonographs; and General Electric's motor, generator, and transformer operations. Wire in all sizes and shapes, coated and uncoated, was one of the city's major products. Innovators like Dudlo's George Jacobs

and G.E.'s James Wood propelled Fort Wayne into the vanguard of American electronic ingenuity.

Fort Wayne's preeminence in the magnet wire field, its climate of invention, its location in the heart of the nation, and its proximity to towns noted for cabinetry skills made it an attractive location for the Magnavox Company. By fortunate coincidence, at the same time that Magnavox wanted to move from its Oakland factory, the Greater Fort Wayne Development Corporation found itself stuck with a new factory on Bueter Road built for a company that had folded only two years after the civic boosters had donated the land and granted a 100 percent construction loan. The 210,000-square-foot plant

suddenly became another compelling advantage, and Magnavox moved east.

Innovations continued in Fort Wayne, with the introduction in 1936 of the first commercial crystal pickup for phonographs. The next year, the company introduced the high-fidelity (hi-fi) phonograph.

For World War II, the plant was converted to military defense production, turning out gun-firing solenoids, interphone systems, radios, bomb directors, radio compasses, and bazooka firing devices. The company's defense work was honored with the first Navy "E" for excellence award given to an electronics firm.

Magnavox organized the Government and Industrial Division in 1951. Two years later, the first practical sonobuoy was introduced. This underwater acoustic sensor was approximately five inches in diameter and three feet long

Left
Using this equipment to develop and manufacture the electrodynamic telephone, Edwin Pridham, Peter Jensen, and Richard E. O'Connor founded the company that would become Magnavox in this Napa, California, building in 1911.

Opposite Bottom
The company built gun-firing solenoids, interphone systems, radios, bomb directors, radio compasses, and bazooka firing devices to aid the Allied war effort.
Below
Magnavox won the coveted "E" designation for its defense production work during World War II.

Below right
Testing the radio units the firm devised for World War I pilots was simply a matter of hooking up the helmets to see if they worked.

and could be launched from an aircraft at up to 250 miles per hour. To slow and stabilize its fall it included a rotochute much like the blades of an autogyro or helicopter. The rotochute and a bottom plate came off when the buoy hit the water, allowing deployment of an antenna and underwater microphone, which picked up noise made by a submarine.

The buoys became more sophisticated in the ensuing years, as transistors replaced vacuum tube technology in the mid-1960s. By that time more sophisticated means of processing sonobuoy information had also evolved. Other improvements include longer life, deeper depths, significantly greater reliability and directionality, and the capability of being launched from jet aircraft at higher speeds and altitudes. At the same time, the average cost of a sonobuoy has dropped from $300 in the first production runs to $150 today. Sonobuoy technology was also adapted for the National Data Buoy developed in 1971 for the National Oceanic and Atmospheric Administration.

Successive military radio contracts throughout the 1950s and 1960s resulted in the production of thousands of specialized radio units, making Magnavox the leading supplier, as well as the leading innovator, in radio technology.

In 1969, the Government and Industrial Electronics Division introduced the MX-902 satellite navigation receiver for position location and ship navigation. Magnavox at its Torrance, California, location is the world's largest supplier of position location systems for navigation, off-shore oil exploration and production, and international mapping and surveying.

The Magnavox Company was purchased by North American Philips Corporation in 1974, and in 1975 the Magnavox Government and Industrial Electronics Company was established as a separate company, a wholly owned subsidiary of Magnavox that is, in turn, wholly owned by North American Philips Corporation.

The firm designs and builds advanced electronic systems for UHF and VHF communications, for environmental monitoring, for antisubmarine surveillance, and for such specialized purposes as countermeasures, computer input-output, and motorcycle ignition. Its products are marketed around the world, but its basic goals are to develop and produce advanced electronic systems in support of the national defense effort.

Today, the Magnavox Government and Industrial Electronics Company employs 3,500 people in Fort Wayne, with 800,000 square feet of engineering laboratories and manufacturing space. A 300,000-square-foot engineering complex next door to the Interstate Park plant will be finished in 1981.

MAY STONE & SAND, INC.

The gravel pit that Bill May took over in 1932 was the oldest in Allen County. Early records indicate that "moulder sand" was taken from the area even before the county commissioners sold it in 1862 to Charles Fairfield, a member of one of Fort Wayne's noted pioneer families. May's big opportunity came because the previous owners had lost the business in the Great Depression. The local bank holding the mortgage on the property agreed to let May operate the business for one year; if May could make the gravel pit pay off, he would then be allowed to buy it on a long-term contract.

The key to saving the business was efficiency through quality control and ready availability of the basic materials. Workers in those cash-short days earned twenty cents an hour and worked 10-hour days, so personnel costs could not easily be trimmed. Machinery innovations would not develop until after World War II.

By the early 1950s, the industry and the company were changing with the shifts in markets. Glacier-polished gravel in paving materials was being phased out, and limestone was becoming increasingly popular as a basic building material. The increased demand for crushed limestone products gave the company a major advantage, because beneath the gravel and sand was enough limestone to last 150 years. Exploratory drilling in 1938 had confirmed the underlay of several hundred feet of extremely hard dolomitic limestone. By 1951, the company had sold enough of the sand and gravel to expose part of the limestone. The stone quarry was started in 1952 — the first of its kind in the United States to obtain limestone by open cut beneath seventy feet of sand, gravel, and clay overburden.

Today the quarry is 304 feet deep, the deepest blue-white limestone quarry in Indiana. Ten miles of conveyor belt carry limestone, sand, and gravel through various crushing and sorting processes that yield fourteen grades of stone and five types of sand and gravel. Nearly 250,000 tons of sand and stone are stockpiled at the main Ardmore plant, with more at the company's Woodburn quarry and DeKalb County sand and gravel plant. Besides construction materials, the firm sells stone for chemical and industrial uses and powder-fine agricultural limestone.

Erie-Haven, a wholly owned subsidiary acquired in 1973, produces ready-mix concrete from cement, sand, and crushed limestone. Formed in 1961 from Erie Materials Company and New Haven Ready-Mix, Inc., Erie-Haven has supplied concrete for Fort Wayne's Anthony Wayne Bank, the City-County Building, Fort Wayne National Bank, expansion projects at all three of the area's hospitals, and numerous new school buildings.

In 1972, May Stone was sold as a wholly owned subsidiary to France Stone of Toledo, Ohio. Paul Seitz succeeded May as president and chief executive officer in 1968.

Top left
In 1955, three years after the May Stone limestone quarry was opened, it looked like this. Today the company owns 200 acres southwest of the intersection of Sandpoint and Ardmore Roads.
Left
Twelve hundred people lined the rim of the quarry in 1962 to watch a blasting demonstration, part of a larger program to inaugurate the company's Rockbusters Club.

MOBILE AERIAL TOWERS, INC.

The product of Mobile Aerial Towers, Inc., was an idea whose time had come. It just took a while to find the best material for its agile, high-reaching truck platforms.

The MAT story begins at Lester L. Myers' airfield shortly after World War II, when the man who was to become the company's president and chief designer decided that there had to be something better than ladders for reaching high places. So Myers designed the jointed-boom-and-bucket and built the first model to paint his hangars and hire out for odd jobs. He became affiliated with C. Gordon Diver and his company, Civilian Building and Supply, on North Clinton Street, where MAT was born in 1950. Roger E. Neff, who was to become chairman of the board and chief executive officer, joined MAT from Civilian, as one of three original stockholders.

MAT, Inc., promoted the concept as much as the product in its early years. The firm's biggest sale in its first decade was thirteen units to the U.S. Air Force. In 1954, MAT left Civilian's building and set up manufacturing and test facilities on North Harrison Street. Business improved, and a few units were sold to electric utility companies between 1954 and 1960, though they were not yet suited to work on energized electrical wires.

MAT recognized the opportunity for a big electric utility market but could not take advantage of it until it could produce a boom-and-bucket of sufficient nonconductive properties to insulate the lineman from the ground when working on high-voltage wires. Early attempts included coating the upper boom-and-bucket with tape, gluing fiberglass to metal buckets, mounting metal buckets on glass insulators, using plywood buckets, and dipping entire platforms in rubber. Nothing really worked until 1960, when structural fiberglass, as strong for its weight as steel and highly nonconductive, was adopted from boat manufacturers.

The electric utility market quickly opened up, and MAT developed a primary market of investor-owned electric utilities. Other markets, in descending order, are rural electric cooperatives, cities (which use MAT's Hi-Rangers for electric line work and for park, traffic, and fire departments), tree contractors, painting contractors, and rental companies. Today the product is well known and accepted.

MAT, Inc., has 275 employees at its Bowser Street plant, once owned by the Bowser Corporation, which moved to Tennessee in the early 1960s. The firm maintains offices in what was Bowser's print shop and also uses a major portion of a large building across the street and four other smaller buildings. The company's entire production and testing is done in the Fort Wayne plant, which also houses one of twenty-three dealer sales offices nationwide, with one dealership in Sweden. Ninety percent of its Hi-Rangers are shipped ready for installation on trucks by the dealers. The majority of MAT's fiberglass is manufactured in Fort Wayne by Plastic Composites, Inc., the first company to make its structural booms.

The product line is designed to work at heights from 35 to 130 feet and features a patented one-hand control in the buckets. Customers can always return their Hi-Rangers to the factory or its dealers for reconditioning and upgrading, and MAT has worked closely with customers and manufacturers' associations to promote safe use of its equipment.

The company's business grew steadily until 1974 to 1976, when electric utilities severely curtailed purchases, but sales are moving slowly upward again as more and more companies realize the functional efficiency of MAT's line of mobile towers.

Left
Mobile Aerial Towers' Unit 1 was used to paint hangars at Lester L. Myers' Fort Wayne airfield shortly after World War II.

Above
The firm's assembly line features single-skill operations to ensure the safety and reliability of its products.

NORTH AMERICAN VAN LINES, INC.

In 1933 a group of local household goods movers banded together in Cleveland, Ohio, to form North American Van Lines, Inc. The original purpose was to provide long distance return loads traffic for the members of the cooperative venture. In the early years, the company's focus was in the Midwest, but by 1940 its operations reached to all forty-eight states. Its organization also changed from a cooperative to a profit-making publicly owned enterprise.

By the mid-1940s, the company became convinced that Cleveland was not the best site for its principal office. After an extensive search, Fort Wayne was deemed the ideal location because of its easy access to highway facilities and Indiana's favorable truck licensing laws. In 1947, northAmerican's headquarters facilities were moved to Fort Wayne at a site just east of the city on U.S. 30.

The firm's growth accelerated throughout the 1950s. It began meeting special needs for international moving by inaugurating air and ocean service. Padded vans were added to the fleet to transport high value items such as computers, medical equipment, and art collections. The company expanded from its household goods moving base to operations as a freight carrier of products from manufacturers to merchants and directly to consumers. Between 1955 and 1961, northAmerican grew again through the acquisition of two trucking companies, one in Grand Rapids and one in Los Angeles.

In 1968, northAmerican was purchased by PepsiCo. The company's trademark was transformed from a cream and red insignia to the now familiar blue and red circles cut by a white arrow. NorthAmerican became an important part of the PepsiCo family of companies, which include such famous brand names as Pepsi Cola, Frito-Lay, Pizza Hut, Taco Bell, and Wilson Sporting Goods.

The firm moved into a new world headquarters building in January of 1978. On a 114-acre site on U.S. Highway 30 West, just west of Interstate 69, the main building has 170,000 square feet of space on one floor. More than 1,200 employees are housed in the principal office, with an additional 300 employees in an adjacent fleet service facility.

With over 8,000 highway vehicles,

Above
NorthAmerican's first Fort Wayne home was this then-modern building on U.S. 30 East in Fort Wayne.
Top right
In January of 1978 northAmerican moved into its new world headquarters building on U.S. Hwy. 30 West.
Right
In 1947, James D. Edgett, northAmerican president; H.A. Weissbrodt, International Harvester Fort Wayne works manager; V.E. Freeman, northAmerican general manager; C.H. Koon, Harvester assistant manager; N.B. Knapke, northAmerican assistant to the general manager; and W.J. Cahill, Harvester Fort Wayne motor truck branch manager, posed with one of the firm's International Harvester trucks.

and agents and employees located throughout the entire Free World, northAmerican has grown to be the seventh largest trucking company in the country. The firm doubled its size from 1975 to 1980, thereby reaching a 10-year goal in half the allotted time.

Although northAmerican recruits personnel on a national basis, many of its executives are longtime natives of the Fort Wayne area, including Kenneth W. Maxfield, chairman of the board and president. These local roots help explain the firm's staunch commitment to community involvement, which is reflected in the company's representation on boards of local charitable, cultural, religious, and financial institutions.

NORTH EASTERN COMPANIES

Joseph L. Zehr's business activities began in 1962 when the Fort Wayne native and recent Goshen College graduate set up his first corporation to develop residential real estate. Encouraged by the interest and support of home builders Chris Stauffer and Delbert Delagrange, he developed some fifty lots his first year. At the same time, he established the first North Eastern Corporation, which started with five employees. On many days, Zehr worked in the office in the early morning and piloted heavy equipment out in the field the rest of the day.

The business grew in complexity as it grew in volume, and Zehr added corporations, partnerships, and joint ventures as they were needed. Maplewood Downs, Oakhurst Park, Bellshire, Blackhawk, and Kern Valley Farms were some of his early developments. Today, his operations range from the acquisition of developable land to the construction activities on the land, and he supervises the separate concerns under his management corporation, North Eastern Management Corp., founded in 1973.

Zehr has built his development operation into the largest development firm in Allen County, an organization that has changed the face of the county with single-family residential units incorporating the latest in land planning concepts. Each week, Zehr studies land acquisition, development feasibility, and financing, estimates cost, makes bids and board presentations, markets his ventures through local real estate salespeople, and attends to the details required by various local bureaucratic bodies, the Indiana State Board of Health, and the State Stream Pollution Control Board.

Current developments include Coventry, a 750-acre PUD in Allen County's southwest section, the county's largest planned unit development (a planner's term meaning a development that sets aside land for common community uses). Other PUDs Zehr has developed are Walden, begun in 1973; Hillsboro, begun in 1975; and Tanbark, begun in 1976. The Village of Buckingham is his most recent development. A step beyond a PUD, it encompasses the mixed land use that will mingle the national headquarters of Hardware Wholesalers, Inc., around an eight-acre lake with single-family homes in the $150,000-plus neighborhood.

Zehr's operation has developed retail commercial buildings, restaurants, a small industrial park, and office buildings.

When elected, Zehr was the youngest life director on the board of the Home Builders Association of Indiana; he serves on the board of the National Association of Home Builders as well. He is also a member of the executive group of the residential council of the Urban Land Institute, a research organization based in Washington, D.C.

Above
A park-like atmosphere prevails in the open space of North Eastern Companies' Heather Ridge subdivision.

Top
North Eastern Companies presented Haverhill in Aboite township in a recent Parade of Homes.

OLD FORT INDUSTRIES, INC.

In 1914, seventeen masonry and plastering contractors pooled their resources to form a general store for building materials. With five employees, a horse-drawn wagon, and $20,000 in capital, they opened the office and warehouse of Old Fort Supply Company, Inc., in a frame building at 705 Clay Street. The supply firm sold mortar, plaster, brick, cement, and other items for the building trades.

After only four years in business, the "lime shop" outgrew its quarters and purchased the former City Carriage Works at 709 Clay Street. The three-story building was remodeled to serve as Old Fort's office and warehouse, the home of the firm for thirty-one years.

Fate occasionally disguises significant events (such as the appointment a young adding machine salesman kept at the expanded "lime shop" on Clay Street in 1923). F. Edwin Schouweiler, a bookkeeper by education, had come to Fort Wayne as a representative for the Thomas W. Briggs Co., a national advertising firm, to sell ads to businesses for publication in the *Journal-Gazette*. Calling on the Burroughs Adding Machine Company, he showed such lively interest in Burroughs' systems that the company hired him on the spot. Six months later, while making an installation call on Old Fort Supply Co., Schouweiler learned of a book-keeping opening and took the job. Five years later, he was named Old Fort's manager.

The general store became a building materials supermarket. The depression years of 1930 and 1931, however, challenged the supply firm and its manager, and reduced the payroll to three — including Schouweiler as manager, bookkeeper, and salesman. Despite the virtual halt in construction, Old Fort managed to mark sales of $39,000 during its darkest year. In 1935, Schouweiler was elected president and acquired majority stock ownership in the company.

The next twenty years were busy ones as the firm matured. The company's first ready-mix concrete plant was built in 1938, followed by a retail-wholesale paint and wallpaper store. The ready-mix operation was expanded in 1943 to serve customers within a 40-mile radius of Fort Wayne. The company's portable concrete plants were the key to large ready-mix contracts during World War II in Pennsylvania and Ohio. Following the war years, sons Edwin C. and W. Dale Schouweiler rejoined the rapidly growing firm. In 1948, Old Fort opened a ready-mix plant in Muncie and shortly thereafter moved into the Dayton, Ohio, market with similar facilities. Later, the company opened a concrete pipe company, Coppco, Inc., in Littleton, Colorado. The 1960s saw the acquisition of Magic City Builders Supply Company, Inc., and Dura Crete Products, Inc., both of Muncie, and the beginnings of the Midwest Aggregates Corporation subsidiary.

Schouweiler has been long active in numerous civic activities, including terms as president of the Fort Wayne Chamber of Commerce and first chairman of the city's United Fund campaigns. The ambitious pattern of growth and development for the future of the Old Fort firm was set by the major trend of the 1970s toward the lawn and garden business.

Today, the corporation, renamed Old Fort Industries, Inc., with main offices at 2013 South Anthony Boulevard and operations in ten states, produces concrete block; ready-mixed concrete; natural resource products, such as crushed limestone, sand, gravel, peat, and humus fertilizer; and machinery, including concrete-block machinery and hydraulic testing equipment. Subsidiary companies include Midwest Aggregates Corporation; Muncie Stone Company; Builders Concrete, Inc.; GOCorp, Inc.; Illinois Brick Company; Anderson Peat; Organic Compost, Inc.; Triple X Products, Inc.; and Wegro.

Below left
Remodeled to serve as office, showroom, and warehouse for Old Fort Supply, which began as a builder's supply store, this building once housed the city carriage works.
Below
Old Fort Industries originally sold materials to retail and wholesale customers. Today, the firm markets a range of building and soil-enrichment products.

PEOPLES TRUST BANK

Fort Wayne was a vigorous city of nearly 50,000 optimistic people in 1903 when Peoples Trust Bank first opened for business at 817 South Calhoun Street. Originally incorporated as "The Peoples Trust and Savings Company," Peoples Trust joined nine other existing banks in serving the financial needs of the city that year and was destined to be the only one of those institutions to survive the Great Depression of the thirties.

In 1903, the city had three hospitals, five "reading room" libraries, eight newspapers, ten parks, and sixteen schools. Fort Wayne was growing with new housing to the south and northeast, particularly in the South Wayne and Lakeside areas.

The last census had reported fewer than 14,000 automobiles in the entire nation. Transportation was provided principally by the horse, the railroad, and the trolley. In Fort Wayne, horses pulled surreys, buggies, and fire wagons over the wood-block paving of downtown streets, and through the unpaved streets and roads that predominated in the rest of the city and county. A five-mile shopping trip was a day's excursion.

The streetcar was an important part of the local scene on which Peoples Trust first opened its doors, and the bank's location, near the Transfer Corner where all streetcar lines crossed, was a convenient one. The speedy trolleys took people from their homes to stores downtown, to Robison Park for polite thrills and romance, and to Centlivre Park for circuses.

In addition, the streetcars carried workers to jobs at the Wayne Knitting Mills, the "Pennsy" shops, Horton Manufacturing, Fort Wayne Electric Works, Packard Piano & Organ Company, Kunkle Valve, Bowser Pumps, and the foundries that had brought Fort Wayne to prominence in manufacturing railroad wheels and axles.

Peoples Trust had its origin in a meeting at the law offices of William P. Breen and John Morris, Jr., where the dozen businessmen present subscribed for 200 shares of stock, providing capital of $200,000 for the new state-

chartered bank. They drafted articles of incorporation, elected a 12-member board of directors, and chose William L. Moellering as the bank's president. Other officers included Robert W.T. DeWald, first vice president; Neil A. McKay, second vice president; and Patrick J. McDonald, secretary-treasurer.

At the close of the first year, the bank had deposits of $384,000 and loans of $415,000. The all-male teller staff worked six day weeks, and on Fridays, "P.J." McDonald walked through the lobby with a money sack, carefully counting out each man's wages for the week.

Five years later, Peoples Trust had grown sufficiently to warrant moving to a six-story building at 913 South Calhoun Street. At a cost of $60,000, remodeling was completed that included, among other features, a special room for ladies' transactions and offices for tenants in the top five stories.

Although progress was steady through the bank's first twenty-five years, by 1928 its twenty-two employees still required only the first floor and basement areas of the building, with the three-man trust department tucked away under the stairway next to the vault. At that time, the bank was headed by P.J. McDonald as president; with August Becker, vice presi-

Above
By the late 1970s, only the bank building remained of the 900 block of South Calhoun Street. To dress up the north side of the building, an artist reproduced the bank's well-known facade. Photo by Gabriel R. Delobbe.

Top
The Peoples Trust moved into its new home at 913 South Calhoun Street (fourth building from right) in 1908.

Above

The bank's six pyramid-style branches won an architectural excellence award from the American Institute of Steel Construction. Inside, customers find a compact service area on the ground floor, bank operations facilities in the basement.

Top

Women began to appear behind tellers' cages in the early 1940s as World War II called men away.

dent; and Donnelly P. McDonald, Sr., secretary-treasurer.

Although the bank itself was doing well, economic storm clouds were gathering above the bustle of Fort Wayne's main streets. Prices for the farmers who banked in Fort Wayne had plummeted in the last years of the decade, and the stock market crashed in the fall of 1929.

As the financial panic of the early thirties gathered momentum, Peoples Trust officers foresaw the need for large cash reserves to meet withdrawal demands and converted huge bond holdings into cash for that purpose. Even during the five-day bank closing, which applied nationwide in March of 1933, McDonald was reputed to have "kept a back door open" for desperate customers. Peoples Bank promptly reopened at the end of the bank holiday, proudly bearing the title of "oldest bank in town" and a reputation for reliability.

The fifties were marked by the growth of branch banking. Under Donnelly P. McDonald, Sr., the bank's first branch was built in Waynedale in 1955, with additional branches added at Southgate Plaza and Bueter Road by 1958. Today, the bank has twelve branches, six of which — using a "pyramid" design — were awarded the Architectural Excellence Award from the American Institute of Steel Construction.

The bank introduced the Peoples Trust Charge Account Plan in the late fifties and was among the first ten banks in the nation to join Interbank, the Master Charge bank card network.

Donnelly P. McDonald, Jr., the third generation of McDonald's to serve as the bank's president, restructured the company in the latter part of the sixties, changing its emphasis from that of a savings or retail banking institution to one that also welcomed commercial and corporate clients. The institution's official name became "Peoples Trust Bank," and a holding company was established to assist in meeting capital requirements needed to keep pace with rapid deposit growth.

A new, 27-story building in Summit Square, just south of the bank's present building, will be completed in 1981, to be jointly occupied by the bank and Indiana & Michigan Electric Company. The poured-concrete structure, designed by the nationally acclaimed architectural firm of Kevin Roche John Dinkeloo & Associates, will have, as its entry-level focal point, a massive, greenhouse-style main banking room.

Peoples Trust Bank entered the decade of the eighties with assets of $445,626,908, and with D.P. McDonald, Jr., serving as board chairman; Hiram Nally as president; and Richard C. Burrows as executive vice president and senior trust officer.

Directors are Harold L. Bobeck, Philip L. Carson, Paul Clarke, David Cunningham, Joseph P. Cunningham, Anthony H. Galpern, Robert I. Goldstine, Richard G. Inskeep, Jon F. Lassus, Alfred Maloley, Donnelly P. McDonald, Jr., Henry J. Moellering, Donald F. Murphy, Hiram Nally, Dr. Levan R. Scott, and Charles H. Seyfert.

PHELPS DODGE

The two Phelps Dodge plants in Fort Wayne, which face each other on New Haven Avenue, are a small part of a large company rich in American business tradition — Phelps Dodge Corporation. Anson Greene Phelps began that tradition in 1834 in New York City when he started a partnership with his son-in-law, William E. Dodge. By the late 1800s, the firm had grown into a major metal importing business with additional interests in mercantile trade, railroads, and lumber.

The company made its first investment in domestic copper mining in 1881 in Bisbee and Morenci, Arizona. The Phelps, Dodge and Company partnership was succeeded by the present Phelps Dodge Corporation in 1908. By 1930, Phelps Dodge had expanded into copper refining, with refineries at Laurel Hill, New York, and El Paso, Texas. The company also built and acquired a number of manufacturing plants; and in 1966, Phelps Dodge Industries, Inc., its wholly owned

PHELPS DODGE COPPER PRODUCTS COMPANY

Phelps Dodge Copper Products Company, the prime mover of Phelps Dodge Corporation's copper, has three plants. They are located in the East, Midwest, and Southwest. The Indiana Rod and Wire Mill began operation in its then newly constructed plant in 1946. At the end of the first year, seventy-five people were employed. More recent employment has run as high as 600 people. The plant was built to produce 11 million pounds of copper rod and wire monthly; rod to supply wire companies in the

Midwest, and wire for use by the Phelps Dodge Magnet Wire Company plant in Fort Wayne.

Current output of copper products far exceeds the tonnage the plant was originally designed to produce. With the expansion of its product line, this plant now supplies companies from coast to coast.

The Indiana Rod and Wire Mill initiated the hot rolling of 600-pound copper wirebars and presently rolls the 600-pound and standard 265-pound wirebars into rod. It pioneered and supplies large shaved rod packages of 4,500 pounds. Rod is both sold to others and used as the starting point for a variety of sizes of round, square, and rectangular copper wire products made

Phelps Dodge Copper Products' Indiana Rod & Wire Mill, built in 1946 to supply companies in the Midwest, now has customers from coast to coast.

at this mill. Rod is rolled to sizes as large as one inch in diameter; wire is drawn to sizes finer than a human hair and is supplied as bare single strands, tinned, or bunched.

Copper has been an important metal in man's life since ancient times. The Indiana Rod and Wire Mill is helping fulfill the ever-increasing need for specific forms of this essential material.

subsidiary, was formed to coordinate and direct all Phelps Dodge manufacturing activities.

Phelps Dodge Industries includes six operating divisions: Phelps Dodge Copper Products Company, Phelps Dodge Magnet Wire Company, Phelps Dodge Cable and Wire Company, Phelps Dodge Communications Company, Phelps Dodge Brass Company, and Phelps Dodge International Corporation.

Phelps Dodge currently employs some 15,000 people and operates four copper mines, four copper smelters, two copper refineries, fifteen copper fabricating mills and plants, and four research and development centers. Phelps Dodge also maintains warehouses and sales offices throughout the United States and has overseas manufacturing associates in more than a dozen countries. Annual sales are about $1 billion.

PHELPS DODGE MAGNET WIRE COMPANY

Phelps Dodge Magnet Wire Company began as the Inca Manufacturing Company in 1929 in the original building of the present Fort Wayne plant, but traces its roots to the former Dudlo Manufacturing Company (1910 to 1927) which started Fort Wayne as the magnet wire manufacturing center of the United States. On joining the Phelps Dodge organization in 1931, the Inca name was revised to Inca Manufacturing Division.

As its magnet wire business grew, the

division's facilities grew. In 1967, a plant in Hopkinsville, Kentucky, was added and a third plant in Newark, Ohio, opened in 1970. While these changes were taking place, the division's name was also undergoing transition. The Inca identity was dropped in 1967, and the Phelps Dodge Magnet Wire name was adopted. Fort Wayne remains the headquarters for the company.

Magnet wire is used for the windings or coils in many electrical and electronic devices. In a motor, the current in magnet wire windings creates the magnetic field that causes the motor to rotate. In residential transformers, the windings lower line voltage to the 115/220 volts standard in home use.

Phelps Dodge Magnet Wire Company's plant on New Haven Avenue began as the Inca Manufacturing Company in 1929. Since 1967, the firm has added two other plants.

Appliances, television sets, and automobile electrical systems also depend on magnet wire to function.

Over the years, many trend-setting insulations, machines, and processes have been developed and patented by the composite talents in the Phelps Dodge Magnet Wire Company. These innovations have established and maintained Phelps Dodge Magnet Wire Company as a leader in the magnet wire industry. Today, Phelps Dodge Magnet Wire is one of the largest manufacturers of magnet wire in the world.

RKO BOTTLERS OF FORT WAYNE

A century has passed since RKO (Radio Keith Orpheum) Bottlers of Fort Wayne began to do business as William Scheele and Son in a 20-by-30 foot bottling plant on Miner Street. Water had to be pumped from a well, carried in buckets to a wooden washtub, and pumped from there into the carbonator. In fact, in 1880, all operations for bottling Scheele Soda Water were performed manually. Even the carbon dioxide for the carbonator was made in the plant through a chemical reaction using marble dust.

BB-shot was the cleansing agent for hand-washing the bottles. Fourteen hours of carrying water and scrubbing bottles would yield company founder, William Scheele, and his son, Edwin, about fifty cases of clean bottles.

Deliveries were made by horse and wagon in the early years, but Edwin's progressive nature induced the firm's purchase of Fort Wayne's first delivery truck, a vehicle reputed to bear up under 1,000 pounds. Scheele was thankful it managed a load of fifteen cases. A lack of legal protection for truckers resulted in as many lawsuits as deliveries, but Scheele persevered and eventually had the pleasure of seeing other companies follow his lead.

In 1923, the business moved from its tiny original location to 1207 North Harrison Street. Then, in 1936, two major events occurred: Edwin Scheele became president after his father's death; and the company became the area's Pepsi-Cola bottler. The business was now leaping toward its eventual 200,000-square-foot facility, not to mention its warehouses in Warsaw and Rome City and a bottling plant in Logansport.

The company was producing 250,000 cases of soft drinks a year by 1955. By the mid-sixties, Scheele's bottling line included Pepsi, Teem, Suncrest, and White Rock products. Mason's Root Beer, Dr. Pepper, Canada Dry, and Nesbitt's products were added the following decade. Annual output jumped to more than six million cases by 1975, when the business was purchased by RKO General, Inc., of New York City, owners of a Dr. Pepper bottling plant in Lima, Ohio, and Pepsi bottling plants in Muncie, Anderson, Toledo, Lima, and Bryan, Ohio, and South Bend and Brookville, Indiana. The company also owns broadcasting interests in New York City.

At the time of the sale, Richard Scheele, Edwin's son and president since 1962, signed a consultant contract agreeing not to engage in the bottling business on his own for ten years. He died in 1976. Robert Stange, who had been Scheele's sales manager since 1952, stepped into his present positions of vice president and general manager.

RKO's acquisition also encompassed Scheele's canning arm, Summit City Canning Company, and its building and maintenance operation, Teem Realty and Rental Company. Today, RKO Bottlers of Fort Wayne bottles Pepsi, Diet Pepsi, Mountain Dew, Teem, Dr. Pepper, Sugar-free Dr. Pepper, Sunkist Orange, and Vernor's Ginger Ale.

Under Stange's leadership, the company has taken special interest in Fort Wayne's youth, sponsoring such events and organizations as the Soap Box Derby, Little League, Boy Scouts, Hot Shot Basketball, Mobile Tennis, and soccer and hockey programs.

Above
In 1880, Scheele's Miner Street bottling plant could only hold four workers plus equipment.
Right
Edwin Scheele's first delivery truck was a one-cylinder Ideal manufactured in Fort Wayne.

SAINT FRANCIS COLLEGE

The Sisters of Saint Francis of Perpetual Adoration found their freedom to teach and care for the needy children of Olpe, Westphalia, severely restricted under the authority of Prussian Chancellor Otto von Bismarck in the late 1800s. When Fort Wayne's Bishop Joseph Dwenger met with Mother Theresia, the order's Superior-General, during a visit to Germany in 1874, he invited her community to establish a branch in Indiana. By December 1875, six sisters — three nurses and three teachers — had settled in Lafayette. They immediately set up a hospital and, within two years, staffed the German Catholic parish school of St. Boniface Church. The Sisters of St. Francis managed eleven hospitals and nine schools throughout the United States by 1890.

St. Francis Normal School, a two-year preparatory school for teaching nuns, emerged in the decade before the turn of the century. Purdue University President James Smart allowed his faculty members to teach courses there beginning in 1891. Two professors, Michael J. Golden and Raymond V. Achatz, also provided administrative assistance, organized the curriculum, outlined courses, and secured lay faculty.

In 1892, the diocesan school board authorized the school to issue teaching certificates. When Indiana passed a teacher licensing law effective in 1923,

St. Francis won accreditation by February. Continuing education courses introduced in the 1920s served as precursors for four-year study. The Indiana Public Instruction Department adopted a four-year educational requirement for teachers in 1936, and the school immediately implemented the required programs.

The school became Saint Francis College in 1939, the same year lay women were first enrolled. In February 1940, Indiana empowered the college to grant degrees in fields besides education. Saint Francis College had outgrown its Lafayette site by 1943, and the imminent need for expansion prompted a move in August 1944 to Brookside, the former John Bass estate on the western edge of Fort Wayne.

The school's new home was a Fort Wayne landmark, and the sisters were careful to preserve its character while adapting the mansion to their needs. At first the structure accommodated the entire college; now it serves as the library. The building has been nominated for a spot on the National Register of Historic Places.

World War II delayed the construction of new facilities. Trinity Hall, which housed residential space, classrooms, a chapel, cafeteria, and the home economics department, was dedicated in October 1949. Today, the campus is comprised of fourteen buildings, includ-

Above

When Saint Francis College moved to Fort Wayne from Lafayette, Indiana, in 1944, this former mansion of industrialist John Bass housed the entire college. The building, which now serves exclusively as a library, has been nominated to the National Register of Historic Places.

Above left

The college's first major construction project began September 18, 1947, with this groundbreaking ceremony attended by Father Seraph Zeitz, college chaplain; Sister Edith, registrar and treasurer; Sister Borgia, superior; Bishop John F. Noll; and Fort Wayne Major Harry Baals.

ing the newest, Achatz Hall of Science, where more than 80,000 visitors have enjoyed "View of the Stars" programs in the Schouweiler Planetarium.

Male students, admitted to late afternoon and evening courses in 1957, gained full-time admission in the fall of 1960. A graduate program was also begun.

About 1,300 students attend Saint Francis College now, some 800 undergraduates and 500 graduate students, with the total enrollment approximately 45 percent male. Programs range from those leading to two-year associate degrees in secretarial studies, business administration, art, accounting, and nursing home administration, to bachelor's degrees in liberal arts, education, business or office administration, nursing, and medical technology to master's degrees in business administration, education, and psychology.

ST. JOSEPH'S HOSPITAL

Only three years after the Civil War, five sisters of a newly established German-based religious order arrived in America to embark on a mission of medical service in Fort Wayne. The venture continues unbroken today.

In 1865, when the city of 26,000 was beset by smallpox, Bishop John Luers stepped forward to champion the cause of a hospital. He commissioned Father Edward Koenig to negotiate with Katherine Kasper, foundress of the Poor Handmaids of Jesus Christ, to teach and nurse area residents and care for the young orphans of the city. On August 13, 1868, the five sisters arrived and began setting up their headquarters in Hessen Cassel, south of Fort Wayne.

While Father Koenig had been completing his task, Bishop Luers was negotiating to buy the abandoned Rockhill House hotel from the estate of the late William Rockhill. Matching contributions from the community, the bishop purchased the 70-room building for $52,000.

The sisters left Hessen Cassel in early 1869 to ready Fort Wayne's first hospital and were still scrubbing on May 4, when the first patient arrived, one of twenty that year. Dr. Isaac M. Rosenthal performed the hospital's first surgery in August. At the time, a week's care cost six dollars, including special diets and drugs.

As the number of patients grew steadily, from 243 in 1871 to nearly 400 in the 1890s, the hospital required several expansions. By 1913, the hospital had become one of the most modern facilities in the Midwest, featuring an X-ray department and criminal detention rooms. In 1918, a School of Nursing was added to the already established clinic for young doctors seeking to study and observe surgery. Long before hospital or medical insurance was an accepted practice, St. Joseph's and seven other Catholic hospitals developed a hospitalization plan which, for $7.20, provided board, care, and treatment for one full year.

In response to continued community growth, the hospital opened a seven-story wing along Berry and Van Buren Streets in 1929, increasing its bed capacity to 270. The staff numbered thirty-five sisters, five additional registered nurses, an X-ray technician, a dietitian, two interns, eighty-five students, and forty-one support service employees.

Through the 1950s, St. Joseph's continued to meet the challenges of its mission in Fort Wayne, keeping pace with medical and technological advances. The more progressive techniques of the day were demonstrated in its 40-seat surgical amphitheater, recovery room, and 24-hour emergency room. The burgeoning case load prompted the hospital's largest expansion project, completed in 1966.

In 1974, St. Joseph's established a seven-bed burn unit, one of only three in the state and the only unit in northern Indiana.

A five-story addition on Main Street was completed in 1980 and provided a new emergency room, laboratory, surgical and recovery facilities, and two patient units.

Today, other major services offered by the 487-bed hospital include coronary, intensive, obstetric, pediatric, psychiatric, and newborn intensive care units; respiratory therapy; social services; outpatient surgery and diagnostic testing; a full range of radiological procedures; and the second largest medical library in the state.

An adjoining medical office building and parking garage, constructed by private developers, are St. Joseph's newest additions. Both structures are evidence of St. Joseph's continuing commitment to providing Christian care and concern for the people of Fort Wayne.

Above
The laboratory was a busy place in the 1940s, reflecting the rapid advance in medical technology since 1869, when the hospital's log listed cases of "fevers, nervous disorders, cancer, bronchitis, and St. Vitus's Dance."

Top
The Rockhill House opened in 1854 as one of Indiana's finest hotels. In 1869, it became St. Joseph's Hospital.

SEYFERT FOODS, INC.

As a boy on a farm near Lebanon, Pennsylvania, Charles H. Seyfert drove so many wagonloads of potatoes to market that he vowed one day to put potato farming behind him. He thought he had the answer in the popular Pennsylvania pretzels that his uncle, Dave Arnold of Fort Wayne, wistfully noted he could not get in Indiana.

With his uncle's comments echoing in his mind, Seyfert set out in 1934 with a mobile kitchen to make his fortune selling pretzels at the Chicago World's Fair. Unfortunately, the fair-goers were not as pretzel-happy as Uncle Dave had been. Nor were the people of Fort Wayne, to whom Seyfert tried to sell his goods on his way back to the farm.

Though the potato wagons held no fond memories, Seyfert decided he could put his knowledge of potatoes to work: He would make potato chips. So on August 20, 1934, Seyfert fired up his first kitchen at 450 East Wallace Street with equipment purchased for seventy-five dollars from a dismantled Pennsylvania potato chip plant. Initially, he was the sole employee and did the chipping, cooking, packaging, and selling. A woman was later hired to do the packaging. Seyfert's early customers were Fort Wayne taverns, where the chips caught on as a perfect complement to beer.

The business grew, consuming 300 pounds of potatoes per week. Seyfert reasoned that with a business of 500 pounds a week "I'd be able to retire." He didn't. Today, the plant takes in between sixty and eighty tons of potatoes per day, to be converted into 24,000 to 30,000 pounds of potato chips for tables within a 150-mile radius in Indiana, Ohio, and Michigan. As an active member of the Potato Chip Institute International, Seyfert worked to overcome the limitations of unpredictable potato varieties and non-airtight packaging. He has also been influential in the development of a wider market range for potato chips and snack foods.

In 1940, the firm outgrew the original kitchen and moved half a block west to the southeast corner of Lafayette and Wallace Streets. That building proved inadequate by 1965, and the company moved to a new three-acre plant at 1001 Paramount Road in Interstate Industrial Park on Indiana 3. Located on a 20-acre site, the plant is the chip industry's largest complete operation under one roof. Thousands of annual visitors watch from a long windowed corridor as the potatoes are washed, sliced, cooked, inspected, and packaged by a combination of automation and handwork.

Seyfert Foods, Inc., also produces cheese popcorn, cheese twisties, raw and roasted nuts, and corn chips. In 1976, Seyfert added innovative equipment to produce another popular type of snack particularly dear to the company president's heart — pretzels. The pretzel machinery, capable of turning out 98,000 pretzels an hour, makes three-ring, one-ring, sticks, and rods.

Seyfert foods arrive on grocers' shelves within days of production. Studies reveal that they are sold within the following week.

Above
Seyfert launched his potato chip business in this building at 450 East Wallace Street.

Left
The pretzels Charles H. Seyfert tried to market in 1934 didn't sell, but potato chips did, and the snack foods entrepreneur was on his way to corporate success.

SOUDER'S FURNITURE AND STUDIO, INC.

The front door of Souder's Furniture and Studio in Grabill is the same one that Henry Souder, local minister and farmer, first opened in 1907 to start his 17-year-old son Elias in business. The 1907 aura is alive today in the sprawling "general" store that is the centerpiece of Grabill's old-time atmosphere.

Henry stayed with the business for eighteen months and then let Elias run the operation alone. The store specialized in harness sales and repair, and Elias also sold gasoline-powered washing machines, horse tanks, and windmills. Souder's was also a cream station, to which area farmers brought their cream for testing and storage until it was delivered to Fort Wayne twice a week.

The arrival of automobiles in Grabill was a sign of changing times, and Elias changed with them. In 1920, he married and bought the old Fair Department Store, which had previously gone out of business. He filled the store with furniture and sold it by going door-to-door in Fort Wayne to tell people about his business. He was the first of many furniture sellers in the small towns ringing Fort Wayne.

The store expanded in the 1930s, as Elias moved into several adjacent buildings. In 1938, Elias brought his wife, Lydia, and their three sons, 14-year-old Henry, 12-year-old Ed, and six-year-old Dwight, into the business as equal partners.

Today, Souder's Furniture and Studio occupies 25,000 square feet of space, encompassing buildings that were once a bank, fire house, jail, saloon, hotel, town hall, Doc Minnick's office, Roth's Soda Fountain and Variety Store, and Grabill's original apothecary shop. The former hotel is the oldest business building remaining from Grabill's turn-of-the-century days; it was bought in 1966, and the empty space between it and the original harness shop was bought and filled in 1969, the only new construction in the facade since 1907.

In addition to furniture sales, the family business includes Souder's General Store and H. Souder & Son, Bookseller. The old-time feeling of the business would not be possible if not for Grabill itself, surrounded on three sides by a settlement of old order Amish and on the fourth by Fort Wayne, its main market area. However, Grabill's historic landmarks received a serious setback in 1976, when two fires destroyed Souder's warehouse and another string of old buildings across the street. The fire left Souder's as the town's only landmark, and Ed Souder called a meeting of Grabill and Fort Wayne businessmen, city planners, and other leaders to assess the damage and set a direction for the future. The meeting solidified Ed's belief in Souder's special tradition, and he resolved to "capitalize on what we've got." He has applied to have the building accepted into the National Register of Historic Places.

After three deaths and one retirement, Ed is the only one remaining from the third generation. Ed's son, Mark, has joined the business as executive vice president, and his nephew, Kevin, has stepped in as vice president, making them the fourth generation of Souder family members to lead the enterprise.

Bottom
In the early 1900s, Hirem "Doc" Racely worked for Souder's harness shop at a salary of ten dollars per week.

Below
Fort Wayne artist James McBride captured the traditional charm and heritage of Souder's Furniture and Studio in this popular rendition of the storefront at State and Main Streets. The windmill decorating the building was taken from the old Souder homestead.

SPEARS-DEHNER, INC.

Since its founding in 1945, Spears-Dehner, Inc., has been a leading highway construction firm. The company played a large part in the construction of the Interstate Highway System.

The firm's first job was actually in highway renovation — a subcontract from John Dehner, Inc., for concrete patching on U.S. 6 near Kendallville. Then the company graded a section of U.S. 20 near Scott. Spears-Dehner was founded in 1945 as a partnership and an expansion arm of John Dehner, Inc., with whom it shares an office building at 1212 Clark Street in Fort Wayne.

The founding partners of the company were Walter H. Meitz, Gaylord H. Spears, and John Dehner. The partnership incorporated in 1946 as Meitz-Spears-Dehner, Inc. Meitz sold his stock and left the firm in 1953, and the company name became Spears-Dehner, Inc., in 1954. The company's officers are now Donald G. "George" Spears, presi-

dent; Edward L. Dehner, vice president; and Gerald G. Dehner, secretary-treasurer. John H. Obringer recently retired after thirty-four years as secretary of the company. None of the founders are living today.

The Spears family has long been involved in highways. Founding partner Gaylord H., who grew up in LaGrange and moved to Fort Wayne, worked for the Indiana State Highway Department as an engineer, traveling around the state from project to project. Later, he was employed by Grace Construction Company. Gaylord's two sons, George and John, were active in the company early on. John Spears joined the firm in 1946. He served as vice president from 1963 until his death in 1978. Upon his discharge from the army, George worked summers for the company while attending Purdue University. After he received his civil engineering degree in 1949, George worked for the Wisconsin

Highway Department for a year and then returned home to work again with Spears-Dehner. The third generation of Spears, James G. and Mark W., have engineering and management roles in the company.

Spears-Dehner's first Interstate construction job was grading and paving a section of I-70 near Richmond in 1959. Other Interstate work has been on I-69, other sections of I-70, and I-65 in Indiana. One of the company's recent jobs was the paving of a section of Route 37 at Bedford, when the heavily traveled road was upgraded from two lanes to four in the 1970s.

Although most of the firm's work has been in the highway construction field, it has also performed heavy and utility construction jobs throughout Indiana. The company has also done subdivision work, such as Brentwood in Fort Wayne, and has combined utility and road construction.

Above
Gaylord H. Spears worked as an engineer for the Indiana State Highway Department before he moved to Fort Wayne and later helped found Meitz-Spears-Dehner, Inc.
Left
Spears-Dehner crews patched a portion of U.S. 6 near Kendallville in 1946. The firm specializes in road construction and rebuilding.

TOKHEIM CORPORATION

In the summer of 1918, a small group of Fort Wayne businessmen gathered each evening and on weekends to renovate two old brick buildings just south of the Wabash Railroad tracks on the east side of town.

Though they all had jobs elsewhere, each had a stake in Ralph F. Diserens's new venture — bringing a gasoline pump company to town from Iowa. The former Wayne Spoke and Bending Company plant had to be ready for the production of pumps as soon as the equipment arrived from Cedar Rapids if the company was to keep its head above water. So the shareholders rolled up their sleeves and went to work, even cleaning the bricks from a still-older wagon shed to build their factory's first addition.

The company, Tokheim Corporation, has gone on to become the nation's leading manufacturer of gasoline pumps and one of the world's foremost designers and producers of systems for moving and measuring liquids. Net sales for 1979 exceeded $101 million.

In 1898, John J. Tokheim had developed his Tokheim Dome Oil Pump after searching for a better method of dispensing kerosene and gasoline at his new hardware store in Thor, Iowa. As a result, he formed the Tokheim Manufacturing Company in Cedar Rapids in 1901, and in 1906 developed a pump with a visible measuring device.

Marketed under the Tokheim Oil Tank and Pump Company banner, that visible electric pump was refined over the next several years, and thousands of models were sold as fast as they could be turned out. The mid-1920s saw major plant expansions, including the creation of a San Francisco sales office in 1923, the first of today's twenty-four district sales offices across the United States, and the introduction in 1927 of the first gasoline pump with a bell to indicate each gallon of delivery and the completion of a sale, a unit so popular that more than 10,000 were sold. Tokheim has since made major contributions to the field, including electric reset mechanisms, money acceptance systems, and the Modular Electronic Marketing System that puts control of an entire gasoline station into one electronic computer.

Tokheim's contributions are not limited to gasoline pumps. The firm has produced materials vital to the nation's defense interests, including the first aerial bombs in 1918 and, during World War II, shells and shot for the United States and Britain. Through diversification, Tokheim product lines today also include meters, automotive fuel pumps, hose reels, die castings, and electronic timers.

Tokheim currently operates plants in Fort Wayne, Albion, and Fremont, Indiana; Lombard and Chicago, Illinois; and Jasper and Newbern, Tennessee. International plants are located in Canada, the Netherlands, South Africa, and Scotland.

Today, the Tokheim Corporation looks forward to future diversification and expansion under the leadership of Joseph J. Guidrey, chairman of the board and chief executive officer, and Richard B. Doner, president.

Above
The Fort Wayne businessmen who bought John Tokheim's pump company also purchased Wayne Spoke and Bending Company's deserted buildings to house their enterprise. Shareholders worked nights and weekends to ready the facility for production.

Top
Motorists liked Tokheim's "visible" gasoline pumps. Heavy demand for them kept the men on the shipping dock busy in the 1920s.

W&W CONCRETE, INC.

After a highway letting in Indianapolis in 1957, Merle Smith, Robert L. Welker, Robert G. Bear, and Elmer MacDonald began a fateful discussion. None of them was in any hurry to go out into the cold night, and conversation naturally turned to business, as three of the friends had concrete and gravel businesses in common. Welker owned a gravel pit west of Fort Wayne in Roanoke; Smith had a concrete plant in Montpelier, and MacDonald was manager of Erie Materials, a Fort Wayne concrete plant. Bear, nicknamed the "mayor of Roanoke," operated the Roanoke Elevator, and took an active interest in his community and its growing urban neighbor.

Talk turned to the lack of a concrete plant in southwest Allen County. Smith's Montpelier concrete plant was not too busy, but someone suggested it would have as much work in Roanoke. Welker casually invited the others to establish a concrete plant next to his gravel business and become a partnership.

And so Smith's plant was moved from Montpelier to Roanoke, MacDonald left his job to be the manager of the 10-employee, four-mixer-truck venture, and W & W Concrete began operation April 22, 1957, at 8031 West County Line Road. Smith soon sold his interest in the ready-mix business, and Bear remained a relatively inactive partner.

Around 1960, the firm won the right to supply concrete for the headquarters building for "Our Sunday Visitor" in Huntington. Additional highway jobs in Huntington prompted W & W Concrete to set up a plant in that city, where it supplied concrete for one of the first "lift-slab" buildings, for which the slab is poured and slowly lifted by hydraulic jacks. W & W also supplied concrete for the First National Bank of Huntington, one of the first hyperbolic paraboloid buildings, plus supplied the concrete for Huntington North High School, and Huntington Memorial Hospital.

In 1963, W & W Concrete took over ready-mix plants in Bluffton and Markle and supplied most of the concrete for the Huntington Reservoir Dam and the

Interstate 69 bridges between Warren to just south of Markle. When the interstate highway was completed in the late 1960s, the Markle plant was put on inactive status. The Bluffton plant provided concrete for the Caylor-Nickel Clinic in Bluffton, the Wells County Hospital, Bluffton High School, and industrial facilities for Owens-Corning, Franklin Electric, and Bachman Pretzels. Although seriously damaged by fire in 1976, the Bluffton operation has been rebuilt. In 1967, the company added a plant in North Manchester, which has furnished concrete for many area schools, including buildings on the North Manchester College campus.

From the original plant in Roanoke, W & W Concrete has supplied concrete for all southwest Allen County schools, the Fort Wayne-Allen County Public Library addition, Northrop High School, and the Archway Cookie plant,

Above
Placing the concrete for Routes 224 and 5 through Huntington in 1963 required two workers per vehicle to unload, one to drive and one to guide the chute. Today, W & W's trucks can be operated by one person.

Top
In the spring of 1957, W & W Concrete's original mixer fleet consisted of these four trucks.

to name a few.

MacDonald and Welker have remained active in civic affairs; both men are past potentates of the Mizpah Shrine Temple. MacDonald served as a state representative between 1965 and 1978, when he was elected a state senator, and in 1980 was a Republican candidate for the fourth district congressional seat.

W & W Concrete now operates four plants and a fleet of about two dozen mixer trucks. Not only does it sell concrete and allied building materials, but it is a partner in Advance Mixers, Inc., which builds front discharge mixers that have simplified concrete pouring.

WAYNE PIPE AND SUPPLY, INC.

In 1896, sawmills, flour mills, feed mills, the looms of Wayne Knitting Mills, even the local electric plant and the pumping stations of Fort Wayne all depended on steam engines for power. And the men who kept the engines running depended on a new shop on Columbia Street.

Now a noted supply house for industrial products and plumbing and heating equipment and materials, Wayne Pipe & Supply, Inc., began as one of the first outlets for oils and greases, lubricating devices, packing, and allied items for steam engines. The initial enterprise was founded by a Mr. Hayner, who had been sent to Fort Wayne by the Atlantic Refining Company of Cleveland, Ohio, with orders to establish a store.

When the refinery decided to divest itself of the store in 1902, E.W. Puckett, newly arrived in the bustling factory town, persuaded a number of local businessmen to buy out the store and incorporate as the Fort Wayne Oil & Supply Company. The new firm continued to carry oils, grease, belting, and the allied items of valves, fittings, transmission materials, tools, and other industrial products.

The company soon outgrew its first location at 220 East Columbia Street and in 1904 moved to new headquarters at 108 West Columbia Street, now part of the Landing.

The first decade of the century was a busy one in Fort Wayne, with numerous new businesses opening and a substantial building spurt downtown. The activity meant increased business for Fort Wayne Oil & Supply, which was constantly adding to the variety of materials it handled. The company established connections throughout the country with leading manufacturers of machinery, pumps, and products for factories and mills. Plumbing supplies were in particular demand, so in 1905 Fort Wayne Oil & Supply purchased the Baltes Supply Company and organized a department called P & H Supply. This newly formed unit of the firm soon became identified with high-quality plumbing supplies carried in sufficient quantities to meet the demands of plumbing and mechanical contractors.

In 1907, the rapidly growing business needed still more space, and a new location was established at 225-227 East Columbia Street. The adjacent building at 229 East Columbia was acquired by the operation in 1914. For many years, the company also maintained a pipe yard and warehouse at 430 East Columbia Street. In 1916, a large warehouse was built on the northwest corner of Clay and Columbia Streets, where the immense stock of steel pipe could be stored under a protecting roof, as well as provide space for the company's stock of boilers, radiators, and pipe covering.

By 1920, the one-time steam engine suppliers were carrying bathroom fixtures, and in 1925, the name was changed to Fort Wayne Pipe & Supply Company. The word "oil" in the name had become misleading as the industry changed and very little oil and grease were sold through industrial distribu-tors.

In 1936, the company purchased a five-story building at 101 East Columbia Street which served as headquarters until 1956, when a modern one-story office, showroom and warehouse facility was constructed on approximately five acres at 1815 South Anthony Boulevard.

Today Wayne Pipe & Supply is one of the largest suppliers of steel pipe in the northern Indiana area. Its unique storage system allows the company to run a rail car directly through the center of the pipe warehouse for easy loading and unloading. A large overhead crane traveling the entire length of the building facilitates the complete unloading of a rail car or truck within minutes. Wayne Pipe officials firmly believe that this and several other stock-handling innovations reflect better customer service and savings to the ultimate user.

The company's computer bookkeeping system is another such program; ev-

Above
These computer operators process and monitor the company's operations using today's most modern methods and machines.

Top left
A Wayne Pipe & Supply, Inc., employee fills an order in Warehouse No. 1. The corporation's shipping department handles a $1.7 million inventory.

Top right
James M. Wilson, president and chairman of the board, is the fifth man to lead Wayne Pipe & Supply since the firm was founded in 1896.

Opposite page
Around 1905, delivery trucks for Fort Wayne Oil & Supply Company's P & H Supply Division were loaded at this warehouse on Columbia Street.

ery phase of the operation is monitored, from inventory to sales order. Day-to-day promotion of merchandise is offered through manufacturer's literature. At a cost of $47,000, the firm also recently produced an 890-page catalog which details its stock of 34,958 items.

Wayne Pipe & Supply now has a total employment of seventy people, an inventory of more than $1.7 million, with annual sales exceeding $9 million. The company contributes an employee payroll of well over $1 million to the

Fort Wayne area economy. Industrial products account for 75 percent of sales volume. Wayne Pipe & Supply is the industrial distributor for fifty-one manufacturers and the plumbing and heating distributor for forty-seven other manufacturing firms.

Throughout the company's history, there have been only five chief executives — E.W. Puckett, C.J. Stier, Julius Schroeder, E.J. Trier, and today's president and chairman of the board of directors, James M. Wilson.

Under Mr. Wilson, the office atmosphere is one of activity comfortably mixed with informal accessibility. He attributes this atmosphere to the fact that "throughout our organization, a spirit of friendly cooperation has been developed over the years. We are a team with each member well-trained, experienced, and competent in his work, willing always to lend a hand where needed." Since 1896, Wayne Pipe & Supply, Inc., has grown because a group of honest, friendly people united their personal efforts to provide a better, more efficient facility for distribution of industrial equipment and plumbing and heating equipment in the Fort Wayne area. Because of that attitude, Mr. Wilson feels the years to come will continue to bring growth and profit.

WATERFIELD MORTGAGE COMPANY, INC.

Founder Richard H. Waterfield was influential in the organization of the Mortgage Bankers Association in Indiana in 1941.

Above
The firm occupied this site at 126 East Berry Street in 1951.

Top right
By 1960, when the corporation moved to 234 East Berry Street, it needed two small buildings to house its growing enterprise.

Richard H. Waterfield arrived in Fort Wayne from New York in 1927 to join his brother, Dallas, in the general insurance business. The following year, after being appointed financial correspondent for Union Central Life Insurance Company of Cincinnati to make real estate loans for its investment portfolio, he decided to enter the mortgage banking business. He opened his first office in the Medical Arts Building, then at Berry and Webster Streets, and in 1942 incorporated as Waterfield Mortgage Company, Inc. For the next twenty-five years, as president and resident agent, Waterfield guided the firm, which today is among the thirty-five largest mortgage banking concerns in the United States, servicing in excess of 75,000 mortgage accounts for 175 institutional investors, involving $1.7 billion. The firm employs approximately 250 people.

The owners have repeatedly declined opportunities to sell company stock and look forward to continued service and prosperity under the present format of a privately held company. The firm maintains operations in Fort Wayne, South Bend, Indianapolis, Kokomo, and Muncie, Indiana; Grand Rapids and Lansing, Michigan; and Akron, Columbus, Dayton, and Cincinnati, Ohio. The Waterfields have tried to allow branch managers and department heads as much autonomy as is practiced in the interest of good business.

At first the company closed loans in the name of the institutional investor and with the investor's funds. Now the corporation closes the loans in its own name and with its own funds, then assigning the mortgage to the institutional investor having contracted to service the loan until its maturity.

Joel K. Bravick joined the company as an attorney in 1961 and in 1967 became president, since Waterfield suffered a heart attack and decided to go into semiretirement. As president, Bravick is in charge of the overall operations of the company. Richard D. Waterfield, executive vice president and son of the founder, joined the company in 1968 and is involved in banking, marketing, and planning functions. Other senior officers include James B. Griffith, executive vice president, marketing; George E. Lowery, Jr., senior vice president, administration; Joseph F. Schrader, senior vice president, commercial loans; and E. Anthony King, executive vice president, insurance agency.

The senior Waterfield comments that he regards the company's activities as "importing." "We import millions of dollars of mortgage funds from all over the United States for use and investment in the areas in which we are active."

WORTHMAN HOMES, INC.

John R. Worthman started a home-building business in 1925. He knew how to work and was able to meet the challenge of survival through the Great Depression by trading services and products to get jobs. Sometimes employees, suppliers, and subcontractors were paid in food, dental, or medical services. Worthman's wife, Alice, took employees' shopping lists to the grocer for whom a new house was being built, and on Friday afternoon, she would deliver bags of groceries to job sites in lieu of cash wages for the week. From these depression-era jobs evolved a custom home-building business that today boasts the best reputation in the area.

Many early Worthman homes were built in Lafayette Place, Southwood Park, and Indian Village. Worthman got into land development when he took over the "suburban" Indian Village, later tripling its size. World War II rationing, shortages, and restrictions confined building to apartments and small

homes, but following the war, Worthman built hundreds of small homes for returning servicemen in North Highlands, Harvester View, Park Place, and other small tracts. In the 1950s, the company returned to designing and building larger, high-quality homes in Worthman communities such as Indian Village, Indian Hills, Woodhurst, Lincolnshire, Timbercrest, Lake Shores, Winterset, Stratton Place in Decatur, Karen Kove at Tri-Lakes, Gatesworth Shores on Crooked Lake, and Northway Place in Huntington.

Worthman's son, Jack, literally grew up in home building. The firm's office was in the family home, with the garage as the shop. Later, Jack studied building at Purdue University and did postgraduate work at the Chicago Academy of Fine Art and Design.

In 1951, Worthman's son-in-law, Ronald E. Flohr, joined the company, bringing both training and experience in business management and accounting to Worthman Homes. Since the death of

the elder Worthman in 1964, Flohr and Jack Worthman have run the firm, which now employs third-generation members from both families.

In the past twenty years, Worthman Homes has expanded into commercial and industrial land development, building apartments, offices, shops, and banks including the Courts of Woodhurst, Candlelite, and the Worthman Office Mall.

Below left
John R. Worthman (second from right) poses with a construction crew in front of this Lafayette Place home being built by his company in June 1926.
Bottom left
Pictured here is one of many homes in Woodhurst designed and built by Worthman Homes.
Bottom right
Today, the firm is active in the design and construction of commercial buildings such as this First National Bank branch in Huntington.
Below
Worthman Homes built this neighborhood on Field Street off North Clinton in 1942. The houses sold for about $6,000.

ZOLLNER CORPORATION

Although Zollner Corporation wasn't "born" in Fort Wayne, it has played an integral role in the city's automotive-related industry as well as its sports life since 1931.

Theodore Zollner ran a machine shop specializing in rebuilding mining equipment engines in Duluth, Minnesota, in the early years of the century. In 1912, he founded the company that became today's Zollner Corporation, one of the world's largest producers of heavy-duty pistons for internal combustion engines.

The Greyhound Bus Company requested that Zollner design and produce a better piston for its buses. The iron pistons of the day were much less effective than the aluminum alloy pistons Zollner and his mechanical engineer son, Fred, designed. As the company's reputation grew, it began specializing in pistons for the trucking industry.

Although iron mines are near Duluth, the trucking industry is not. By 1931,

the Zollners had decided to leave Duluth for an area closer to the truck and automotive industries. On a visit to Fort Wayne that year, the elder Zollner was shown a site by Al Schaff of the Greater Fort Wayne Development Corporation. The site was just north of the International Harvester plant, one of Zollner's major customers. Three days later, Zollner returned to the site with his son, and they signed an agreement to develop the location at 2425 South Coliseum Boulevard.

About fifteen employees moved from Duluth to Fort Wayne with the Zollner family and the company. Forty-nine years later, Zollner's pistons are still molded from aluminum alloy. The metal enters the plant in the form of ingots and leaves as a variety of finished pistons ranging from 1.5 to 9 inches in diameter. Zollner pistons have been used in trucks, buses, cars, tractors, industrial and marine engines, and other

internal combustion power units, compressors, and pumps.

Zollner's original fifteen employees have grown to 1,600, many of whom have long tenure with the company, which offers good benefits and attitudes coupled with no shutdowns and small, infrequent layoffs. Executives important to the company include Janet Fisher, Blayne Osborne, Lou Bowser, Ron Burgette, Paul Schirmeyer, and Marjorie Bowstrom, assistant chairman of the board and assistant chief executive officer under Fred Zollner.

In 1952, Fred took over the leadership of the company from his father, who died later that year. Fred, who graduated from the University of Minnesota in 1927, has been the guiding light of the company's growth years, manifested by periodic plant expansions that have yielded nearly half a million square feet of office, engineering, and manufacturing space. The 1956 addi-

tion was a completely mechanized permanent mold foundry that enabled the company to make its own castings for the first time.

District sales offices are in Birmingham, Michigan, and Oakbrook, Illinois. A wholly owned subsidiary, Zollner Canada, Ltd., in Leamington, Ontario, is a smaller version of the home plant and attests to Zollner's international reputation. Its major customer remains the trucking industry.

The corporation has a history of supporting local civic, social service projects and fund drives, but it is no doubt best remembered for the professional softball and basketball teams Fred organized in 1939 and 1940, which ushered in Fort Wayne's golden age of professional sports.

After only one year, the Zollner Pistons basketball team moved into national competition in 1940, and home games were played in the North Side High School gymnasium. The Pistons' Bobby McDermott, hired away from the New York Celtics in 1940, was the leading scorer for the National Basketball Association. He encouraged other talented players to come to Fort Wayne and was recognized as the best long-shot artist in the game. The Pistons' rapid-pass style transformed the game and won league championships in 1943, 1944, and 1945. In 1946, the season ended with the Pistons' sweep of the professional teams in a play-off tournament at Chicago Stadium. Rochester won the league title in 1946, but the Pistons won the world title in the Chicago Pro Invitational. The team's last Fort Wayne hurrah was in 1955, when it met the Syracuse Nationals in the national play-offs. No play-off games were played in Fort Wayne, because the National Bowling Congress had booked Memorial Coliseum. Indianapolis became the home game city. Syracuse won the series in the seventh game after a flurry of questionable calls. The Pistons moved to Detroit for the 1957 to 1958 season.

The Zollner Pistons softball team, which today would be termed a fastball team, so dominated the professional circuit that they eliminated their own competition. Organized in 1940, the team disbanded in 1954. It consistently won the National Fastball League Championship with an .869 winning percentage. Initially, the team played at Municipal Beach, now City Utilities Park, but relocated to Zollner Stadium on North Anthony Boulevard in 1947. Zollner Stadium was sold in 1958 to Concordia Lutheran High School. All of the adjoining land owned by Zollner has been donated to Concordia and Indiana Vocational Technical College. During both sports' dynamic seasons, thousands of Fort Wayne youngsters attended Zollner Pistons' games as members of the Knot Hole Gang, established by Fred.

Top
Fred Zollner has been the guiding light behind the growth of the Zollner Corporation, a leading manufacturer of heavy-duty aluminum alloy pistons, founded in 1912 by Theodore Zollner.

Left
Zollner's original Fort Wayne plant (encircled, left), built in 1931, has been integrated into later extensive expansions. A close-up of the front of the modern structure is seen (far left).

ACKNOWLEDGMENTS

The author is grateful for the help of numerous individuals and organizations in getting together the materials and seeing through the completion of this book. They include Edwin C. Metcalfe, president, and D.J. Petruccelli, executive vice-president, and others of the Fort Wayne Chamber of Commerce; David Carto; Helen Colchin, Don B. Rust, Robert H. Vegeler and Rick Ashton of the Public Library; Teri Davis Greenberg, Katherine Cooper, and Randall Smoot of Windsor Publications; the staffs of the Fort Wayne Park Board and the Allen County-Fort Wayne Historical Society, the Allen County Planning Commission, *The News-Sentinel,* the *Journal-Gazette;* and photographers Alan Vandever, Carl Hartup, John Sorensen, John Stearns, Argil Shock, Greg Dorsett, Dean Musser, Jr., Mike Hanley, Dailey Fogle, Harry Grabner, Gabriel Delobbe, Robert Bastress, and others current and from the past. Many people and events played important roles in the life and times of Fort Wayne but are not mentioned in this volume because of space limitations, a condition the author regrets.

INDEX

Numbers in bold face indicate illustrations

THIS BOOK WAS SET IN
PALADIUM AND SOUVENIR TYPES,
PRINTED ON
80lb. ENAMEL
AND BOUND BY
WALSWORTH PUBLISHING COMPANY.
COVER AND BOOK DESIGN BY
ALEXANDER D'ANCA
LAYOUT BY
LISA SHERER AND MELINDA WADE